PRAISE FOR THE *VANISI*

"Coming from a former sc̶h̶o̶o̶l̶ ̶b̶o̶a̶r̶d̶, ̶t̶h̶i̶s̶ ̶b̶o̶o̶k̶ ̶d̶e̶f̶t̶l̶y̶ current educational trends as well as reforms. . . . I would recommend this book as part of any school board's arsenal and required reading for any up and coming leader in the educational system!"

—**Jeff Campbell**, director of youth services,
Children's Home Association of Illinois

"As a superintendent of two rural districts in Central Illinois, this book has provided a greater understanding of the relationship between the superintendent and board of education. Board governance is a critical piece in the success of public school districts, and Dr. Rice presents very compelling information on how boards of education are key to student achievement. I would highly recommend this book to all superintendents, board members, and to anyone interested in the mechanisms of school board governance."

—**Bill Mulvaney**, superintendent, Armstrong Township
High School District #225 and Armstrong-Ellis
Consolidated School District #61, Illinois

"Dr. Rice provides readers with a thoughtful analysis of the critical role public school boards play in our society and what we must do to ensure their success in meeting the future challenges of P-12 education. This book contains important lessons for everyone interested in preserving and advancing our public schools."

—**John A. Dively**, Jr. JD, EdD, associate professor,
Eastern Illinois University

"In the world of constantly changing issues, school board leadership is more challenging today than ever. In too many cases there are no easy solutions to those challenges. The list continues to grow as the complexities of running a non-revenue generating school: long meetings, information overload or insufficient disclosures, communally voiced frustrations and fears, media frenzies over closing buildings or reductions in staff. It is not surprising that Patrick Rice's book *Vanishing School Boards* is an important read. Fundamental to local control of a community's children is the elected and supported board structure. Sitting board members will find this enlightening and supportive, superintendents will discover vital information, college courses on local governances or board relationships will have found a much needed textbook."

—**Donna McCaw**, EdD, professor emeritus, Western Illinois University, author, educational consultant, and national professional development trainer

"This is one of the few books that educators will find that is based upon research from an individual, Dr. Patrick Rice, who clearly understands the importance of school board governance. His background in education validates his expertise in the dynamics of local school boards, [shows] the current threat to their ability to drive academic achievement of students, and shares how superintendents can effectively foster and nurture the appropriate training that will make school boards [transform from] good to great."

—**Jean Chrostoski**, superintendent, Goshen County School District #1, Torrington, WY

"As a public school administrator for over twenty years, I have found that federal and state agencies, along with corporations and their privately funded think tanks, are enacting 'educational reforms' that systematically strip away local decision making and undermine the very existence of public education. Dr. Rice does a great job at using extensive research to discuss issues concerning current education reforms, why school boards are necessary more now than possibly ever, and how we as representatives of the public should stand together to support more local control and less intervention from those who profit from the constant scrutiny we face in the global market today. People who read this book will better understand the politics of education and why we must continue to promote local decision making and the work of local boards of education."

—**Dr. Steve Webb**, president, Illinois Association of School Administrators; associate professor in educational administration and leadership, McKendree University; and superintendent, Goreville, Illinois C.U.S.D. #1

"Dr. Rice has written one of the most thought provoking books of our century for the board of education. His book provides board members with an in-depth examination of how local school boards and their governance has been under constant fire in the handling of education issues facing our times. This masterpiece provides a litany of solutions on how board members can take our school districts to the next highest level of academic greatness by having a laser-like focus on student achievement through their own participation in professional development, establishing on-going positive relationships with their CEO, and embracing transparency and continuous community engagement."

—**Dr. Valorie M. Moore**, superintendent, Brookwood School District 167, Illinois

"What an awesome read! This book outlines the framework of where public schools have been and where they are headed. Dr. Rice has eloquently compiled research on everything from school governance, educational reforms, need for school boards, and relativity of school board governance, to student achievement and so much more. Anyone who believes education is the cornerstone of our democracy and must be preserved will want to read this book. I wish I had a book such as this when I began my service as a school board member in 1995."

—**Carolyne D. Brooks**, president pro-tem, West Richland Community Unity School District #2, Noble, Illinois

"The role of the school board in the governance of America's schools is a longstanding tradition and one that ensures that local values and interests are incorporated into local schools. This book identifies and explores the forces and trends that are slowly putting state and national interests ahead of local control. One can grieve these developments and watch our schools become nothing but big government schools, or take steps to actively strengthen the viability of local boards of education. At risk is the very nature of the type education our children will receive and perhaps even the preservation of our democracy."

—**Michael A. Jacoby**, EdD SFO, CAE, executive director, Illinois ASBO

"In this timely book, Dr. Rice thoughtfully describes the role of school boards in education and carefully defends their historic and contemporary relevance at a time when school boards are under increasing attack. He offers a number of important strategies for strengthening school boards through professional development, systemic evaluation, and enhanced relationships with school personnel, especially administrators. *Vanishing School Boards* is an important read for anyone who values community involvement in education and wants to keep the public, democratic mission of schools alive."

—**Kathy Hytten**, professor of educational leadership and cultural foundations, University of North Carolina at Greensboro

Vanishing School Boards

*Where School Boards Have Gone,
Why We Need Them, and How
We Can Bring Them Back*

Patrick Rice

ROWMAN & LITTLEFIELD EDUCATION
A DIVISION OF

ROWMAN & LITTLEFIELD
Lanham • Boulder • New York • Toronto • Plymouth, UK

Published by Rowman & Littlefield Education
A division of Rowman & Littlefield
4501 Forbes Boulevard, Suite 200, Lanham, Maryland 20706
www.rowman.com

10 Thornbury Road, Plymouth PL6 7PP, United Kingdom

British Library Cataloguing in Publication Information Available

Library of Congress Cataloging-in-Publication Data

Rice, Patrick.
  Vanishing school boards : where school boards have gone, why we need them, and how we can bring them back / Patrick Rice.
    pages cm
  Includes bibliographical references.
  ISBN 978-1-4758-0814-8 (cloth : alk. paper) -- ISBN 978-1-4758-0815-5 (pbk. : alk. paper) -- ISBN 978-1-4758-0816-2 (electronic) 1. School boards--United States. 2. School management and organization--United States. 3. Educational change--United States. I. Title.
  LB2831.R54 2013
  379.1'531--dc23
                                    2013031866

♾™ The paper used in this publication meets the minimum requirements of American National Standard for Information Sciences—Permanence of Paper for Printed Library Materials, ANSI/NISO Z39.48-1992.

Printed in the United States of America

Dedication

To my grandmother Millie Sanders, who understood the principle that God often chooses the foolish things of the world to confound the wise. And to my parents Wilkie and Laverne Rice, who instilled biblical values in my life.

Contents

Foreword

Our public schools have the responsibility to provide an educational program that assures each and every child an equal opportunity to achieve his or her full potential. Securing this mission can be very challenging due to the many changing variables that impact our society. Local school boards have a historical origin that is strongly based in representing the needs of the local constituents in assuring that a positive directional vision for the schools will be secured through local control and quality decision making. Given the present political, economic, and philosophical instability confronting our communities, our states, and our country, the local school boards' responsibility to provide strong collaborative leadership and guidance is greater than ever.

In his book *Vanishing School Boards*, Dr. Patrick Rice discusses why the school board as a local institution is critically important to the overall success of the public school. Dr. Rice composed much of his text from his firsthand experiences in observing and providing assistance to numerous local school boards through his work as a director of field services for the Illinois Association of School Boards. He has been a teacher and a building principal, and he has taught at the university level.

This book clearly explains how local boards of education serve as the collected representation of the beliefs and values of their constituents and therefore are essential to the continued existence of local control of the schools. In order to keep our system of local school boards viable and safe from the challenges of deactivation, he discusses the need to secure a stronger understanding of the function of local control and how it can and should influence the design and development of the educational program. Dr. Rice also shares data from research showing how local school boards can have a positive impact on changes in curriculum design and student performance.

Dr. Rice has clearly defined the distinct differences in the roles of the school board and the superintendent. He provides a strong emphasis on the importance of the relationship between the school board and superintendent. Dr. Rice indicates that the critical responsibility for building a strong collaborative existence between the office of the superintendent and board of education belongs to the school superintendent. Dr. Rice articulates how a high-quality relationship developed and nurtured by the superintendent directly relates to the overall success of the school's initiatives and the successful pursuit of the district's stated mission and vision.

Professional development for boards of education has and continues to be a major contributing factor to the efficient and orderly operation of the board of education. However, it can be a challenge to gain commitment from lay board members to invest in this very important responsibility of their office. Dr. Rice identifies that the school superintendent must own the responsibility for securing quality professional development for board members and provides in his book suggestions on how to secure commitment and engagement.

Dr. Rice is to be commended for pulling together a summary of research along with some excellent suggestions on how to strengthen and enhance the operation of our local school boards. He indeed has provided a contribution to the strong argument for the continued existence of this very important local institution.

—Dr. Nick Osborne
Associate Professor–Educational Administration,
Eastern Illinois University
Field Service Director, Illinois Association of School Administrators
Former Superintendent, Mount Vernon City Schools, District 80

Preface

Changes are occurring rapidly in public education. The U.S. educational system is going through a period of significant transformation, especially in the area of local control. These changes both overtly and covertly threaten to privatize the educational system through an increase of state and federal control. Some of the changes appear to be as still waters, but there is a lot of turbulence underneath.

David T. Conley, professor of Educational Policy and Leadership at the University of Oregon, expressed this sentiment best when he wrote in his book, *Who Governs Our Schools? Changing Roles and Responsibilities*, "Almost every state has been evolving from a local control of governance and finance . . . to a state system of finance, specified standards and content knowledge, and statewide tests and assessments. During this time, the federal role in education policy has become increasingly activist and, when viewed from the local perspective, intrusive" (Conley, 2003).

This book, rooted in the research literature, offers a framework for understanding how the concept of local control is being redefined and how public schools have been under attack. It is extremely challenging to determine who actually governs public schools in light of increasing state and federal authority, and more importantly, the role of school boards in the governance process. As a result of so many players in the educational marketplace, solutions concerning how to promote a quality education have led to a defragmentation of reforms with little or no consensus.

This book will inform the educational practitioners (superintendents, school board members, and education instructors) and the public why it is important that public schools are governed by local school boards. In order for school boards to survive, these audiences must create a united partnership to practice good governance principles and promote student achievement.

THE STATE OF EDUCATIONAL REFORM

The call for increased state and federal involvement in public school operations and governance comes from a variety of sources: the media, corporations, philanthropists, politicians, think tanks, researchers, and others. Collectively, these voices are demanding changes and call for "educational reform." Even the federal government is joining the ranks in school reform initiatives.

Although the federal government has been involved in education in various capacities since the Soviet launch of Sputnik and the civil rights era of the 1960s, the federal government's role in public education is steadily accelerating. It is without question that the passage of No Child Left Behind legislation and the Race to the Top federal grant fund have threatened the long-term survival and concept of local control.

In fact, the federal role in public education has been the driving force for reforms in areas such as charter schools, common standards, merit pay, teacher evaluations, and principal preparatory programs, and the pace of this force is steadily accelerating. Most of these reforms are based upon corporate-driven initiatives. With the support of organizations such as the National Education Association, the U.S. Department of Education was launched under President Jimmy Carter in 1980. At that time, it was the department's stated goal not to supersede local control.

Conservative lawmakers who opposed the formation of the U.S. Department of Education warned of a federalization of education in areas such as curriculum and personnel. Conley (2003) warned that federal educational policy would have "diverse ambitious goals that pay lip service to local control but have a series of confusing and often contradictory effects on the functioning of schools."

With so much federal involvement in public education, it is becoming increasingly unclear as to what role the school board can or should play in deciding what a quality education is. For instance, many states have adopted the new Common Core Standards in part due to federal pressure, but it will be challenging for local districts to develop their own assessments and curricula to meet the common standards. Illinois is one of several states that have redesigned student-learning standards and assessments based upon Common Core Standards, thus establishing a new statewide curriculum.

With the uniform standards and national assessment tests based on those standards, we'll have a national curriculum for the first time ever. This is a takeover of public education and the destruction of local control under the guise of "reform." In essence, local control will mean the ability to make decisions consistent with broad state and federal educational goals (Conley, 2003).

Superintendents have as much to be concerned about regarding the state of education as do school boards. More and more attention has been given to the performance of individual schools compared to that of the overall district. For instance, President Obama is seeking to increase his Race to the Top fund to service individual school reforms. Some of the reforms are so prescriptive that they threaten to change the superintendent's role from an educational leader to that of an educational manager. Nevertheless, superintendent effectiveness increasingly will be called into question if individual schools fail. In many ways, this ties the superintendent's success to the success of the building principal since the principal is the educational leader of the school.

Increasingly, superintendents are discontented with the continuous flow of new mandated reforms initiated by state and federal lawmakers. Due to the fact that many districts are already strapped for cash, many of these new mandates requiring financial resources are unfunded, making it difficult for superintendents to prepare their budgets. Furthermore, superintendents find it challenging to attempt to implement so many mandated reforms and still serve as effective instructional leaders. Because of factors such as these, superintendents are becoming more aggressive in communicating their message to state and federal officials regarding the negative impact of school mandates.

School boards should play a decisive role in determining what reforms are needed in their district to ultimately enhance student achievement. Local school boards and superintendents should be key players in promoting student achievement. When boards engage in training and maintain a good relationship with the superintendent, student achievement soars (Land, 2002; Rice, 2010).

School boards were established to collaboratively govern public schools compared to operating by top-down policies given to them by legislators who have no knowledge of local conditions and who fail to engage parents and community members in their decisions. More importantly, local school boards play a key role in the mission of schools, which is to assist in preserving our democratic republic by maintaining individual freedoms while simultaneously forging unity. To foster unity, the board assists in balancing community values of liberty, equality, and prosperity because public education has always reflected the values of our republic (Boyle and Burns, 2011).

Unfortunately, the tide against local control is rising quickly as states such as Louisiana, Michigan, and Tennessee are creating entirely new districts for low-performing schools (Samuels, 2011a). It is unclear if community stakeholders will have any role. A similar approach was put into place in New Orleans after Hurricane Katrina with the creation of the Recovery School District. Although some academic improvements were made, the district faced numerous complaints, such as not being responsive to the needs of parents (Samuels, 2011a).

WHERE ARE THE SCHOOL BOARDS?

Why have school boards vanished from the discussion of promoting student achievement and educational reform? The answer is twofold. There are many school boards that have not been successful in their governance role in conjunction with outside attacks. Concerning failures, school boards have not taken responsibility for their actions and behavior and have failed to market themselves, while others have governed in a laissez-faire manner in regard to implementing appropriate education reforms to raise student achievement. School boards have been under attack from the media, politicians, and special interest organizations, which in part exploit public education for political and financial reasons.

The intentional or unintentional consequences of these forces have led to a failure for the school board to convince communities why they are still essential. As Arnold Fege, director of Public Education

Network, noted in an article entitled "The Perception Challenge," that "The public school establishment has not done a very good job of marketing itself, providing counter viewpoints and a vision of itself. If we come out and try to respond, it's translated into whining and apologizing for a bad school system." Failure to establish a vision of their own role may also be the result of boards substituting their primary purpose of focusing on the values, mission, and goals—a proactive vision—for one that is reactive and subject to defending results and rationale used in decision making.

Role confusion between the board and administration may be due to the nature of the basic requirements to become a board member in most states, coupled with the school board's failure to commit to professional development. When school boards pursue training and professional development, they perform more efficiently and effectively, thus positively impacting student achievement (Adamson, 2012).

Because many school boards have taken a tepid approach to professional development, educational critics wonder if board members are committed to their job. If boards are going to be a player in establishing the aims of public education and not considered obsolete, they need to take responsibility for their governance, market themselves, and understand the importance of how board training can help in that mission.

A variety of sources are calling for school reform, which impacts how boards govern their districts. Although school boards in some ways created the climate by failing to establish the vision and to provide alternative viewpoints, various stakeholders have capitalized on these weaknesses by controlling the message of educational reform. Because school boards left the door open for others to define the aims of public education by being neither clear on their message nor visible, they allowed citizens to view schools through the lens of the media, politicians, and special interest groups.

AUDIENCE

This book is geared to several audiences. First, it should be extremely valuable to *superintendents*. Because superintendents are the school board's primary employees, this book offers guidance as to how superintendents can promote training with their boards in a manner that does not compromise the employer/employee relationship. In other words, superintendents must promote professional development in a manner that is not perceived as dictating to their employer. Few superintendents are taught how to work with school boards, although their success is dependent on the board's success.

According to Don McAdams (2003), president of the Center for Reform of School Systems, "Effective superintendents know that in addition to everything else they do, they must assist in leading the board to take advantage of professional development opportunities. It is a paradox. The superintendent works for the board, yet the superintendent must accept responsibility for educating the board and showing the board how to lead."

Superintendents and school boards can create and maintain a healthy relationship by understanding each other's roles and responsibilities. In an effort for the superintendent to motivate board members to pursue training, this book builds a case for the need for continuous training. The bottom line is that most superintendents want to be successful and work harmoniously with their boards.

Secondly, this book is also valuable to *school board members*. It will explain why school boards were created and their importance, the school board member role and duties, the need for training, and why citizen/school boards are the most effective means of building and maintaining community support for and control of local schools.

In an effort to minimize the confusion about how to improve public education, local school boards need to be reinvigorated. If school boards are fully empowered, they will bear the ultimate responsibility as it relates to student-achievement outcomes. Because such has not been entirely the case in public education, this book also provides a look at how current educational reforms have led to frightening levels of discontent among educational practitioners due mostly to faulty research and politically motivated agendas aimed at eroding support for public education.

Because most of the information regarding school-board governance is fragmented and the public often does not fully understand the governance structure of schools, this book coalesces various sources of information in order to make effective arguments concerning why school boards are important and what they must do to ensure their vitality.

Thirdly, this book should be helpful to *educational administration professors* who are not only teaching future superintendents about best practices in school management but are also equally concerned with teaching those future superintendents about school governance and the role of the school board. Future superintendents must understand how to work with and support their board as if their success depends on it—because it does.

Finally, this book should be valuable and insightful for citizens and parents concerning the state of public education and their role in preserving local control of their school district. It is imperative that the public be educated about its role in preserving its voice in local public education.

Michael Rochholz, board president of Schoolcraft Schools in Schoolcraft, MI, in an article entitled "The Problem School Boards Have with the Public" (2012), stated that

> The education landscape has turned into a free-for-all for politicians, billionaires and movie producers who seem insistent on creating new, unproven systems of education choices and assessment. The only way this will be reversed is if regular citizens stand up for public education and learn what they must know to participate and insist on policies that reflect community realities and the needs of all children. It is time for people to stop believing that standardized tests scores mean much, or that media spin is accurate.

When these combined audiences understand what is at stake for each of them and begin to collaborate together to advocate for local school governance, it will be possible to slow or even to stop the tide of private, state, and federal control that is eroding confidence in the U.S. public education system.

BOOK ORGANIZATION

This book will explain why school boards are needed and how to improve their work. In addition, this book will discuss the need for school board training, board member perspectives and concerns about training, and the role the superintendent should play in promoting and engaging in board training. Chapter 1 explains several problems commonly attributed to school boards. Chapters 2 and 3 examine the educational foundation that has been used to define a quality education and various educational reforms.

Chapters 4 and 5 provide four compelling reasons concerning the need for school boards. Chapters 6, 7, and 8 explore various reasons why citizens run and/or serve on the school board, why school board members should participate in board training, and school board members' perceptions and attitudes concerning school board training. Chapters 9 and 10 review the role of the superintendent in school board trainings, key training areas for the school board, and how the superintendent can build and maintain superintendent-board relationships to ensure good governance. Chapter 11 examines why school board evaluations are necessary to ensure good governance. Finally, chapter 12 explores how to build community support for professional development and local control of schools.

Part of the overall aim of this book is to inform superintendents how they can promote and participate in school board trainings and the benefits of doing so. Primarily, it is due to the fact that the superintendent's success is correlated with the success of his or her school board. By promoting training, the superintendent will further understand how to work with his or her school board and how to maintain a healthy relationship with the school board by understanding the roles and duties of each, a necessary element of effective governance. More importantly, school boards face the challenge concerning how to redefine themselves if they are to remain viable in public education in light of increasing state and federal involvement.

Because this book addresses the needs and challenges of school boards nationally, various board member survey results are cited throughout. The majority of the surveys originated from state associations of school boards and the National School Board Association. See the appendix for a brief description of the research methodology associated with the surveys.

AUTHOR'S REFLECTION

As I grow older, I have discovered the difficulty of aging. The world with which we were acquainted slowly dies. The songs, trends, and community with which we are familiar slowly evolve and do not look the same. Logically, things evolve and should evolve. Traditions, values, and beliefs often change from generation to generation, which makes our country great.

Nevertheless, there are some values that should never change, such as statements in our Declaration of Independence: "We hold these truths to be self-evident, that all men are created equal, that they are endowed by their Creator with certain unalienable rights, that among these are Life, Liberty and the pursuit of Happiness." We always must realize this value or face the consequence that our country will fail to honor our great heritage of diversity.

Similarly, we must continue to cherish and value our public schools and ensure that we always keep the public in public schools throughout all generations. This value should never change, and everyone should have a right to a free and appropriate education based in part on the values of the local community. If our citizens become less educated, the consequence will be a failed democracy. As a product of local public schools, I understand firsthand the value of public schools, and this compelled me to write this book.

The current system of school board governance dates back two hundred years to Massachusetts, when local citizens decided that the administration of towns and schools should be separate (Danzberger, 1994). Since that time, the belief in local control has been questioned and has faced strong opposition (Rice, 2010). There has been active involvement from courts, Congress, the president, mayors, governors, and business leaders in the governance process. As a result of too many players in the educational marketplace, it is unclear who actually governs public education and who ultimately should be held accountable.

A number of theories attempt to explain this invasion. Research indicates that school board governance has declined for factors such as the increasing number of state and federal mandates, private markets, not engaging in professional development, failure to provide leadership for school reforms, failure to engage the community, failure to properly understand role and duties, and the micromanagement of the superintendent. Whatever the reason(s) associated with the decrease in school board governance, the reality is that school boards are being redefined and fighting for their long-term survival.

This book illustrates the need for trained school board leaders to oversee the governance of public schools. When school boards engage in professional development and are held accountable for governing effectively as a team as well as maintaining a good relationship with the superintendent and engaging the community, student achievement soars. More importantly, there is a clear sense of accountability. Superintendents view the school board favorably, and communities serve as partners with their schools.

The bottom line is that research clearly indicates that this model works best when these conditions apply. However, if we continue to allow the role of the school board to deteriorate and/or if we experiment with other forms of school governance, there is a strong likelihood that overall school governance will continue to be chaotic, parents and other community stakeholders will increasingly become dissatisfied, there will be rampant turnover of qualified teachers and administrators, and private companies will continue to line their pockets with money.

There are few books that address school governance from the standpoint of who should be in charge of public schools. While offering great insights, these books leave it to the reader to form conclusions as to who should govern public schools. According to Kirst (2004), the country has to decide if it wants more state and federal control, little or no state or local control regarding educational curriculum, or some sort of market-based (business) model such as school vouchers and merit pay.

This book provides the answer to this question by presenting compelling reasons why locally elected school boards, if trained and held accountable, should be in charge of public schools based upon research, national surveys, and my insights as an educational practitioner.

ACKNOWLEDGMENTS

First and foremost, I would like to give thanks to my Lord and savior Jesus Christ for all of His blessings and grace. Special thanks to my family including the love of my life Crystal and daughters Diamond and Emerald. To my siblings: Wilkie, Daryl, William, and Sheila. To my cousin Ladonna Akins and lifelong friends Daimon Jones, Dorian Prophet, and Leo Smith.

Special thanks to the numerous professionals who aided me in the creation of this book, including Diane Cape, James Russell, Cathy Talbert, Dr. Dean Langdon, Jenny Harkins, John Cassel, Dr. Freddie A. Banks, Harry Mosley, Bill Mulvaney, Jeffery Campbell, Dr. Kevin Settle, Dr. Thomas Alsbury, and Dr. Nick Osborne.

Special thanks to my lifetime pastor Dr. Norman E. Owens and his wife Charlotte, Pavey Chapel C.M.E. Church, and Hopewell Baptist Church. Also, to my fraternity Alpha Phi Alpha Fraternity, Inc.

CHAPTER 1

Why School Boards Are Under Siege

Public schools have always been viewed through a microscopic lens by public and private interests. But today's teachers, administrators, and school boards have been under a siege of escalating criticism by a public demanding better returns on their educational investments of tax dollars.

Right or wrong, and regardless of how hyperbolic some of the allegations are, such criticisms have prompted state and federal lawmakers and agencies to reform teacher and administrator programs of study, to change how teachers and administrators are evaluated, and to push for uniform academic standards (Common Core Standards) intended to raise student achievement. Many states are now adopting the Common Core Standards and are linking student performance to teacher and administrator evaluations.

While most reforms have been aimed at professional educators, direct reform of school boards has been largely overlooked (Goodman and Zimmerman, 2000). That may be because little is known about school board governance. As noted by Howell (2005), "It is hardly an exaggeration to note that more is known about the operation of medieval guilds than about the institutions that govern contemporary school districts." The roles and duties of the school board and the qualifications needed to become a school board member are spelled out by law, yet the ninety-five thousand men and women who fill these positions toil rather anonymously until a classroom crisis or unpopular decision brings their policy-making role into question.

Most school board members prefer the relatively low profile of their altruistic work. The position is seldom seen as a political stepping stone; in fact, state school board associations data suggest that most school board members simply desire to give back to their communities. It is possible that lawmakers are not as critical of school boards because they have discounted the role of these local citizen representatives in the face of increasing state and federal involvement in public education. Regardless, it is clear that school boards are being left out of the national conversation concerning public education reform.

Although the discussion of school boards has been less vociferous than the discussion of teacher and administrator performance, there have been some overlapping concerns. Danzberger (1994) and Land (2002) pointed out several criticisms of school boards, including:

- Failing to provide leadership needed for reform
- Micromanaging district administrators and other personnel
- Failing to work with other social agencies
- Lacking accountability
- Failing to maintain a working relationship with the superintendent
- Lacking motivation for professional growth
- Failing to assess their performance
- Failing to obtain ongoing professional training
- Failing to govern effectively

All of these issues may have some merit, but a crucial problem facing many school boards is the tendency to micromanage the superintendent, staff, and operations. Normally, this occurs when school board members do not properly understand their roles and duties. As a result, these board members spend less time on their primary function of adopting policy and setting goals that fulfill the district's mission and more time dealing with administrative concerns (Land, 2002; Todras, 1993).

Another crucial problem facing boards is dealing with difficult board members. Difficult school board members bring the school board bad publicity and loss of credibility when the community perceives the board acting as the negative ones do.

Many critics believe that school boards were important in the eighteenth century when public schools were smaller and were often extensions of the local community church. They hold that the current system of governance is a carryover from an earlier time rather than a relevant solution in a complex global society (Rhim, 2013).

Proponents, on the other hand, would argue that school boards are important. As a nation committed to representative democracy, proponents believe that school boards, which are supported by local tax dollars, empower the community to direct the aims of public education. In other words, this nation has always believed in the concept of the words spoken by Abraham Lincoln in his Gettysburg Address that "Government of the people, by the people, and for the people shall not perish from the earth" or a popular slogan of the American Revolution proclaiming, "No taxation without representation."

School boards are stewards of the community because they are charged with making decisions on behalf of the community that reflect the values of the community. As with other representative bodies, school boards may periodically not make the very best governing decisions, but this alone is not a valid reason why they should not govern over public education. As Alsbury (2008) noted, "Indeed, if all our representative bodies were threatened with dissolution based on poor performance or general dissatisfaction, our democracy itself might not survive."

For example, in 2012 various polls indicated that the U.S. Congress's approval rating was at historic lows. Despite this reality, it may not be wise to dissolve Congress due to the potential impact it will have on our democracy. After all, according to Winston Churchill, "Democracy is the worst form of government, except for all those other forms that have been tried from time to time."

Regarding the argument that local lay people should not govern education, it must be noted that public school governance is similar to the governance structure of our nation. For instance, the U.S. military is governed by people who may or may not have military training, including the president, who is the commander in chief. Despite this fact, the U.S. military is considered to be second to none. Just as the commander in chief relies on the information from his or her generals to make decisions to govern on behalf of the country, the school board relies on the superintendent to govern on its behalf as trustees for the community.

THE DISSATISFACTION THEORY

Like most popularly elected officials, school board members generally believe that the electoral voting process is an accurate predictor of their effectiveness and tenure in office (Rice, 2010). However, it is a mistake for school board members to believe that elections alone are good indicators of their effectiveness. More often than not, voters are disengaged from the work of school boards until their work is interrupted by a negative event of great magnitude. When this occurs, it is referred to as the "Dissatisfaction Theory."

Alsbury (2004) stated, "The Dissatisfaction Theory presumes that democracy is a measure of whether citizens have a relatively unencumbered opportunity to participate. Using this definition, a system could be described as democratic and have neither vast participation by citizens nor responsiveness by the school board." As Alsbury alludes, many citizens do not vote in their school board races.

Moreover, the Dissatisfaction Theory takes over when the timing of an election is connected to local negative events. While voters can choose at any given time to be involved in school board governance, they generally choose not to do so except when they become dissatisfied with the school board. When citizens become dissatisfied, their only choice is to use the ballot box to voice their disapproval.

Reasons for Voter Dissatisfaction

There are many reasons why citizens can become dissatisfied with the incumbent school board. The school board members and superintendents in Rice's study (2010) cited superintendent-board collaboration, physical sports (e.g., funding issues), finance (negative fund balances), and lack of communication as the leading four causes of voter dissatisfaction. Ideally, there should be equal concern with issues more aligned to student achievement; nevertheless, the luxury of having school boards is that the local community can have a voice regarding a whole spectrum of school issues.

Increasingly, voters would like school board members to seek out professional development in the areas of educational governance and want them to be held accountable in their service. It is important to note that in many cases, voters are not familiar with the requirements for one to become a school board member unless the governance cycle is interrupted by a negative event (Dissatisfaction Theory), as noted by Yackera (1999). Qualifications to become a school board member in many states include general requirements, such as being a U.S. citizen, a resident of the state, and a registered voter. A detailed list of various state qualifications is located in chapter 7.

When voters become aware of the qualifications to become a board member, the research is insufficient to conclude that voters favor additional qualifications to ensure that board members are knowledgeable of their role and duties. Nevertheless, research is clear that voters would like to see school board members engage in professional development once elected to make certain that board members have the skills necessary to govern over the school system (Yackera, 1999).

And when school board members engage in professional development, public support of the school board increases. If school boards fail to engage in professional development and do not market themselves better, the perceived need for school boards will continue to deteriorate, and more citizens may favor alternatives as to who should govern public education.

SCHOOL BOARD MEMBER TURNOVER AND THE ELECTION PROCESS

It is vital that school board members understand how participating in training opportunities can limit school board member turnover. When school boards understand their role and duties and govern accordingly, community dissatisfaction is limited, which is a factor associated with school board member turnover that ultimately negatively affects student achievement. For instance, on the average in Washington State, there is a 30% board turnover during each election with 25% due to political reasons and retirement (Alsbury, 2004).

Voter dissatisfaction with the school board and/or the district could lead to changes in the district's direction. Often when voter dissatisfaction reaches its acme, a correlation exists between politics and the operation of public schools, such as school board member elections and their impact on the operation of public schools. Politically motivated school board turnover often results in superintendent administrative changes, which impact key areas such as student achievement.

For instance, according to Alsbury (2008), newly elected superintendents hired as a result of vast changes on the governance team often are not clear about the goals of the board and frequently do the following:

- Change the organizational structure in areas such as personnel, programs, finance, curriculum, student assessment, and facilities
- Authorize job reassignments
- Transfer staff to alternate grade levels
- Transfer school administrators to alternative buildings and positions
- Facilitate school reconfiguration

These changes inhibit the goal-setting process that shapes the district's improvement plan and damage morale of district administrators and staff. Besides negatively impacting student achievement, this type of political turnover also brings about instability in the delivery of education.

SPECIAL INTEREST GROUPS AND THE ELECTION PROCESS

Public school advocates are concerned with the role special interest groups play in local school board elections and their influence on state and federal legislators. Wealthy donors such as former New York City Schools Chancellor Joel I. Klein and powerful groups such as StudentsFirst have spent large amounts of money in school board races hoping to advance educational reforms such as charter schools (McNeil, 2013b). In 2011, over two million dollars was spent on school board elections in Denver, Colorado; Wake County, North Carolina; and Fairfax County, Virginia, and $5.2 million in the Los Angeles Unified School District by special interest groups (Stover, 2012a).

Filmmaker Robert Greenwald appeared on the cable TV network MSNBC's Ed Shultz's show August 15, 2011, to discuss how the Koch brothers financed school board elections in Wake County, North Carolina. The Koch brothers own Koch Industries, a U.S. private energy conglomerate with subsidiaries in manufacturing, trading, and investments. The program reported that the Koch brothers financed candidates who were opposed to utilizing busing as a tool to desegregate schools.

Special interest groups are increasingly lobbying state and federal lawmakers as well. Stand for Children, a political action committee based in Oregon, collected approximately $3.5 million for legislative races in Illinois and issued candidates' donations ranging from $10,000 to $175,000. According to Johnson (2011), Stand for Children founder Jonah Edelman bragged on camera about how simple it was to persuade Illinois lawmakers with monetary donations.

Although there is nothing wrong with wanting to be involved in the educational process, there is concern about how special interest groups attempt to influence the process, such as using large monetary incentives. Throughout Illinois, many educators believe that Stand for Children influence assisted in the passage of Senate Bill 7, which makes it harder for Chicago teachers to strike by eliminating the fact-finding process, minimizing tenure rights, and linking teacher performance to student performance (Wheeler, 2011).

Although most school board candidates primarily finance their own campaigns, followed by receiving donations from friends and family, increasingly school board candidates in urban cities are becoming dependent upon donations from teacher unions, special interest groups, and corporate sponsors (Alsbury, 2008). This door, which is open to special interest groups, will, if left open, leave elected school board members vulnerable to the aims of such interest groups as those who advocate for vouchers and charter schools.

The Supreme Court ruled in 2010 that corporations, unions, and private individuals can donate freely to political campaign elections (Liptak, 2010). This practice, some may argue, suggests that democracy is for sale within the United States, as corporations may find it easier to mobilize and finance sympathetic candidates who serve their best interests.

Even the 2012 presidential election tested the influence that special interest groups have on the election process. Super political action committees spent more than $840 million on the presidential election (Beckel and Russ, 2012). *Time* magazine (August 2012) captured the peculiarity of the 2012 presidential campaign in its front-page headline entitled "For Sale: Asking $2.5 Billion—How to Buy the White House."

Conservative and "progressive" candidates who believe in social justice and equality get the advantage of this spending, as many of them favor student vouchers, charter schools, merit pay for teachers, and turnaround models of school reform (Barkan, 2011; Greenblatt, 2011; Stover, 2012a). Educators should wonder if education reform will be based solely on the strength of special interest groups and on the financing that supports them, and how local communities can successfully mobilize against them. The only way to ensure local success is through the leadership of locally elected school boards.

THE ESCALATION OF STATE AND FEDERAL INVOLVEMENT

Another major problem facing school boards is the escalation of federal and state involvement in public education. State involvement in schools in many ways is directly tied to the expanded federal role in education. Prior to 1960, most state boards of education were small in size and primarily operated to ensure local district compliance to state and federal law (Conley, 2003).

According to Conley (2003), although the federal government has significantly expanded its role in public education, the government cannot implement any reforms without the support of the state to implement and/or monitor reforms. Thus, federal monies poured into various states to carry out federal reforms such as Title 1, special education, bilingual and migrant education, vocational education, and other school improvement initiatives.

Similarly, state boards of education cannot efficiently carry out any reforms without the support of local school districts. For any reform to be successful, it is vital that local districts take a lead role in guiding and facilitating the process. To implement reforms successfully and to foster creativity, a strong relationship is vital among the state, federal, and local government. States and federal governments can learn what is working from various districts and what changes may be needed in various policies to assist local districts (Conley, 2003).

As noted earlier, many states are carrying out reforms and other mandates on school districts on behalf of the Federal Department of Education, especially when there are financial incentives. In light of this, legislators in various states sponsor hundreds if not thousands of educational bills independent of federal influence, many of which are unfunded and become law. How can districts operate and school boards govern effectively when they are constantly bombarded with new mandates requiring time, money, and other resources from local districts?

Truthfully speaking, this does not mean that certain mandates do not have validity. However, states and the federal government are too far removed to know what is best for each school district and are not able to monitor their own policies. For example, in less than three months, the Illinois General Assembly introduced dozens of bills in 2013 impacting public education, including bills to (www.ilga.gov):

- Require school boards to redefine "zero tolerance"
- Require school boards to adopt a policy limiting tackling in football practice
- Require coaches to complete a sudden cardiac arrest training course
- Require a school district to utilize a certified nurse if the nurse will provide any recommendations on a student's Individualized Education Program
- Require school districts to include a storm shelter
- Require school districts to provide twenty minutes of recess per day in grades K through 5
- Require that class sizes be no more than twenty-seven
- Require school boards to report to local responders any renovations or floor plan changes in the district's buildings
- Require guidance counselors and school teachers to receive in-service on mental illness

Sadly, these are some of the bills that originated in Illinois in less than three months, simultaneous to school district budgets being cut. If this transpired in three months, what other bills could originate and potentially pass in Illinois during the remainder of the fiscal year? Unfortunately, Illinois is symbolic of what is occurring in other states as well.

Local superintendents and highly effective school boards understand the value and importance of collaborating with various stakeholders to address educational concerns. Unfortunately, what is troublesome in the current reform movement is that it is based upon a top-down model where the federal government directs the states, which, in turn, direct local districts that often have little to no input. All too often, many superintendents and other educators view the federal role as intrusive and counterproductive in fostering creativity (Kay, 2011).

Similar to superintendents and local school boards, states are increasingly seeing the federal government role as an intrusion on states' rights regarding oversight of education, even though the U.S. Constitution cedes to states the authority to regulate local education. Yet in many ways, the federal government has been circumventing this authority under the guise of providing for the general welfare of U.S. citizens.

In a recent example, the U.S. Department of Education pondered the idea of allowing individual school districts to file for No Child Left Behind (NCLB) waivers rather than the states that oversee them (McNeil, 2012a). State educational chiefs were appalled when they heard of this consideration at a meeting of the Council of Chief State School Officers, and they informed the Education Secretary that this authority should rest with the state rather than with individual districts.

Is it undemocratic for the U.S. Department of Education to directly oversee districts and bypass state and local communities without giving voice to the people in those affected communities? Right or wrong, it is evident that Secretary Duncan believes that the U.S. Department of Education should directly oversee or monitor some public schools as the department will issue out more than four hundred million dollars in Race to the Top competitive grant funds for districts. To qualify, local districts have to submit individualized classroom instruction plans as well as college and career readiness plans to the Department of Education that align with the department's educational reform agenda.

Ideally, the federal government can set various conditions when states apply for and accept federal monies. However, considering that most states have been operating in the red, many of them believed they had no other choice but to submit to additional federal regulation. Some would call this coercion. Interestingly, U.S. Supreme Court Justice Samuel Alito lectured and posed a question to White House officials during a debate concerning at what point the federal government acknowledges that it is being coercive. Alito posed a question to federal attorneys when he stated,

"Now, this is a great offer, and we think you will take it," Justice Alito said. "But of course, if you take it, it's going to have some conditions because we are going to set rules on teacher tenure, on collective bargaining, on curriculum, on textbooks, class size, school calendar, and many other things. So take it or leave it." The states could say no, but they would have to pay the federal education tax plus come up with their own money to replace the federal dollars they declined, the justice added. "Would that be the point where financial inducement turns into coercion?" (Walsh, 2012)

Because the federal government has the power of the purse, should it be able to dictate to states without collaboration? Most think not.

Increasingly, more states are forfeiting their role to the federal government to increase student achievement because states are bankrupt of ideas as to how to meet increasing targets set forth in NCLB. As a result, the federal government is significantly impacting many districts across the country as states submit plans to the government for approval concerning who will teach in their schools, how students will be tested, how teachers may be fired, and which schools may be closed down due to policies originated by bureaucrats and politicians from Washington (Ramirez, 2010). It appears that the federal government is happy with this arrangement and continues to intercede in state and local educational politics.

Public education advocates have been quite critical of the role Secretary Duncan has played in advancing the federal reach into local education. Public education advocates believe that Secretary Duncan has not only advanced the federal role but in many instances has overstepped his authority. For example, Secretary Duncan pressured Washington, D.C., mayor Vincent Gray to keep Kaya Henderson as the district's chancellor and urged the Detroit City Council to place a question on the ballot entailing handing over control of the city schools to the mayor (McNeil, 2011a). Is this the appropriate role for the Secretary of Education and the Department of Education, or should these decisions be left up to local communities? Most educators prefer the latter.

Associations such as the National School Boards Association (NSBA) have voiced dissent directly to Secretary Duncan, warning of a federal overreach into local control during the association's annual legislative conference in Washington, D.C. Members present at the conference complained to Secretary Duncan about the department's enamored support for charter schools compared to public schools, the issuing of waivers to NCLB with stringent strings attached, and the undermining of local control. In a cavalier fashion, Secretary Duncan informed the conference participants that he would stand firm regarding all of his past initiatives originating since his first term (McNeil, 2013b).

In view of Duncan's statement, critics of the department's educational agenda deserve to have their voices heard. Their voices should be heard concerning why the department is investing in teacher evaluation systems, the use of which use is not supported by research. Critics' voices should be heard concerning why the department favors charter over traditional public schools when charter schools have not made substantial improvements. Their voices should be heard concerning why states must apply for waivers from NCLB with stringent strings attached when the Department of Education readily admits that it is impossible for states to meet the requirements of NCLB.

Because the NSBA feels that its message of local control has fallen on deaf ears with the Department of Education, the NSBA has drafted legislation recognizing the role of local school boards and local districts in designing, developing, and delivering educational services for U.S. students (NSBA, 2013). By allowing school boards to continue to govern over public education, the public voice will be heard as school boards provide an accessible level of government (Alsbury, 2008).

Understanding the Impacts of Bureaucracy on Education

It is impractical for state and federal governments to continue to make decisions regarding public schools without the input of local school boards. The state and federal government must realize their limitations in attempting to reform schools and the chaos this has caused in public school governance. To alleviate this problem, state and federal governments must work with local school boards in establishing common educational goals. For instance, it may be beneficial for the federal and/or state government to provide limited oversight and direction to schools by investing in educational research while local school boards can ensure the application of that oversight.

If state and federal governments continue in not soliciting school boards' input into educational decisions, state and federal mandates may be enacted to the letter, but the spirit of the law will be missing, yielding its own consequences regarding the effectiveness of these mandates (Conley, 2003).

Because of the increasing bureaucracy in education, many people are beginning to wonder if local control is slipping away given the increase in state and more specifically federal mandates. To illustrate this point, Matt Winkle, a board member from Batavia, IL, noted the impact of federal mandates on his district. Winkle (2010) made the following statement: "Local boards are paralyzed by legislation resulting in the outsourcing of major decisions to higher levels of government. Power is becoming more and more centralized, and decisions are being pushed further from the point of impact. Boards are relegated to fine-tuning the lens, while state officials and the feds decide what the big picture is and where the focus should be."

With so much interest and shared responsibility, conflicts in educational governance are bound to emerge as well. In 2004, a conflict emerged in Florida as a result of a federal court ruling regarding desegregation in schools and public school choice provided by NCLB. The federal court had a bone of contention in attempting to achieve racial balance and remain in compliance with NCLB (DeBray, 2005).

There are several other conflicts as well. NCLB is at odds with the federal Individuals with Disabilities Education Act in that NCLB imposes uniform requirements for all students to reach proficiency by 2014. Ninety-five percent of students in all of the testing school subgroups must take the test in order for adequate yearly progress (AYP) to be valid. The conflict arises as special education students are subjected to the same standards as nondisabled students, and these scores determine if a school will be eligible in making AYP (Kraus, n.d.).

THE PRIVATIZATION OF PUBLIC EDUCATION

An increasing number of education advocates believe that business leaders are manufacturing a crisis in education in order for their companies to profit from the solutions available from efficiency-producing entrepreneurs. McKenzie and Scheurich (2004) described these intentions like this: "Capitalism has become hyperaggressive in its search for lucrative new markets, and it is now trying to colonize what were once considered public (democratic) spheres of social activity, like schools."

In their search for potential new markets, such businesses cater to parents as consumers by offering them more "choice" in the form of vouchers and specialized charter schools. In short, business reformers lure parents by appealing to their individual needs and freedoms. The challenge private enterprise poses to school boards is that school boards attempt to govern based primarily on equality values because they have to accept all students.

The incentive for private firms to become primary education providers is simple: profit. But is that what public education has become? Urschel (2003) characterized this as follows:

> Choice writ large is the value of consumerism; entrepreneurial capital; investment in my future, not yours; investment in my children, not other people's children. We have made the consumer king! Consequently, the lines are blurring between what is public and what is private. We are transforming public education from a public good into a private individual good. We are witnessing and participating in the "Pepsi-ization" of public education!

Yes, parental choice should be respected and considered, but the institution of locally elected school boards is the only means available to promote what is collectively best for the public good.

Advocates of public education view "parent trigger" as the newest scheme to privatize public schools. States that have parent trigger laws allow a majority of parents to significantly reform a school often through private charter conversion. Private foundations such as the Walton Family Foundation have financed parent groups whose aim is to spread the concept of parent trigger. Although California was the first state to adopt a parent trigger law, to date more than a dozen other states are considering parent trigger laws (Ujifusa, 2013a).

When individual freedoms outweigh equality freedoms, it is extremely difficult, if not impossible, to accommodate both in a single mission. Boyle and Burns (2011) offer a hypothetical example of a liberty-centered vision of public education:

- Dismantle federal and state laws regulating education
- Tax credits for public, private, or home schooled students
- No federal or state intervention regarding homeschooling
- Do away with mandatory attendance laws
- Allow private companies to manage schools
- Maximize parental choice
- Empower parents to approve books and reading assignments
- Empower parents to teach their children values and sex education
- Allow parents to decide how their educational tax dollars should be spent

How Private Companies Profited from Public Schools Not Making Adequate Yearly Progress

Private enterprise has made hefty profits from public education since the passage of NCLB, which requires districts not making AYP to pay tutorial aid, costing districts millions of dollars. AYP is the term used to describe specific, gradual steps taken to reach 100% proficiency in reading and math as measured by a multiple choice style test.

According to NCLB legislation, each school and each subgroup within the school (such as minority populations, special education students, and English-as-a-second-language students) must be 100% proficient by 2014. This federal requirement literally means that if even one student does not meet standards by 2014, the entire school is regarded as failing.

According to the NCLB legislation, districts that do not make AYP for two years must offer and pay for Supplemental Educational Services. While such tutorial programs are designed to provide academic assistance to at-risk students, many reports have surfaced of tutors with inadequate experience, providers demonstrating poor coordination with teachers, companies lacking oversight by state educational agencies, and companies rating their own performance (Jacobson, 2011). Ironically, school districts were forced to spend money on tutorial programs with no accountability rather than providing greater accountability, which was one of the primary purposes of NCLB.

Private Investment in Public Education

Instead of local school boards facilitating the discussion concerning the overall direction of public education, the conversation is increasingly dominated by influential private stakeholders. Philanthropists such as the Bill and Melinda Gates Foundation, the Eli and Edythe Broad Foundation, and the Walton Family Foundation spend over four billion dollars annually to promote public education "reforms" (Barkan, 2011; Greenblatt, 2011).

Often these philanthropists supported the following reforms, with little or no input from the community: corporate connected charter schools, voucher programs, mayoral control, high-stakes standardized testing for students, merit pay for teachers based upon student test scores, terminating teachers and administrators, closing down schools when test scores do not improve, increasing the number of teachers with alternative certification, and longitudinal data collection based upon teacher and student performance (Barkan, 2011; Greenblatt, 2011).

Instead of wealthy, powerful "venture philanthropic" individuals and organizations dictating to middle- and lower-income communities about how to improve their schools, perhaps their money will be better spent in ensuring the elimination of poverty and creating economic opportunities to get Americans back to work. In fact, research is crystal clear that poverty is a major factor in overcoming the achievement gap (Payne, 2003). When poverty exists among families, the cycle often continues.

This "venture philanthropic" influence is not limited to financial contributions. The federal education department not only embraces the involvement of the Gates Foundation as an active partner to reform public education, it has even hired Gates staffers to assist (Hong, 2009). Margot M. Rogers, former assistant to the director of education for the Gates Foundation, later served as chief of staff to Education Secretary Arne Duncan. James Shelton, formerly a program director for the Gates Foundation, currently serves as the Assistant Deputy Education Secretary for Innovation and Improvement.

Moreover, Secretary Duncan hired those coming from the staffs of other "venture philanthropic" advocacy groups and school management organizations they fund for top positions in the Department of Education (Schniedewind and Sapon-Shevin, 2012). Some critics have reason to believe that corporations and foundations are playing a major role in developing the nation's educational strategy and believe that Bill Gates is actually managing the Department of Education (Greenblatt, 2011).

A similar argument is made by Joanne Barkan in her article "Got Dough? How Billionaires Rule Our Schools" (2011) and by Ginger Wheeler in "School Reform: Beyond Silver Bullets, Capes" (2011). Both conclude that today's reformers are more likely billionaires and political appointees—not educational professionals and researchers—often with little actual experience in the classroom. Unfortunately, voters have limited access to the private foundations, politicians, and other organizations that are determining the fate of public education (Ravitch, 2010).

Market Ideology versus Public Values

Despite the concerns associated with market-based systems to reform public education, support for these systems has accelerated and been supported by federal and state policy. Michael Engel (2000), author of the book *The Struggle for Control of Public Education: Market Ideology vs. Democratic Values*, states, "Behind the façade of progressive rhetoric, advocates of these corporate models have succeeded in imposing their definition of school reform through federal and state policymakers. As a result, communities lose control of their schools, teachers lose control of their work, and students lose control of their futures."

Engel quoted Jonathan Kozol in his argument that "The struggle for control of public education is a highly charged, politically important work, written with clarity and courage, in defense of public education as a legacy endangered by the juggernaut of corporate control."

It would be naïve to suggest that there have not always been capitalistic interests in public education. But educational practitioners wonder why there is a need to invest in new systems rather than improving the current systems or why voters are told that student achievement can only be achieved through market-based approaches such as competition (charters), privatization, and school choice (Benjamin and Trout, 2011).

This reality exists because most critics of public education are seeing less value associated with education as a public, democratic good compared to its purpose as a private, economic good. That's why Boyle and Burns (2011) noted that democratic values are necessary for defending public schools:

Alexis de Tocqueville predicted that private interest would more than ever become the chief, if not the only, driving force behind all behavior in modern society. Our contemporary debate and discussion about public education focuses more on education as a private, economic good than as a public good. This focus encourages us to see public education as an economic investment; to emphasize individual student achievement, albeit in aggregated form; to think of ways to privatize public schools; to operate public schools and classrooms in accord with market principles; and to seek to give education a competitive edge.

To solve this dilemma between these two competing purposes, U.S. voters have to determine what kind of society we hope to become. If we believe that public education should be a public democratic good based in part on community expectations, then locally elected school boards are vital because they govern public education as trustees for the community. If we believe that public education should evolve into a private economic good, then we have to do away with laws regulating education and simply allow the market to have full access to our schools.

SUMMARY

Teachers and administrators have been at the heart of the discussion concerning educational reform efforts. While the role of the school board in the educational process has been less frequently discussed than that of teachers and administrators, there have been some concerns regarding their lack of commitment to professional development and their micromanagement of the superintendent.

School board members as elected officials must understand the concept of the Dissatisfaction Theory if they hope to remain in office. Dissatisfaction Theory presumes that all citizens have the opportunity to participate in a democracy (election), although their participation varies based upon the significance of local negative events that resonate with them.

In view of this reality, school boards can be proactive by engaging in professional development so that they can be better prepared to develop policy to manage the affairs of the district and to deal with voter discontent. If school boards do not pursue training to enhance school board governance, they may continue to see their role diminished by state, federal, and other governance systems as school boards fail to justify their involvement in educational matters. Also, if school board members fail to take advantage of training opportunities, they are at a higher risk for school board member turnover, which leads to superintendent turnover as well.

There are several other problems that impact the role of the school board. Within the last decade or so, special interest groups and private enterprise have played a major role in educational reform issues. The Bill and Melinda Gates Foundation, the Eli Edythe Foundation, and the Walton Foundation spend a yearly average of four billion dollars seeking to influence public education. Although all stakeholders should have a voice in the educational process, it is unhealthy for those groups or individuals with financial resources to dominate the conversation of school reform efforts.

Despite the traditional problems that have always confronted school boards, school boards are faced with a new challenge of how to govern in light of increased federal and state involvement. Due to the efforts of special interest groups and private enterprise, state and federal lawmakers have increased their involvement in public schools, often resulting in bureaucracy and a misunderstanding of roles and duties between the school board and the state and federal government.

Interestingly, although lawmakers are primarily responsible for creating the bureaucracy in public schools, most have supported the creation of charter schools based on the premise that charter schools need to be exempt from much of the state and federal bureaucracy in order to increase student achievement outcomes for students. If having a locally determined mission and freedom from state and federal mandates is the answer, why not give all public schools these options as well?

QUESTIONS FOR REFLECTION

1. List and describe various problems confronting school boards.
2. What is the Dissatisfaction Theory, and why should school boards be aware of this theory?
3. How does school board member turnover impact student achievement?

4. Should special interest groups be allowed to influence the educational process? If so, to what extent? Are there any possible disadvantages?
5. Should state and federal officials implement educational reform measures without the support of local school boards?
6. Explain how federal policies and oversight have created significant governance issues for local districts.
7. What is meant by education being a private, economic good compared to a public, democratic good?
8. Describe how private investments influence public education policy in the United States.

CHAPTER 2

A Look at What Comprises a Quality Education

If asked, most Americans would agree that all students need a quality education to become productive and viable citizens. This is such a simple premise, but it begs many complex questions:

- How do we determine what a quality education looks like?
- How do we determine student success?
- Who decides what is needed to improve public education?
- What regulations or standards are needed to assure that all states, districts, schools, and classrooms are complying?

It appears that the federal government is deciding what a quality education looks like, and, with decreasing input from states and even less from local school boards, it is attempting to answer the remaining questions as well.

Many local school boards disagree with the federal definition and goals for "quality education." According to a nationwide survey entitled "School Boards Circa 2010: Governance in the Accountability Era" (Hess and Meeks, 2010), local school board members have very different priorities on how to increase student achievement. In fact, many school board members rate strong leadership and professional development as more important factors in boosting student achievement than touted reforms such as charter schools, performance pay for teachers, and year-round school (Samuels, 2011d).

Superintendents are just as concerned that state and federal legislators have stifled, rather than supported, local district innovation (Kay, 2011).

These superintendents believe districts should be focusing on the four Cs: critical thinking, communication, collaboration, and creativity.

Districts that have made significant achievement gains based on the four Cs have local initiatives such as student understanding by design, curriculum mapping, professional learning communities, project-based learning, and various locally designed rubrics to gauge and improve learning. More importantly, these reforms were formulated by partnering with stakeholders from the community and supported by local boards (Kay, 2011).

THE EMPHASIS ON READING AND MATH

In defining a quality education, it appears that the Department of Education believes that students need to be competent only in reading and math to be successful, productive citizens. With the emphasis on reading and math, little or no attention has been given to other subjects such as social studies, science, music, and art. According to Diane Ravitch's 2010 book, *The Death and Life of the Great American School System: How Testing and Choice Are Undermining Education*, quality education should include a strong liberal arts curriculum.

Schools need to be in the business of educating the whole child, which includes community expectations. To foster quality education, we need local community input facilitated by school boards that sit in trust for the community and not an educational achievement blueprint dictated by politicians, many of whom are influenced by powerful foundations. With so much emphasis placed on reading and math, our students are ignorant about current events, science, world governments, economics, world cultures, and other important human contributions to the arts.

School boards are becoming increasingly hesitant to allow their educators to teach subjects besides math and reading because of state and federal mandates (Ravitch, 2010). Sadly, most public schools had to defund programs in areas such as the vocational education, art, music, and sport programs on which many communities base their pride and identity. As a former student of East St. Louis District 189, I know firsthand how the district and the community were proud of their stellar athletic programs and jazz bands, to name a few. In fact, I attended East St. Louis Lincoln Senior High School, a predominantly black high school that was well known for its jazz band, basketball, and track programs.

With the emphasis on reading and math, athletic and music programs were defunded in East St. Louis District 189 as well as in other cities. Sadly, programs such as these motivated students to be more engaged academically at school, because students could not participate if they failed to maintain a passing grade point average.

It has also been my experience that rural schools witnessed defunding of vocational education, which was significant to various rural communities (carpentry, farming, mechanics, and welding). By shrinking the curriculum, educators fear that students will become increasingly disinterested in public education.

No Child Left Behind (Adequate Yearly Progress) Waiver Process

Education Secretary Arne Duncan noted that 80% of the country's schools will not make adequate yearly progress (AYP) based upon No Child Left Behind's (NCLB's) faulty assessment measures in meeting AYP targets. What is interesting about this confession is that Secretary Duncan is willing to offer states relief from key aspects of the law by offering waivers—if states agree to specific federal provisions, including curricular decisions.

On September 23, 2012, President Obama outlined the procedures to qualify for NCLB waivers. In exchange for relief from some NCLB requirements, the government will require states to adopt standards for college and career readiness, focus improvement efforts on 15% of the lowest performing schools including personnel changes, and align teacher evaluations to student performance (McNeil and Klein, 2011).

Due to federal demands, many educators believe that their states are being pressured to accept the federal provisions of centralizing educational decisions because there is no way of succeeding with existing NCLB regulations. Besides, many states are so financially strapped that they are in no real position to turn down federal funds. Once these funds are accepted, the federal government will regulate vital educational decisions previously reserved for state and local school boards.

Without question, many educators see federal waivers as a tool to coerce states to go along with the Department of Education by enabling them to request exemptions from an AYP goal, which Secretary Duncan admits is unrealistic. According to Duncan, if states fail to obtain a waiver, more than 80% of schools will not succeed in reaching AYP. As a penalty, schools will be required to spend money on tutorial services, school choice, and school restructuring measures.

Educators in Illinois are watching more and more of their schools fail to reach AYP. For instance, 99% of Illinois high schools failed to make AYP in 2011 (Rossi, 2011). Overall, more than 720 schools are on the state's academic watch list for failing to meet AYP targets. Simultaneously, several of these schools are on the state honor roll for making improvement gains (Dunn, 2011). However, according to NCLB, these schools are regarded as failures despite the gains that were made.

Due to various state and federal mandates, districts that continuously miss AYP targets face severe sanctions such as closure or transformation into a charter school. Conflicts like this emerge when there is too much government bureaucracy. In an effort to minimize bureaucracy, local school boards should continue to work collaboratively with the state board of education to identify schools that are doing well and/or need improvement and offer resources to assist accordingly.

The government must realize its own limitations and exhibit more faith and trust in those who govern closer to the people. Without this realization, more bureaucracy will be added to an already complex governing system.

The debate concerning how to reform the Elementary and Secondary Act, which contains the NCLB Act, has created some interesting bedfellows. The National Education Association (NEA), which supported Obama's presidential election and has traditionally supported the Democratic Party, agrees with the Republican Party concerning key changes in the Elementary and Secondary Act. Specifically, the NEA agrees with Senator Alexander that districts should be allowed to submit plans to their respective states rather than to the U.S. Secretary of Education concerning how to turn around low-performing schools.

According to Alexander, school districts should be accountable to their state department of education rather than follow prescriptive measures established by the federal department. The NEA and GOP also supported the dismissal of an amendment sponsored by Democrats that would have mandated states to craft teacher evaluations based in part on student performance (Klein, 2011a).

As states try to become compliant with federal and state mandates, more and more districts are pursuing waivers, leading to protests by some states. States such as Montana are becoming defiant in complying with the government's goal of meeting 100% by 2014. State Superintendent of Education for Montana Denise Juneau informed the U.S. Department of Education that she refuses to raise the state AYP goal to meet the unrealistic AYP requirements of the NCLB law (Associated Press, 2011a).

Nevertheless, in the spirit of compromise with the department, she agreed to raise the standards minimally so that the impact would not be as intense (Klein and McNeil, 2011). Other states that have protested include Idaho and South Dakota. Idaho's education chief, Tom Luna, informed the U.S. Department of Education that Idaho has no intention of complying with the current AYP law, waiver or no waiver (McNeil, 2011b).

Should other states follow Montana's and Idaho's example and denounce meeting such unrealistic AYP benchmarks, waiver or no waiver? Some appear to be leaning that way. Minnesota is another state seeking a waiver of NCLB requirements. To date, half of Minnesota's schools have not made AYP, and seventy-one of those are in corrective action due to the unrealistic goals of NCLB (Albert Lea Tribune, 2011).

Michigan and Tennessee are also seeking waivers from the government (McNeil, 2011b). As a consequence, states are expected to intervene with struggling schools, but most states are experiencing financial difficulties that will limit their involvement in their schools.

THE EMPHASIS ON TESTS

There have been positives and negatives associated with standardized tests. Supporters believe that tests promote accountability and measure student and teacher progress. However, critics believe that standardized tests narrow the curriculum, are not valid indicators of student and teacher performance, and demoralize the teaching profession. Practitioners, specifically teachers, see little benefit to standardized tests and do not believe they are an accurate indicator of what students know. Most teachers believe that many students do not take standardized tests seriously, especially in a culture that links tests to student and teacher performance (Rebora, 2012).

Regardless of which side of the fence one may be on regarding standardized tests, it is undeniable that tests are primarily used to gauge student learning and in some cases student promotion. Increasingly, more states are retaining third graders in an effort to assist struggling readers based upon a single state test. Oklahoma is one of several states that recently adopted reading policies that retain third graders if they cannot pass a state-mandated test (Robelen, 2012). Since the passage of NCLB, annual state spending on standardized tests has risen from $423 million to almost $1.1 billion in 2008 (Vu, 2008).

During the summer of 2011, educators, parents, and other educational activists marched to Washington, D.C., to protest the educational policy of the federal Department of Education and specifically its emphasis on test-based accountability. Teachers and other organizers who attended the rally voiced concern that current U.S. educational policy restricts educators from teaching anything besides how to prepare students to fill in bubbles on mandatory state tests. Equally important, organizers believed that teachers are constantly singled out as the scapegoat for society's ills (Robelen, 2011a).

Does standardized testing actually limit the curriculum as argued by the protesters? Since 2001, school districts have reduced instruction in science, social studies, and the arts in order to increase instructional time in reading and math (Ravitch, 2010). When the curriculum is narrowed, it leads to a "creativity crisis" among students because students have been conditioned for rote learning (Zagursky, 2011).

Among the protesters were many who supported President Obama's bid for the office of president, including actor Matt Damon, who has expressed his hope that the Obama administration will change direction from Bush's NCLB and the overreliance on test scores. Sadly, organizers were disappointed that Obama not only did not change direction from the Bush policies regarding education, he actually exacerbated them (Robelen, 2011a).

School boards are also voicing concerns regarding the overusage of standardized tests to gauge student learning. Over 525 Texas school boards signed a national resolution indicating that standardized testing has narrowed the curriculum, encouraged teaching to the test, reduced the love for learning, and helped drive students and educators out of the profession. Texas school boards believe that there should be multiple forms of assessment to monitor student learning rather than a single indicator test (Parents for Public Schools, 2012).

Tests should be used primarily as assessment tools to improve instruction rather than as a punitive approach for educators and a determinant to school closings. When tests are used in this fashion, it encourages cheating (Toppo, 2011). In addition, because standardized tests have been used for stringent accountability purposes instead of as assessment tools, people who question the validity of tests to gauge student learning and teacher performance are often accused of taking a pacifist approach to improving schools (Foster, 2012).

Research has shown that students may make gains on a standardized test because those students are trained to take a specific test, but core knowledge often is not transferred to other tests such as the federal National Assessment of Education Progress test, for which students did not prepare (Ravitch, 2010). The 2001 Brookings Institution study also found that standardized tests are unreliable in determining student performance. The study noted that over 50% of yearly standardized test score improvements did not lead to long-term changes in student learning (Olson, 2001).

Regardless of whether or not standardized tests are accurate indicators of student learning, state and federal pressure has led districts to teach shortcuts and other schemes in an effort to post gains on a standardized test. Philip Roby (2011), executive director of the department of secondary schools at the National Catholic Educational Association, noted the pressure teachers and administrators are under to post gains on standardized tests:

> To increase overall test results, a common scheme is to give special focus to students who score at percentages just above or below the passing rate on pretests. By focusing on these subgroups, and by teaching to the upcoming standardized tests, teachers, instructional coaches, and school

administrators do everything they can to coax and drill pupils to the passing point. Schools that show marked improvement are often held up as models of success, regardless of whether students retain the information they were tested on.

In addition to this testing strategy noted by Roby, some educators are being in-serviced to teach students to look for repeated words in a text to determine the main idea of the reading passage. Is this true learning or simply beating the system? Regardless of the reality, the fact is that we are a test-crazy society and are demoralizing our youth. For instance, educational reformers frequently compare the United States to other countries, such as South Korea, that are perceived as outperforming U.S. students in the area of math. In light of this reality, public school reformers advocate for more rigorous testing to determine if U.S. students are making additional gains in math.

However, reformers should note that the government of South Korea is banning after-hours tutoring because of concerns that the overemphasis on testing is demoralizing and decreasing innovation of their youth (Rebora, 2011). State Superintendent Chris Koch of Illinois agrees with the argument that students in the United States are overly tested. Koch stated, "I would argue probably in the United States, we're testing too much. Countries that are exceeding us [in international tests] are not testing every child every year in every grade. Instead, they are choosing to put their education resources elsewhere" (Rossi, 2011). If we continue to demoralize our students by overemphasizing tests, the outcome will be detrimental to the future of our country.

Testing and Preschoolers

Due to the emphasis on high-stakes standardized tests, preschool advocates are concerned that such tests will be used with preschoolers to determine the success of new Race to the Top early learning competitive grant dollars (Kelleher, 2011). Preschool advocates' concerns may be well founded. The Department of Education released Head Start grant rules November 9, 2011, which took effect December 9, 2011.

According to the rules, preschool grant programs are required to formulate and implement school-readiness goals, which include an emphasis on reading, cognition, and general knowledge; approaches to learning, physical well-being, and motor development; and social and emotional development (Sparks, 2011b).

Besides dealing with the implementation and assessment of readiness goals, the federal government now requires Head Start providers to compete for grant funding. Providers who have been in operation for decades are now being told they do not qualify because of minor compliance issues. As with closing down schools associated with the Department of Education school reform turnaround model, the closing down of these centers has made it more challenging for parents to find quality preschool services in their communities (Samuels, 2013).

Educators are in a state of uncertainty in deciding how to balance the department curricular guidelines and at the same time tending to students' developmental needs such as play, the arts, social skills, and integrated instruction. Educators believe that a child's developmental needs are just as important as a student learning the alphabet. Educational experts believe that it is misguided to test children to a narrowly defined curriculum because of children's irregular development cycle (Zubrzycki, 2011).

Ironically, many politicians who advocate for rigorous testing often send their children to private schools that place a tremendous value on extracurricular activities. Alan Jones, a retired principal and current educational consultant, noted how the Sidwell Friends School, a private school in Washington, D.C., which President Obama's children attend, emphasizes students' developmental needs as well as their academic needs. While researching Sidwell, Jones (2013) commented:

> Sidwell students, it seemed, experienced an instructional program that allocated appropriate time for each discipline to be taught well; engaged in instructional activities that were problem based and interdisciplinary; participated in a rich extracurricular program; and were supervised by administrators and teachers who place children's social and emotional development on an equal footing with their intellectual growth. I saw no mention of test scores, adequate yearly progress, or data-driven instruction.

This is one example out of many of how various legislators prescribe a different school from the schools that their children attend. Unfortunately, many poverty-stricken schools receive a scripted curriculum and limited educational offerings, while those in wealthy schools receive more innovative teaching strategies and enrichment opportunities (Schniedewind and Sapon-Shevin, 2012). As noted, schools should be allowed to be holistic in their approach toward educating children.

As a consequence of promoting rigorous learning for primary students, as of 2009, 30% of elementary schools eliminated recess, whereas 40% significantly reduced recess times. According to Elder and Obel-Omia (2012), restricting recess negatively impacts involuntary attention. Involuntary attention entails the mind's reaction to rapid changes in the environment compared to directed or voluntary attention, where the focus is on concentration.

To be generally healthy, children need the opportunity to interact freely with different environments, which leads to more focused concentration in more controlled environments. Comparatively, most adults require work breaks in order to stay productive with specific job tasks, something we are taking away from our youth. When children buy into the message that it is all about the tests, this creates severe stress among children exhibited by crying and vomiting (Ohanian, 2002). More importantly, some children view themselves as incompetent and inferior if they do not meet the minimum testing assessment goal.

Although the vast majority of educators support recess, educators also support educational standards but believe that a balance should exist between the two. Educators believe that standards should not be so narrowly defined as to concentrate solely on reading and math instruction. Edward Miller, a senior researcher for the advocacy group Alliance for Childhood, summed it up like this:

> We feel that the early education [K-12] standards—particularly the kindergarten standards, but also the early elementary standards—in the common core [standards] are a disaster, and are going to greatly worsen what is already a crisis situation in early-childhood education. I am not opposed to the idea of standards. We know a lot about what children need to be successful. But it has very little to do with very narrowly defined bits of knowledge. If you expect every five-year-old to be able to read and drill them on reading skills, the ones who don't get it are defined by the schools and by themselves as failures. (Zubrzycki, 2011)

As a former principal, I am convinced that we create special education students by introducing concepts before students are ready to handle them. By the time students are mentally ready, instruction is usually no longer being provided at that age group, and students are placed into special programs. In reality, the problem is actually developmental.

As a society, we must understand that learning is not all about tests and we should also be concerned about student social skills and other methods to measure student growth and performance. More importantly, parents tend to be more involved in their child's education at this age level, and they should be empowered to work with their local districts to meet their learning needs rather than adhering to top-down state and federal decisions.

FEDERAL AND STATE INVOLVEMENT IN TEACHER/ ADMINISTRATOR LICENSURE

Teacher Licensure

In addition to reforms like the Common Core Standards, White House education officials also seek to reform how teachers are licensed through grants such as the proposed Presidential Teaching Fellows grant program (Sawchuk, 2011a). Additionally, the federal government has pressured states to ratchet up their requirements to ensure that teachers are highly qualified, as noted in NCLB. As a result, states such as Illinois have made it difficult for potential teachers to enter the profession by administering rigorous basic skills tests.

By shrinking the teaching workforce in public schools, this inevitably impacts local districts because it poses a challenge in recruiting teachers. For instance, community graduates who were initially interested in the field of education to give back to their community may now be disinterested due to the rigorous requirements. This is relevant because most educators understand that the relationship between teachers and students is a key factor in promoting student achievement.

College professors, educational professionals, and teachers in Illinois are concerned that the basic skill tests are anything but basic because most students, comparatively speaking, will have to score a thirty or higher out of thirty-six possible points on the ACT to pass the exam. For instance, the basic skills pass/fail rate of students enrolled in colleges of education during the school years of 2008–2009 and 2010–2011 for the state of Illinois according to All Education Schools (2011) is as follows:

- During the 2008–2009 school year, the combined pass rate was 86% compared to 23% during the 2010–2011 school year.
- During the 2008–2009 school year, Caucasian students' combined pass rate was 91% compared to 27% during the 2010–2011 school year.
- During the 2008–2009 school year, African-American students' combined pass rate was 59% compared to 5% during the 2010–2011 school year.
- During the 2008–2009 school year, Latino students' combined pass rate was 70% compared to 9% during the 2010–2011 school year.
- During the 2008–2009 school year, Asian students' combined pass rate was 80% compared to 20% during the 2010–2011 school year.

There is nothing wrong with ensuring that we have a qualified workforce of teachers. However, we must not be swayed by the phrase "highly qualified teacher" without realizing what that phrase encompasses. For instance, NCLB was an attractive name for Bush's legislation to reform education. Many lawmakers were so dazzled by its name and its implication that perhaps they did not understand that it was based upon unrealistic expectations such as mandating that students be 100% proficient in reading and math by 2014.

Increasingly, more politicians and "experts" equate advanced education and a high grade point average with teaching excellence, but this is faulty thinking. For starters, a student's grade point average is difficult to analyze due to variations in course content and the rigor of classes from both high school and college. In addition, commonsense thinking may imply that the more intelligent or knowledgeable the teacher is, the better teacher he or she will become. However, this theory has not been supported by sound research (Sawchuk, 2013a).

As a former administrator, I've unfortunately seen too many people who were bright and wonderful students but who simply were not effective teachers. To become a great teacher, a student does need to know not only content but more importantly how to relate to and reach students (Payne, 2003). The bottom line is that there are multiple factors that constitute a good teacher.

The National Council for Teacher Accreditation and the Teacher Education Accreditation Council, both of which accredit U.S. teacher colleges, are merging and have plans to create more rigorous standards and admission policies for applicants desiring to become teachers (Sawchuk, 2011a). As teacher candidate requirements increase, many educators believe that more and more individuals will be discouraged from wanting to become teachers, particularly minority individuals. For instance, based on federal data, minority teachers currently make up about 17% of the teaching profession due in part to the rigorous demands of becoming a teacher.

The number of minority students nationwide vastly outnumbers minority teachers. This discrepancy must be addressed in order for all students to succeed. Although all students can benefit from learning about racial and cultural diversity, having minority teachers is extremely beneficial to minority students. The National Collaborative on Diversity in the Teaching Force (2004) noted the following benefits of minority teachers:

- Enrich diverse students' learning because of shared racial and cultural identities
- Serve as cultural brokers by assisting students in navigating their school environment and culture, as well as increasing the involvement of parents

Increasing diversity among our nation's teachers will also help to eliminate the achievement gap (Sawchuk, 2013a). A key factor in doing this successfully is establishing and maintaining a caring relationship with students through the use of role models with whom students can readily identify.

As noted, although some states have placed rigorous demands on who can become a teacher, the same does not hold true for most charter school teachers. In many states, charter school teachers are exempt from the licensure requirements for public school teachers. For instance, Governor Walker of Wisconsin proposed lifting a requirement that teachers at charter schools be licensed and believes that charter school teachers should have minimal qualifications such as only a bachelor's degree (Fiori, 2011).

Due to intense certification requirements to become a public school teacher in addition to meager salaries, the teacher pool is shrinking in public education. Is this a plot to manufacture a crisis in education so that the public can support alternatives such as charter schools and alternative certifications? In answering this question, one must wonder why reforms exist that will significantly decrease the number of potential public school teacher candidates. How will this impact public education? For starters, public schools will lack a diverse workforce. Therefore, students of color will be less likely to see teachers who look similar to them.

It is faulty to assume that the most advanced students should become teachers, and that will foster an increase in student achievement. Can we reasonably expect our top-tier students to become teachers and to work in large urban districts and that their knowledge base alone will increase student achievement? Is it fair to expect that these teachers can improve student achievement when most of these potential teachers have not had any ties to such communities beforehand? One must realize that good teachers possess more than a knowledge base, although this is an important variable. Good teachers understand the cultural and societal issues in the communities in which they work, and they foster good relationships with community stakeholders.

As I've mentioned before, good teachers must have more than a strong academic background. They must be able to relate to all students and to the community at large. Equally important, there has been little attention given to teaching practices that are beneficial to students of diverse racial, ethnic, and cultural backgrounds (Hawley and Irvine, 2011).

For teachers to be effective, they must be culturally responsive to all students. However, if the federal government and states continue to push for teachers who are at the top of their class academically and disenfranchise others from becoming teachers, we will lack diversity in our schools and will not be able to guarantee that future teachers will be culturally responsive.

Research is clear that student achievement will falter if a teacher cannot relate to the community or develop a caring relationship with his or her students (Hawley and Irvine, 2011). Derek Roguski and Hannah Sadtler, who came to New Orleans as a part of Teach For America (TFA, an organization that recruits college graduates and other professionals to teach for two years in urban and rural communities), developed a support group called New Teachers' Roundtable. Roguski and Sadtler founded the group to assist teachers in understanding their experiences and roles in the city schools of New Orleans.

The pair was motivated to create this group after they realized they were ill prepared to teach in the classrooms to which they were assigned and had no connection to the cultural differences of their students, which impacted their students' learning needs (Zubrzycki, 2013). On the other hand, teachers such as Neha Singhal, who worked for TFA, indicated that TFA taught its teaching recruits to stay within their teaching perimeters and did not allow discussion of students' cultural and diversity differences sway them from that mission (Schniedewind and Sapon-Shevin, 2012). As with Roguski and Sadtler, teachers need to understand students' cultural backgrounds in order to make a difference in the lives of students.

With so much emphasis placed on teacher quality, many are led to believe that improving student achievement is solely the responsibility of teachers compared to other stakeholders. Although we should not discount the impact and role of teachers, there are many other factors associated with improving student achievement. Comparatively, we cannot fault the farmer for poor crop yields without considering variables such as weather. Certainly, teachers play a role in promoting student achievement but they should not be held solely responsible for it.

When parents, students, teachers, and administrators are asked who is responsible for student achievement, we see a variety of responses:

- Parents say the teachers
- Teachers say the parents
- Principals and administrators say both teachers and parents (Cantor, 2012)

As David Cantor (2012), the managing director with the Glover Park Group, a strategic communications firm in Washington, D.C., noted, "We need to accept that we are asking people throughout the education system to do more. But in many cases, these are people who feel they are already putting in extraordinary time and effort." As a result, teachers and administrators are getting burned out.

Educators are expected to carry out a wide range of programs such as standards-based grading and instruction; Common Core Standards; common grading; end-of-course assessment; conversation, help, activity, movement, participation, and success (CHAMPS); creating independence through student-owned strategies (CRISS); love and logic; pyramid to intervention; response to intervention; learning targets; data walks; teacher-principal evaluation project (TPEP); school improvement plans (SIP); academic collaboration time (ACT); positive behavioral intervention and supports (PBIS); Smarter Balanced Assessment Consortium; and Partnership for Assessment of Readiness for College and Careers (PARCC) (Barnoski, 2013).

Educational critics need to stop pointing fingers and begin working collaboratively with all stakeholders to address common educational problems. With all of these programs that educators are expected to implement, it is easy to understand why they are feeling frustrated and discouraged.

Principal Licensure

In addition to teachers, principals have also become the target of certification reforms. Educational reformists believe that teachers cannot be properly evaluated for their performance if principals do not possess the skill and experience to evaluate and remediate teachers. Reformists believe that administrator evaluations are needed to ensure that principals promote student achievement, safe schools, and teacher satisfaction (Samuels, 2011d). Concerning the federal government, the Obama administration seeks to clarify how states define what it means to be an effective administrator according to their blueprint for the reauthorization of the Elementary and Secondary Education Act (Samuels, 2011d).

Various states and individual districts, such as Delaware and Florida's Hillsborough County, have focused their efforts on principal evaluations. Delaware's evaluation framework for principals includes many components such as the ability to analyze data and how to remediate teachers. Florida's Hillsborough County district evaluation system focuses on test score improvement for at-risk students and on evaluations from teachers (Samuels, 2011d).

In addition to Delaware and Hillsborough County, Florida, other states are formulating procedures as to how principals are evaluated. For instance, on June 1, 2010, Governor Quinn of Illinois signed Senate Bill 226 into a state law, which will revise the process of how principals are certified. Specific changes include the following: allowing nonprofit organizations to certify and facilitate endorsement programs without working with state colleges and universities; requiring existing college and university principal programs to be reaccredited to meet new state guidelines; and establishing a principal's endorsement requiring four years of teaching experience, a master's degree, and successful completion of a principal preparation program (Illinois General Assembly (n.d.)).

Why all the changes? Governor Quinn indicated that the revisions were necessary in order to be eligible to compete for Race to the Top funds from the Obama administration. Due to principal certification changes, universities in Illinois have experienced declining enrollment in their preparatory programs for principals.

Special interest groups hope to have their say concerning how principals are trained as well. Principal programs in Denver and in Georgia's Gwinnett County school system are receiving $75 million from the Wallace Foundation over a five-year period aimed at training, evaluating, and supporting principals (Samuels, 2011d). Legislators and special interest groups are having their say regarding teacher and principal effectiveness, but where are the local superintendents and school board voices? Superintendents and local school boards should play a major role in determining what constitutes an effective teacher and/or administrator.

Besides teachers and principals, superintendents are confronting changes in the manner in which they are licensed as well. Since 2000, several states have made changes regarding the certification process for superintendents. Ironically, these states permit others to become superintendents regardless of whether they have a background in education. One of the most notable examples is the state of Tennessee. Qualifications to become a superintendent in Tennessee include being a citizen of the state and possessing a college degree (Alsbury, 2008).

Politicians may not want to discuss the role of school boards in areas such as teacher and/or administrator quality directly due to various reasons. For instance, politicians can control the overall goals of education while paying lip service to the importance of school boards and not have to come under attack for doing away with or limiting local control. If local control is removed, our children's future will be left in the hands of entrepreneurs and politicians, many of whom are influenced by powerful foundations (Ravitch, 2010).

As previously noted, school boards rather than lawmakers should decide teacher and administrator quality. School boards are entrusted to represent their communities and to hire teachers based upon the superintendent's recommendations, which are reflective of community expectations.

THE PUSH FOR COMMON CORE STANDARDS

Common Core Standards promoted by the federal government through state application for Race to the Top funds and NCLB waivers have reenergized debates about who defines what a quality education is. The intent of Common Core Standards is to provide a clear understanding of what students are expected to know, which is reflective of real-life experiences needed for success in college and careers. Moreover, Common Core Standards can ensure uniformity in student learning despite issues such as student mobility and can serve as a basis for uniform assessment among U.S. public school students.

Common Core Standards were promoted by the Obama administration, but were created and promoted by the National Governors Association and State Educational Chiefs with funding provided in part by the Bill and Melinda Gates Foundation, which has significant ties to the Department of Education. Furthermore, corporate-driven public school reformists support the standards. To date, a majority of states have endorsed the standards.

Educational leaders are concerned that the creation of uniform standards among states will result in a shared national curriculum, facilitated and sponsored by the federal government and other special interest groups with little input from local communities (Gewertz, 2011). For instance, the national planning committee, which designed the standards, included no classroom teachers and was dominated by employees from major testing companies (Schniedewind and Sapon-Shevin, 2012). Educators believe it is absurd to have outsiders, many of whom never worked with school-aged children, develop standards for students.

Public school advocates believe that the Common Core Standards will be used by the private sector to access public funds. In particular, these opponents highlight the special role Bill Gates has played in promoting these standards. They maintain that Bill Gates has provided funding and/or other support services to the National Governors Association, State Education Chiefs, and the Department of Education to advance the agenda of the United Nations Educational, Scientific, and Cultural Organization, with which Gates signed an agreement aimed at promoting shared educational objectives and/or promoting global competiveness with other nations. They argue that this agreement will benefit Microsoft technologies (Ujifusa, 2013b).

Public school advocates also question the purpose of demanding that every student in the state function the same with teachers pressured to teach from a scripted curriculum. Opponents of the Common Core Standards believe that schools are increasingly being utilized to prepare workers for corporations and assist companies in better competing internationally. Schniedewind and Sapon-Shevin (2012) stated that "If these standards are more economic than educational in their inspiration, more about winning than learning, devoted more to serving the interests of business than to meeting the needs of kids, then we've merely painted a twenty-first-century façade on a hoary, dreary model of school-as-employee training."

Public school supporters believe a more sinister role exists in the creation of the Common Core Standards and other "educational reforms." They believe that the creation of uniform standards and common assessment tests will deprofessionalize the teaching profession. Schniedewind and Sapon-Shevin (2012) noted the following:

> One goal of a market-driven approach to education is to deprofessionalize the teaching profession, and its pay, by making teaching a routine job rather than a field that requires a comprehensive education and ongoing professional development. Rather than being public intellectuals who

teach young people how to think critically, solve problems creatively, and engage deeply with ideas, teachers will only need to follow a scripted curriculum geared toward passing standardized tests. Teachers will be trained quickly, paid little, and burn out, thus maintaining a revolving door of educators. Low salaries will help cut costs. But teacher unions are in the way, so neoliberals have mounted a massive public relations campaign claiming that they are an impediment to reform.

Do Common Core Standards and other "educational reforms" championed by market-driven reformers assist in deprofessionalizing the teaching profession? Although the jury may still be deliberating in reaching a verdict, it seems highly plausible. Organizations such as TFA streamline the process for individuals to become teachers. Often, their students learn their profession in a five-week training module and students are taught to believe in business principles such as merit pay, charter schools, tenure, dismantled unions, standardized testing, and teacher accountability (limited due process rights).

TFA sends a third of its teachers to work in privately run charter schools (Simon, 2012a). Ironically, charter school teachers are 230% more likely to leave the teaching profession compared to traditional public school teachers (Schniedewind and Sapon-Shevin, 2012). With such a high turnover rate, it is undeniable that the teaching process in many charter schools has been deprofessionalized with the assistance of corporate-funded organizations such as TFA.

Furthermore, TFA sends students with little classroom experience (fifteen to twenty classroom hours) into various schools to replace tenured teachers that have been laid off. As a result of students' lack of classroom experience, and the fact that TFA students are expected to work in low income schools with an array of learning issues, they often leave the profession prematurely. Despite how TFA aids in the deprofessionalizing of the teaching profession, it often receives private and public grants to continue its mission. Secretary Duncan remarked that TFA made teaching "cool" again and in 2010, TFA received a fifty-million-dollar grant from the Department of Education (Simon, 2012a).

Few educators believe that the creation of uniform standards is a benefit for students. Although some educators may support the creation of common standards, most educators disliked the process utilized by the Obama administration of using Race to the Top funds and waivers as an incentive to persuade states to adopt the standards or the clandestine matter in which they were created (Ujifusa, 2013b). More importantly, because Common Core Standards will impact many students throughout the United States, input from local communities can substantially enrich the curriculum.

Regardless of whether the Common Core Standards are a good idea or not, local communities need to have input about how students will be educated within their borders. Local school districts should be empowered to complement the uniform standards by adding their own meanings as well.

Gewertz (2011) cited Neal P. McCluskey, a policy analyst at the Cato Institute in Washington, as saying, "The whole point of having national standards is to drive curriculum." Currently, the government is funding the development of common assessments to measure the standards that will lay the foundation to forming a national curriculum without regard to the diverse needs of communities. To date, the Obama administration has spent over $360 million in the development of such assessment tests.

The push for Common Core Standards does not appear to be lessening, and in the future there is likely to be a national curriculum. According to the Constitution, education is a power reserved to the states, not to the federal government. Ironically, the law does not permit the U.S. government to create a national curriculum, but the Obama administration has been clever in pushing this agenda. On the other hand, lawmakers are concerned about the possibility of having a national curriculum that Congress did not authorize and often debate this issue rigorously when discussing the reauthorization of NCLB (Whitehurst, 2010).

SUMMARY

The federal government has taken the lead in determining what constitutes a quality education. Since the passage of NCLB, the government's focus has been on reading and math—and more recently on Common Core Standards. With so much attention on reading and math, students are ignorant about current world events, science, and world government.

Regarding Common Core Standards, many educators believe this is the doorway to a national curriculum measured by common assessments as well. As a result of this top-down approach from Washington, many districts are hesitant to develop their own mission because they believe lawmakers will provide schools with a common mission as well.

Increasingly, standardized tests are the yardstick to determine student academic success. The overreliance on standardized tests has created multiple other problems such as test-score validity and whether test scores should be used to measure teacher and administrator performance. Research suggests that student test scores should not be used to measure teacher performance. As noted earlier, experts such as the Economic Policy Institute warned about using tests to measure teacher academic performance due to the number of variables involved. Despite various warnings, the federal government has pressured states to link the two if they are to be eligible for a waiver from NCLB.

Federal and state lawmakers are increasingly changing how teachers and administrators are certified and trained. Some of the requirements are so intense and cumbersome that many educators believe it will lead to a teacher and/or administrator shortage, including disenfranchising minorities from becoming educators. For instance, the current revised basic skills test to become a teacher in Illinois is so intense that few students have been able to pass it compared to previous years. Those lawmakers and other stakeholders who favor beefing up the requirements are under the impression that academic content as measured by a standardized test is the formula that makes great teachers.

QUESTIONS FOR REFLECTION

1. Identify and describe the concerns associated with a curriculum primarily focused on reading and math.
2. Describe your thoughts regarding the Obama administration's conditions in order for states to obtain a waiver from NCLB guidelines. Are these conditions fair or unfair? Please explain.
3. Identify and describe the pros and cons of utilizing standardized tests to gauge student learning.
4. How are standardized assessments impacting preschool programs?

5. Explain how the federal and state governments have impacted the licensure process for teachers. What have been the results of such efforts?
6. How have state and federal lawmakers impacted the licensure process for administrators?
7. Identify the pros and cons of the Common Core Standards. Describe your thoughts regarding whether or not market-driven reforms such as Common Core Standards assist in deprofessionalizing the teaching profession.

CHAPTER 3

Understanding the Reform Movement

Since the launch of Sputnik into space by the Soviet Union, there have been a number of educational reforms with the intention of ensuring that all students receive a quality education. The difference between today's reforms and previous reforms is that the federal government and private enterprise are becoming increasingly aggressive and more assertive than in years past, citing global competiveness.

The Department of Education currently funds more than sixty education programs that not only provide funding but also impose additional rules and regulations on state education departments and local districts (Ryan, 2004). The assumption that schools are failing and public education doesn't work has made education reform a staple platform issue in most political campaigns, from local to state and even presidential elections.

Legislators, philanthropists, and business leaders are ringleaders in supporting a variety of reforms to address failing schools. As noted, current efforts to increase student achievement include merit pay, vouchers, Common Core Standards, charter schools, and teacher and principal evaluation systems linked to student achievement data. Most of these reforms have been encompassed in school turnaround models for schools deemed as failing and embraced by corporate-driven educational reformists.

Sadly, these reforms have excluded the input of local school boards and their superintendents, and most have originated outside of local communities. As Schniedewind and Sapon-Shevin (2012) noted in their book *Educational Courage: Resisting the Ambush of Public Edu-*

cation, "High-stakes testing, voucher programs, corporate-connected charter schools, test-driven teacher evaluation, merit pay, mayoral control, and national standards put private corporations at the helm of education, rather than our public."

Various politicians and the White House have prompted reforms as well. The federal government promoted its reforms such as common standards by enticing cash-strapped states with monetary assistance (Whitehurst, 2010). Politicizing the educational agenda has led to the expansion of charter schools and vouchers. This has led to U.S. schools going through a period of segregation, desegregation, and resegregation based on race and economic class (Boyle and Burns, 2011). Resegregation is now a national issue, but lawmakers have not been vocal about how various legislative polices impacted the resegregation of schools.

It is this author's contention (and one shared by many others) that such a lack of confidence in public education is unwarranted. In fact, although urban school districts are the subject of vast reforms, many urban districts have made significant gains in math scores from 2009 to 2011, according to the most recent National Assessment of Educational Progress (NAEP) test results (Robelen, 2011b). For instance, the NAEP's website reports the following urban city scores (based on a scale between 0 and 500):

- Austin fourth graders (245 in 2011 from 240 in 2009)
- Baltimore fourth graders (226 in 2011 from 222 in 2009)
- Philadelphia fourth graders (225 in 2011 from 222 in 2009)
- Charlotte eighth graders (285 in 2011 from 283 in 2009 and 279 in 2003)
- Chicago eighth graders (270 in 2011 from 264 in 2009)
- Detroit eighth graders (246 in 2011 from 238 in 2009)
- District of Columbia eighth graders (255 in 2011 from 251 in 2009 and 243 in 2003)

Student achievement in math is important because math is less reflective of a student's socioeconomic background than is achievement in language arts. For example, it is difficult to reinforce good grammar learned at school if broken English is used in the home. These math assessments provide relevant data that many inner-city schools are making progress. According to the NAEP test results, fourth and eighth graders have continued to make significant strides since the 1970s.

Besides test scores, school dropout rates fell to less than 10% compared to being in the double digits in the past two decades (Smith, Turner, and Lattanzio, 2012). And the nation's graduation rate has significantly improved as well. The 2010 freshman graduation rate increased to 78.2% compared to 71.7% in 2001 (Adams and Sparks, 2013). In regard to international comparisons, since 2011 the United States ranks above the national average of participating nations as measured by Trends in International Mathematics and Science Study and the Progress in International Reading Literacy Study.[1]

Admittedly, all schools, whether public or private, should seek ways to make themselves more efficient in their delivery of quality education. Although there are various ways in which schools can improve, no school can reach its full potential independent of the board governance team. To improve schools in the best way, we need first and foremost to ensure that districts are governed and operating properly. If not, then most externally driven reforms will likely die because they lack support from the local community (Nemir, 2010).

The fundamental problem with most school reform measures is that educational reformists have put the cart before the horse by not addressing school board governance. As Lee and Eadens (2013) noted, "School boards have been virtually overlooked and from recent sweeping accountability movements such as No Child Left Behind. Much is expected of school districts, individual schools, teachers, and administrators, but those who potentially most impact the quality of a school system, in regards to policy, seem to have been almost ignored." In order to improve public schools, it is imperative that a locally elected, qualified, and trained school board be made accountable for student achievement outcomes that are staff-driven and community supported.

---

[1] Trends in International Mathematics and Science Study and the Progress in International Reading Literacy Study are two assessment tests used internationally to assess achievement. U.S. fourth-grade students outperformed many of their counterparts in other nations as compared by Progress in International Reading Literacy Study (Robelen, 2013). Moreover, according to the Program for International Student Assessment, U.S. schools that had less than 10% poverty outperformed their counterparts in high-performing nations (Schniedewind and Sapon-Shevin, 2012).

This chapter is intended to explore current popular reforms aimed at providing a quality education for all students. More importantly, this chapter seeks to illustrate how these reforms have not truly assisted in providing a quality education but have instead damaged staff morale and the delivery of quality education. This chapter serves to enhance the discussion and debate of why school boards should be the drivers of any needed school reforms because they serve as trustees for the community.

TURNAROUND MODEL OF SCHOOL REFORM

School boards and superintendents are not alone in their criticism of the Department of Education and its approach to defining quality education and turning around student achievement. Alan Blankstein, president of the HOPE foundation (an educational consulting organization), and Pedro Noguera, professor of Education at New York University, recently panned President Obama's reliance on unresearched, market-driven turnaround models (Blankstein and Noguera, 2012). Obama's plans, they said, encourage states to address the bottom 5% of their schools by pressuring districts to close down underperforming schools, convert them to charters, or, in some cases, make wholesale changes in staff and administrators (Hammond-Darling, 2012).

The most egregious example is the state of Illinois, which is contemplating legislation that would remove school boards and further suspend their elections in districts with the lowest 5% of student achievement. Unfortunately, the legislation being considered makes the assumption that districts identified as "5% of lowest achievers" have school boards that are guilty of dysfunctional, unethical, or illegal governance practices without taking other variables into consideration such as mobility, lack of parental involvement, and high poverty rates (Illinois Statewide School Management Alliance, 2013).

When reformers mention failing schools, typically they are referring to large urban cities that have more minority students, lower household incomes, and a wide range of serious social issues (Stover, 2011a). This trend is commonly referred to as the "95/5 dilemma," wherein 5% of failing schools are defining the educational expectations for the successful 95% (Benjamin and Trout, 2011).

In the business community, concentrating on specific areas to deny services or increase costs is commonly referred to as "redlining." Sociologist John McKnight coined this phrase in the 1960s when banks drew a red line on a map to highlight the areas in which they would not invest. By redlining specific school districts, business and real estate investors will very likely not invest in those communities.

Using only school districts with significant social and economic challenges, the reformists—led by legislators, philanthropists, and business leaders—are making broad assumptions and proposing a cookie-cutter model to address them (Rose and Gallup, 2010). As Cuban (2004) noted, "They [educational reformists] apply uniform approaches to dissimilar problems. They take power away from local school boards and educators, the only people who can improve what happens in the classrooms, and give it to distant officials, who have little capacity to achieve results."

The process of firing teachers and administrators, transforming schools to charters, and closing schools to remedy failing schools should be carefully assessed because it is highly disruptive to the community. Often, schools are the major institution in the community (Schniedewind and Sapon-Shevin, 2012). Teachers, parents, students, and other stakeholders are usually highly vested in their schools, and the closing of public schools is, in many ways, viewed as destroying key components of the community.

More and more parents are rejecting the notion of using turnaround models to help strengthen public schools when these models are put into practice. Some parents are very candid in their belief that they have been hoodwinked into believing that these models are the best tools to reform public schools, specifically regarding minority communities. Turnaround models have primarily targeted inner-city schools and not their suburban counterparts.

Citizen and parent groups in Chicago, the District of Columbia, New York, Newark, and Philadelphia have filed for a moratorium regarding the use of school closings and have voiced dissent regarding other turnaround models with the U.S. Department of Education's Office for Civil Rights. Citizen and parent groups voiced several complaints, such as the lack of transparency in districts using these models, the U.S. Department of Education involvement with private interest groups including charter school operators, and the use of turnarounds as a primary intervention (Zubrzycki, 2012a).

According to Schniedewind and Sapon-Shevin (2012), civil rights groups have challenged the manner in which the market-driven reforms have negatively impacted students of color. They stated that

> The NAACP, the Lawyers' Committee for Civil Rights Under Law, and Rainbow/Push Coalition, criticized Race to the Top legislation for emphasizing competitive incentives that leave the majority of low-income and students of color behind. It also critiqued the shutting down of low-performing schools, rather than doing more to close gaps in resources and to end racial segregation in schools.

Interestingly, Secretary Arne Duncan, who oversees the U.S. Department of Education, is a primary ringleader in supporting these reforms.

Districts should not rely on turnaround models because such models do not get at the heart of the problem that primarily caused the school to fail. The Academy @ Shawnee, located in Louisville, Kentucky, participated in the "turnaround model" of school reform and has been visited by Secretary Duncan. In reforming the school using the "turnaround" model, the school was given a $1.5 million grant, a major staffing change, uniform learning standards, and assistance from key educational experts, but the school remains at the bottom of the state list of low-performing schools (Klein, 2012a).

There are many factors that must be considered as to why a school or a district is failing. To turn schools around successfully, the complete school system should be analyzed to find specific causes. Blankstein and Noguera (2012) noted the following in failing schools:

- Variety of students who have unmet social needs
- Discipline issues
- Low staff morale
- Tardiness and absenteeism
- Lack of collaboration
- Little to no parental or community engagement

As noted by Blankstein and Noguera (2012), a commonality in major urban districts is a high poverty rate. Can school districts change poverty rates? Obviously not, but districts that are prepared to address the specialized needs of students in these areas can impact the quality of local education. And it is the quality of local schools that is rated as the single most important factor in determining real estate values and enhancing economic investment and development opportunities.

THE CONNECTION BETWEEN THE REFORM MOVEMENT AND GLOBAL COMPETITION

According to Cuban (2004), politicians, corporations, private foundations, and other educational reformists often cite low worker productivity and decreasing global competition as primary reasons to intervene in public education. Due to this compelling belief, the federal role in public education has been expanding at alarming rates. Since 1989, the following reforms have occurred in public education (Fuhrman, 2004; Klein, 2011c; Whitehurst, 2010):

- In 1989, George H. W. Bush convened the nation's governors to draft national educational goals.
- In the 1990s, Congress authorized goals supported by President Bill Clinton that aligned standards to specific outcomes.
- In 2001, Congress passed No Child Left Behind (NCLB) supported by the Bush administration. At the time, NCLB was the largest expansion of the federal role in public education.
- In 2009, President Obama authorized the spending of over $4.35 billion dollars to spur innovation and reforms in public education by competing for Race to the Top (RTT) grant dollars under the leadership of Secretary of Education Arne Duncan. States were awarded points if they agreed to the Department of Education's aim to promote charter schools and privatization of education, performance-based standards, merit pay, and nationwide standards.

RTT was the first federal initiative through which the Secretary of Education could influence public education to such an extent without the support of Congress. Whitehurst (2010) remarked that "It is a mistake in principle—and a danger in reality—to allow any U.S. secretary of education this much policy discretion when doling out large sums of money." Klein (2011c) cited Republican Representative John Kline of Minnesota, chairman of the House Education and the Workforce Committee, as saying, "I think many of us would say, maybe you don't need to be accountable to the secretary of education."

Although low worker productivity and global competition are two primary reasons that educational reformists offer as excuses to intervene in public education, are these reasons valid? According to Cuban (2004), youth unemployment has increased and decreased in inconsistent ways since the Great Depression. While employers often indicate that workers have low levels of productivity because they have insufficient basic skills, these employers seldom identify the specific knowledge and skills in which workers are deficient. This is primarily due to the fact that employers are more interested in employee attitudes and behaviors than in the latter's math and science skills (Cuban, 2004).

Common sense suggests that youth need guidance to be successful in the workplace and should know the importance of good work ethics such as arriving to work on time. As a former administrator in the city of Mt. Vernon, Illinois, I am impressed by the work of the Jefferson County Development Corporation (JCDC) directed by Mary Ellen Bechtel, of which I was a member.

JCDC's mission is to support the retention and expansion of area business. The JCDC, in collaboration with local business, education, and workforce professionals and health care organizations, created the World Class Workforce program. The purpose of this program is to foster individual awareness and responsibility concerning the importance of the shared success of the individual, employer, and community (www.jeffcodev.org). To foster this awareness, individuals take the following pledge:

> I pledge, as a member of the World Class Workforce, to be a valued team member in my workplace and community. I understand that my attitude, performance, and character make a difference. I recognize that the choices I make impact on my success, my employer and my community.

As noted in the pledge, the JCDC believes that workers must understand the correlation that exists between their work ethic and/or behavior and their success, as well as that of the employer and community.

Perhaps other cities should role-model JCDC's efforts in designing similar programs targeting the appropriate work behaviors that interest employers the most.

What are the facts regarding whether insufficiently educated workers slowed U.S. production and threatened our global status? Cuban (2004) cites the following facts:

1. The United States enjoyed almost a decade of economic prosperity in the 1990s.
2. U.S. productivity has increased—not decreased—in the past 15 years.
3. Between 2000 and 2002, the U.S. economy weakened, but the World Economic Forum noted that the United States had the world's second highest economy.

If the U.S. economy was primarily based upon student achievement outcomes, these facts suggest that public schools should be championed by legislators and other reform advocates. In truth, our country's economic gains are not as heavily influenced by student achievement outcomes as they are by monetary, trade, and industrial policies, as well as by key decisions made by the president and Congress and the federal departments of the Treasury, Commerce, and Labor (Cuban, 2004).

LINKING STUDENT AND TEACHER PERFORMANCE

A central theme of concern in promoting student achievement is guaranteeing that quality teachers are in front of the classrooms. To ensure that this happens, a good teacher evaluation is critical. If teacher evaluations are to be effective, it is vital that teachers and administrators view the evaluation process as a tool to improve instruction rather than as an "I got you." What are the components of an effective teacher evaluation instrument? There are many components that educators will note such as teacher preparedness, group work, and teacher lessons designed to stimulate critical thinking skills. Most educators view these as more reasonable evaluation areas than unproven methods such as linking teacher performance to student performance.

Although there is scant research indicating the effectiveness of evaluation systems based upon teacher and student performance, this method of evaluation is gaining in popularity as business leaders, philanthropists, and legislators have endorsed it and made it a central reform issue. The White House followed suit, making this is a key part of President Obama's educational reform agenda. Advocates of this process believe newly designed evaluation systems will identify not only quality teachers but a majority of teachers who they believe are subpar.

Yet results in states such as Michigan, Florida, Tennessee, and Georgia, among the first in revamping their evaluation systems to meet federal guidelines, documented that 94% or better of their teachers were effective. Rather than looking for a smoking gun indicating that many teachers are subpar, many reformists should view this as evidence of teachers' hard work and dedication (Sawchuk, 2013b).

A statement from the Economic Policy Institute (EPI), a nonprofit think tank known for its statistical research, cautioned against reliance on student test scores in determining teacher effectiveness due to the variables involved and, more specifically, recommended that scores not be a factor in making personnel decisions (EPI, 2010).

The EPI's position provides insights as to why there are no effective evaluation systems in use for districts to model due to the variables involved. Consequently, states are beginning to move in that direction with support from the federal government. Although the Department of Education pays lip service to being data driven, it has not provided any data to support the use of connecting the two.

States are facing major hurdles in attempting to create data systems to link teacher and student effectiveness. Several states are under pressure from the Department of Education to connect the two based on a combination of RTT funds and NCLB waivers. To date, all twelve RTT state recipients have experienced significant problems in creating these new teacher evaluation systems. This includes states such as Maryland, Massachusetts, and Ohio, which are implementing RTT somewhat better than the other nine states. This serves as testimony to the EPI's recommendation (McNeil, 2012c).

Tennessee is another state that knows firsthand how tedious it is to attempt to link teacher performance to student performance. Newspaper reporter Michael Winerip in Tennessee reported that following the rules for these new evaluations has become overly excessive in regard to staff resources in attempting to make such a system work.

Tennessee was named one of the first states to win Obama's RTT grant funds totaling $501 million and promised to create a new evaluation system based on linking student and teacher performance. Tennessee's revised evaluation assessment bases 50% of a teacher's evaluation on observations, 35% on student growth (including value-added), and 15% on other measures (Heitin, 2011). Tennessee's evaluation instrument created several problems, such as determining how to measure nonacademic classes.

In his 2011 article entitled "In Tennessee, Following the Rules for Evaluations Off a Cliff," Michael Winerip cited respected principal Will Shelton, principal of Blackman Middle School. Shelton, who believes in classroom observations to measure teacher effectiveness, claims Tennessee's process for teacher observations is overbearing. "I've never seen such nonsense," he said. "In the five years I've been principal here, I've never known so little about what's going on in my own building." According to the state-enforced rules concerning teacher evaluations in Tennessee, principals are required to do several observations yearly for all teachers, without respect to tenure or experience.

Specifically, Shelton has sixty-five teachers and, according to the new evaluation rules, a formal evaluation process includes the following: preobservation, which takes twenty minutes, formal observation, which takes fifty minutes, postobservation, which takes twenty minutes, and the completion of the rubric, which takes forty minutes (Winerip, 2011).

Shelton's concerns reflect those of other administrators such as Timothy Setterland, principal at Collierville High School in Tennessee, who also believes that it is a tremendous amount of work to conduct teacher evaluations (Heitin, 2011). Admittedly, these two principals feel that there are advantages to the evaluation process, but not in its current form. Furthermore, the process should not build a culture of distrust between teachers and administrators.

Besides the sheer volume of conducting this evaluation process, many Tennessee administrators and teachers believe that the evaluation model is not a fair way to measure teacher performance. For instance, the state's evaluation instrument allows evaluations for math specialists to be based on their schools' English scores, first-grade teachers can be evaluated based on the schools' fifth-grade writing scores, and nonacademic teachers can be assessed by the school's writing scores as well (Winerip, 2011).

Obviously, this system is absurd, as one's job performance is based solely upon the performance of another educator. Additionally, this system creates conflict between the school's staff in part because one can be evaluated solely based upon the work of another teacher rather than building a culture of collaboration and responsibility as with Professional Learning Communities.

Initially, Tennessee educators were hopeful that their system of evaluations would not spread to other states, because Tennessee was one of the leading pioneers of RTT; however, the damage has been done. In April 2013, the National Education Association (NEA) filed a lawsuit on behalf of three affiliates of its Florida chapter along with seven teachers concerning teacher appraisal irregularities. The NEA believes that teachers are being held accountable for students they do not instruct, which is a violation of teachers' constitutional rights (Sawchuk, 2013b).

In an effort to link teacher and student performance, states such as New York have gone so far as to publically release significant amounts of data that evaluate teacher efforts to boost student test scores (Banchero, 2012). Several things are disturbing about this. First, the data New York released were based on limited figures such as the number of students and school years. Apparently critics in New York believed that this approach would shame teachers into leaving the field without giving them ample opportunities to improve if they were found to be in need of assistance (Banchero, 2012).

New York's decision to release this data was faulty and irresponsible. Data could easily be misinterpreted, especially by individuals without educational acumen. For instance, if data were released that hypothetically showed that 20% of Ms. Jones's students did not succeed on state tests, one may believe Ms. Jones to be a bad teacher. However, let's suppose that Ms. Jones's class had high absenteeism, a number of students with special needs, a high poverty rate, several students with limited English language skills, or a combination of all of these factors. With limited data and without asking the right questions, one would reach a faulty conclusion in evaluating her performance. Unfortunately, this was the result in New York.

When New York City's education department decided to release test score data to the media identifying teachers by name, teacher Pascale Mauclair was identified as the city's worst teacher as cited by the *New York Post* (Hammond-Darling, 2012). The bad news spread as other journalists questioned her skill and dedication and even informed her father that she was the city's worst teacher. Does this sound like teacher bashing? Obviously yes, and what is so ironic about this story is that Mauclair is known as an effective teacher even though the faulty data showed a different picture.

For starters, Ms. Mauclair received stellar A ratings from the city's rating system and earned high evaluation marks from her principal and peers as well as a reputation for working well with immigrant students who are deficient in speaking English (Hammond-Darling, 2012). If more and more teachers receive poor evaluations for working with challenging students, teachers may be hesitant to teach classes that desperately need their expertise.

Regardless of whether the process of linking student and teacher performance is fair or not, critics are concerned that other states may follow suit because the Department of Education has pressured states to align the two. Rather than relying on a system that gauges teacher success based on student performance, we need to rely on other proven variables and focus on collaboration and professional development for teachers. If we concentrate on the latter, this approach would negatively impact teacher collaboration as teachers would be more interested in how they rank compared to their relationship with other teachers.

It should be apparent that educators need to define what a good teacher evaluation looks like and not politicians without educational acumen. Instead of using an overreliance on performance measures, experienced administrators believe that they should look at multiple indicators to determine who is and is not an effective teacher. For starters, many administrators support the following variables to gauge teacher effectiveness (DuFour et al., 2006; Koppich and Humphrey, 2011; Valentine, 2005):

- Joint administrative and peer evaluation process.

- Formal peer assistance and review process. Many educators believe that it may be a disadvantage for a single person (e.g., principal) to provide support and monitor performance effectively.
- Administrator walk-throughs and/or pop ins.
- Professional Learning Communities (collaboration with colleagues and administration).
- Individual teacher professional development plans that identify goals and objectives (may include a portfolio that includes student work, phone logs to parents, etc.).
- Community and school participation.
- Professional engagement participation.

Although all twelve states have experienced problems in meeting provisions of the RTT grant, Secretary Duncan is determined that states will fulfill their grant obligations regardless of existing research or problems experienced by the RTT states (McNeil, 2012c).

To date, there are no indications that Secretary Duncan is willing to rethink his plans of how to identify quality teachers without student growth being a significant factor. Perhaps Secretary Duncan should take the EPI's recommendation to not attempt to link teacher and student performance and instead work with RTT states to utilize other, more appropriate factors in determining teacher effectiveness.

Despite the EPI's advice, the Department of Education still favors a top-down governance model. For instance, instead of collaborating with states to develop systems to gauge teacher effectiveness, the department has warned various states to deliver on their promises of creating an evaluation system that links student and teacher performance.

More specifically, the Department of Education has placed Hawaii on a high-risk status and limited its access to the remaining RTT funds for failure to do so (McNeil, 2012c). If Secretary Duncan gave states the leeway to be creative rather than coercing the process, states might make greater progress in finding innovative ways to boost student achievement.

Although states agreed to create new teacher evaluation systems, one should note that states primarily agreed to compete for RTT funds due to budget shortfalls. As noted earlier, Whitehurst (2010), a senior fellow and the director of the Brown Center on Education Policy, reaffirmed how Duncan gained support for his reforms by enticing cash-strapped states to compete for their share of over five billion dollars in federal funds set aside for the American Recovery and Reinvestment Act of 2009.

Ironically, the Obama administration talks frequently about the need to hold teachers accountable but has not been willing to hold Secretary Duncan accountable. As mentioned earlier, all twelve RTT states have struggled with the implementation of their educational plans, but Obama's budget calls for a three-hundred-million-dollar increase to the five billion dollars the department had previously received for RTT (Klein, 2012a). Whitehurst (2010) believes that it is unwise to allow any Secretary of Education the authority to single-handedly influence educational policy by utilizing vast amounts of tax dollars in discretionary educational spending.

THE FACTS ABOUT UNIONS, MERIT PAY, VOUCHERS, AND CHARTER SCHOOLS

There are many educational reformers who seek to overhaul school systems—to push their agenda rather than finding other meaningful ways to support existing educational infrastructures. The great majority of current popular reforms are based on shallow research and have not included input from school boards. The reformists attempt to sell these reform measures based on the following ideology:

- Unions are the primary cause of low student achievement because they protect novice and inept teachers.
- Merit pay will encourage teachers to work harder.
- Vouchers will allow students to attend high-performing schools.
- Charter schools are needed to reform public schools.

When reformers utilize shallow academic research to justify their involvement in public schools, it takes attention off the real problems impacting public education such as teacher retention. Due to the flood of federal and state mandates, teachers are increasingly losing their desire to teach. Various research studies reflect that many first- and second-year teachers leave the profession, especially in large urban districts (Wheeler, 2011).

According to the twenty-eighth annual MetLife Survey of the American Teacher, only 44% of teachers are satisfied with their profession compared to 59% in 2009 (Heitin, 2011). American Federation of Teachers (AFT) president Randi Weingarten believes that this attitude among teachers reflects shrinking educational budgets and the bashing of teachers by politicians and by special interest groups. Interestingly, Weingarten noted that the survey finds that 77% of teachers feel that they are respected as professionals in the community, which reflects the belief that most communities are proud of their schools and teachers (Bushaw and Lopez, 2011; Heitin, 2011).

Serious school reform models must consider a variety of essential factors to bolster student achievement. It is unwise to take such a complex problem and reduce it to one or two areas such as teacher effectiveness. When teachers are unilaterally blamed for poor student achievement without regard to other variables such as social conditions, then teacher satisfaction will continue to decrease, leading to more teacher turnover. Blaming teachers limits future prospects of those interested in becoming teachers.

In order to impact student achievement positively, we need to look at a variety of variables. For instance, the Chicago Consortium on Chicago School Research analyzed twenty years of school improvement research and concluded that a reliable recipe to bolster student achievement must include the following (Wheeler, 2011):

- Quality instruction that is properly aligned per grade level
- Strong leadership
- Parental involvement
- Student-centered learning environment
- Professional and knowledgeable staff who have a responsibility to the entire school

When elements such as these are missing from the equation, it is doubtful that significant improvements will occur in education. More importantly, districts that have had significant increases in student achievement were governed by school boards that targeted these areas.

If power continues to be centralized at the state and federal level, it is doubtful that the state and federal officials can lead in these areas, as they govern at a distance compared to local school boards.

TEACHER UNIONS

The premise that teacher unions are solely responsible for undermining student achievement because of things such as tenure rights is faulty. Are there problems with some teacher unions? Yes, but they do not bear ultimate blame for poor student achievement. All too often, politicians have played political football with teacher unions to score political points.

Politicians who blame teacher unions should understand that not all states are unionized or are "right-to-work" states. States that have "right-to-work" laws primarily prohibit agreements between labor unions and employers that require workers to pay union dues as a condition of their employment. On the other hand, school districts in states such as Arizona have discretion on whether to recognize unions.

Right-to-work states have not seen high increases in student achievement compared to unionized states (Ravitch, 2010). Ravitch (2010) argues that teacher unions in southern states have either been weak or nonexistent, yet this has not increased student achievement. Likewise, states such as Massachusetts and countries such as Finland, which maintain active teacher unions, have been successful in promoting student achievement.

Teacher Tenure

Educational critics argue that, regardless of teachers' performance, it is difficult to dismiss teachers who have tenure and who are members of an active union. It is important to realize that tenure was not designed to guarantee employment for substandard work, as the film *Waiting for Superman* depicts.

The reality is that unions such as the AFT are willing to work with districts in streamlining the process of terminating ineffective teachers (Sawchuk, 2010b). However, teachers should have due process to ensure that any terminations are fair. Unions have been necessary to ensure that teachers are not dismissed for reasons such as disagreeing with administrators, joining what is seen as a wrong religion, or refusing to donate to certain politicians, all of which are significant factors in some areas (Ravitch, 2010).

Educational critics have continuously argued that teacher unions protect tenured teachers regardless of their performance and cite how difficult it is to remove teachers once they are tenured. On the other hand, union officials highlight the fact that administrators are the ones who conduct teacher evaluations and approve which teachers are ultimately tenured. Regarding terminating a tenured teacher, many administrators will tell you that if teachers are given effective evaluations from their administrators, if the evaluations document poor performance, and if administrators have the support of their local board, then any teacher could be removed for poor performance.

Union Infiltration

Teacher unions feel that they are being negatively targeted in many other ways besides revising evaluation assessments. Teacher union advocates believe that unions are being infiltrated by so-called grassroots groups pretending to give voice to teachers in issues such as school policy but in actuality are fronting for special interest groups, most of which are anti-union.

Ironically, these organizations are comprised of teachers, many of whom who are dissatisfied with union leadership. For instance, United Teachers Los Angeles was originated by a group of teachers unhappy with the union's failure to propose policies regarding teacher evaluation and professional development. And New York City's Educators 4 Excellence organization does not collaborate with New York City's United Federation of Teachers (Sawchuck, 2011d).

Other special interest groups include the Joyce Foundation, the Bill and Melinda Gates Foundation, and the Denver-based Rose Community Foundation. These organizations support new teacher advocacy groups such as United Teachers Los Angeles, Teacher Plus Policy Fellow (Boston, Chicago, Indianapolis, Los Angeles, and Memphis), New Millennium Initiative (Denver, Hillsborough County, IL, San

Francisco Bay Area, and Seattle), and New York City's Educators 4 Excellence (Sawchuck, 2011d).

Teacher union advocates believe that special interest groups provide financial incentives to these new advocacy groups simply to support their reforms, disrupt union activities, and weaken their membership. For instance, to be eligible for membership to New York City's Educators 4 Excellence (financed by the Bill and Melinda Gates Foundation), teachers must sign a declaration of support for linking teacher evaluation to student performance and teacher tenure reforms, both supported by the Gates Foundation (Sawchuck, 2011d).

Unions and Private Enterprise

Public school advocates believe that teachers and unions are being used as scapegoats to conceal the fact that corporations are creating higher unemployment through outsourcing jobs compared to a shortage of skilled workers. High unemployment leads to a variety of societal issues that impact student achievement for which teachers often are blamed. For instance, America has been hard hit by transitioning from a manufacturing economy to a service economy.

According to Hasan (2010), industries such as leather, textiles, footwear, and clothing have been primarily outsourced to other countries, which has resulted in the loss of hundreds of thousands of American jobs, especially skilled and semi-skilled. Service jobs, on the other hand, do not pay as much and require fewer technical skills.

During this transitioning to a service economy, America outsourced four hundred thousand manufacturing jobs, and this is expected to reach a total of 3.3 million by 2015. U.S. investors and shareholders reap financial benefits from outsourcing; however, the poverty that this system creates does not help restore the U.S. economy but instead exacerbates decreasing local, state, and federal taxes, which are needed for public services (Hasan, 2010).

Furthermore, outsourcing leaves fewer people who can afford to purchase the products being manufactured. Hence, manufacturers are cutting their profit margins by reducing the pool of potential purchasers. Turning a deaf ear to this problem and blaming educators is not the answer.

Former teacher Anthony Cody echoes this reality when he noted in *Education Week* (2010) that "The truth is that poverty and unemployment yield hopelessness in our communities and in our schools as well. People who have lived in multi-generational poverty often see no way out, and children are very sensitive to this. Teachers in our schools do their best to inspire our children to lift their aspirations upwards, but we do not succeed with all of them."

Although the jury is still out regarding how the public ultimately feels about unions, the Phi Delta Kappa/Gallup Poll notes that the public supports teacher rights in collective bargaining and maintains a high trust level for teachers (Bushaw and Lopez, 2011). Thus, critics of teacher unions must be careful not to stereotype all unions based on the notion that there are in reality some teachers who are not suited to be educators. But as noted by the AFT, many unions are poised to work with administrators in streamlining the process of terminating such teachers.

How Unions Are Impacted by Legislative Reforms

As the public school teacher pool shrinks due to rigorous demands, many critics believe this will lead to an increase in alternative certifications so others can enter the teaching force. For instance, if one has a degree in English, one may be eligible to teach, although lacking educational pedagogy as with traditional teachers. Public school reformers believe that a teacher's academic skill level will improve teaching and learning.

On the other hand, public school advocates see alternative certifications as a tool to diminish the role of unions and create conditions to further privatize the market. According to Lieberman (1994), public unions exist solely to control wage rates and other terms and conditions of employment. Teacher unions such as the NEA and AFT survive because they realize that producer competition (e.g., alternative certifications) will hurt unions through contracting out services or organizing nonunion workers, which may or may not be beneficial to consumers.

If unions such as the NEA and AFT did not have any say in the hiring and/or dismissal of employees, they will eventually lose membership and perhaps cease to exist. To prevent this, the NEA and AFT attempt to eliminate producer competition in a variety of ways such as supporting legislation requiring all teachers to be certified (including private schools), placing limitations on school boards to contract out services, engaging in collective bargaining contracts that mandate that school boards negotiate wage rates between teachers and support personnel, and opposing vouchers or tax waivers to parents who wish to enroll their children into private school. Public school advocates believe that market competition (global economy) has hurt unions in the private sector by contracting out jobs coupled with the organization of nonunion workers.

Unions are feeling the effects of antiunion organizations and legislators who wish to take away collective bargaining rights for teachers. The NEA, the largest teachers' union, has seen a one hundred thousand–person decline in membership since 2010 (Sawchuk, 2012). States such as Wisconsin, Ohio, and Tennessee have introduced legislation attempting to restrict unions from collectively bargaining. Wisconsin and Tennessee were both successful in stripping teacher bargaining rights, although many citizens have been adamant in attempting to repeal the law.

As a consequence of Tennessee's legislation, union membership in Tennessee and other states has declined since lawmakers stripped unions of the right to collectively bargain (Associated Press, 2011b). On the other hand, both Democrats and Republican voters in Ohio were heavily opposed to the law and struck down legislation prohibiting teachers from collectively bargaining (McNeil, 2011d).

MERIT PAY

Many reformists are promoting the idea of merit pay to boost teacher effectiveness. In short, merit pay is basing an employee's salary in part on his or her performance or the offering of financial incentives to boost teacher performance. Often, test scores are utilized as a basis for merit pay for teachers, a practice that many educational experts deem as unreliable due to the number of variables involved (Economic Policy Institute, 2010).

A rigorous three-year, in-depth study of teachers in Tennessee clearly shows that merit pay is not a factor in promoting student achievement and has little, if any, impact (Sawchuk, 2010b). According to the study conducted by researchers affiliated with the National Center on Performance Incentives at Vanderbilt University, teachers in one group were offered incentives of up to fifteen thousand dollars if they raised student math scores, but the control group was offered no incentives. During the three years of the study, both groups' scores were similar. To prove the validity of this experiment, the study was widely and positively appraised by various scholars.

The Rand Corporation also investigated the system of merit pay in New York and concluded that it did not improve student achievement or teacher job satisfaction. According to the Rand Corporation's report, most teachers viewed merit pay as having been money received for work that they would have normally performed with or without incentives (Sparks, 2011c). Due to research findings indicating that merit pay was ineffective in New York, the state canceled its merit pay program.

Most teachers work hard, are motivated by making a difference in the lives of students, and are not overly influenced by monetary incentives. Critics and other stakeholders should proceed with caution in attempting to fuse business practices with public education.

American Pulitzer Prize–winning columnist and former assistant managing editor for the *Washington Post* Eugene Robinson describes merit pay tied to students' test scores as a racket in his article "The Test Score Racket." Robinson's response came after the indictment of Beverly Hall, the former superintendent of the Atlanta public schools who was charged with facilitating a cheating scheme with thirty-four teachers and principals that won her over five hundred thousand dollars in bonuses. Teachers and principals who worked under the tutelage of Hall also received bonuses and promotions based on student test scores (Robinson, 2013).

Robinson realizes and notes how there have been many other reports of cheating scandals throughout the nation, often the result of an obsession with testing to determine student achievement. And creating a situation in which teachers are more apt to cheat than students indicates how the overreliance on testing has negatively impacted teachers and administrators.

Based upon current research, merit pay is not the answer to promoting student achievement. To enhance student achievement, teachers must not only maintain high expectations for students but also demonstrate that they care about the lives of their students as well (Payne, 2003). High-stakes testing implies that teachers care only about test scores and not about students as individuals.

As Robinson (2013) stated, "But even absent cheating, the blind obsession with test scores implies that teachers are interchangeable implements of information transfer, rather than caring professionals who know their students as individuals. It reduces students to the leavings of a No. 2 pencil." Tests should be utilized as diagnostic tools to aid in guiding curriculum changes rather than as a punitive approach.

Professional Learning Communities

Rather than relying on merit pay to boost teacher effectiveness, wise administrators understand that there are other, more reliable ways to foster teacher effectiveness. Superintendent Sheldon H. Berman of Eugene, Oregon, and past superintendent of the Jefferson County schools in Louisville, Kentucky, notes the success he has had implementing professional learning communities (PLCs) (Berman and Camins, 2011).

According to Dufour et al. (2006), a PLC is a group of educators (administrators and teachers) who work collaboratively in ongoing processes to increase student achievement. Components of a PLC include shared mission, collaborative culture (focus on learning), collective inquiry, action orientation (learning by doing), commitment to continuous improvement, and results orientation. Educators in a PLC school develop common formative and summative assessments, and rely on shared curricular and teaching methodologies to bolster student achievement.

Merit pay has been known to create friction among teachers. A sure way to create a conflict among people is to point out differences among them. In a merit pay system, teachers may be unwilling to work together as a team, might hoard resources, and/or could even feud over which students they have to instruct. Rather than relying on a system of merit pay that may destroy collaboration with staff members, PLCs promote collaboration.

As a former principal, I assisted in implementing PLCs at J. L. Buford Intermediate Center in partnership with Eastern Illinois University. I am convinced that our implementation of PLCs led to an increase in student achievement, as reflected in our local and state assessments.

There may be some positives and negatives in regard to all educational reforms, but one thing is clear: all reforms and any attempts to transform teacher practice will fail if teachers are not given the opportunity to plan and strategize together. Research is clear that districts that practice the tenets of PLCs foster student achievement. For instance, in Houston public schools, the administration worked hand in hand with teachers to create Individualized Professional Development Plans that included teacher goals for the academic year and the support that teachers would receive to achieve those goals. As a result of the district engaging in collaboration, the district made improvements in areas such as teacher evaluations (Grier, 2011).

There are other success stories of districts utilizing PLCs in schools. School District 54 in Schaumburg, Illinois, was increasingly the target of community dissatisfaction with its schools due to low student achievement over the course of several years. Also, staff morale was dwindling and, while teachers worked hard, they did not see any positive results (Myers and Rafferty, 2012).

The district responded by implementing PLCs after a thorough review of research. District administrators worked hand in hand with the teachers' union to promote collaboration, and the results were amazing. For instance, the district moved from 241st out of 740 Illinois schools to 65th in 2011. And in 2011, seventeen out of the district's twenty-seven schools met or exceeded state standards (Myers and Rafferty, 2012).

In regard to merit pay, many administrators are pessimistic that merit pay and/or linking teacher performance to student growth can exist without disrupting the unity of the teaching staff. When districts rely on these two models to bolster student achievement, it has the opposite effect. More importantly, educational research does not support its use. Simply stated, to measure teacher effectiveness properly, administrators have to look at several variables rather than just single indicators such as test scores.

Variety of Variables Affecting Student Achievement

Variables such as student attendance, students with disabilities, English-as-a-second-language students, student motivation, homeless students, poverty, and student mobility are usually not factored in when determining student achievement. Because of these factors, tests are not reliable in determining teacher quality as it relates to student assessment, and utilizing tests to evaluate teachers would be unfair to teachers. Nevertheless, the federal government is continuing to fund states' efforts to develop data-based systems that align student achievement (based in part on standardized tests) and teacher performance to measure teacher effectiveness.

Teachers who are performing poorly should be properly evaluated and given additional resources so they may improve. If they do not improve, dismissal may be warranted. No matter how one views merit pay, it is not the answer to promoting a quality education. As noted before, many teachers are motivated by their desire to make a difference in the life of a child, not merely because they will receive a monetary reward.

The Phi Delta Kappa/Gallup Poll indicates that the American public feels that teachers should be evaluated by a multitude of factors including experience, academic degrees, and principal evaluations, and is less interested in utilizing high-stakes testing as a measurement of teacher performance (Bushaw and Lopez, 2011).

Nevertheless, the Obama administration advocates for the belief that student tests should be used significantly to determine teacher effectiveness. As a result, critics have contended that Obama's approach to merit pay does not align with public opinion. More importantly, the results of one of the most rigorous studies ever conducted of performance-based pay in Tennessee showed that merit pay had little effect on student achievement (Sawchuk, 2010b).

The Importance of Collaboration

As previously noted, staff collaboration is a fundamental element in boosting and sustaining student achievement. Angelis and Wilcox, both investigators of the Know Your Schools for New York project, studied schools that consistently outperformed their counterparts over an eight-year span. The investigators noted that in all of the high-performing schools they studied, collaboration and community engagement set them apart from their counterparts. Educators in those schools believed that the collaboration among teachers, administrators, parents, and staff was a key in promoting student achievement (Angelis and Wilcox, 2011).

Districts that collaborate with staff and/or promote the concept of PLCs often are supported and encouraged by the local school board. This is yet another reason why we need school boards. Effective school boards understand the reality of why collaboration is important and are instrumental in securing community support in that partnership.

Collaboration is beneficial in many other areas as well, such as labor–district relations. School boards and superintendents who have utilized the collective bargaining process as a tool to better relationships with the union have had positive results. School board governance teams that work collaboratively with their unions experience an increase in student achievement. Also, they experience a better-prepared workforce because teachers feel empowered as a result of being consulted and listened to (Sawchuk, 2011d). For instance, teachers in the Hillsborough County district feel empowered because the district conducts monthly meetings with teachers to discuss a wide range of issues from the curriculum to school calendar planning (Sawchuk, 2011d). When teachers feel supported and collaboration is present, student achievement soars.

Despite success stories regarding this form of collaboration in districts such as Hillsborough, educational critics such as Michelle Rhee, the former chancellor of the District of Columbia schools, believe that collaboration is overrated (Sawchuk, 2011d). Ironically, Rhee faced heavy parental opposition during her tenure because community stakeholders did not feel she listened to their concerns.

Upon leaving her post in the District of Columbia, she was offered a job by the Department of Education, which may be an indicator of what the department values. This attitude goes against the nature of locally elected school boards. As trustees, school boards take pride in the fact that they serve on the community's behalf and often allow for public input concerning the governance of its schools.

The U.S. Department of Education has sent out mixed messages regarding its belief in collaboration. The department has publicly advocated for collaboration between labor and management, but its actions have been quite contrary. For instance, in February 2011, the U.S.

Department of Education hosted a conference on labor management collaboration with the NEA, AFT, and groups representing various administrators. Additionally, the department encouraged collaboration in districts by requiring the administration to obtain union support prior to the processing of the RTT application (Cavanagh, 2011b).

Although these are examples of collaboration, there are also many examples when the department did not favor collaboration. For instance, the Obama administration supported the firing of every teacher in the Central Fall High School district in Rhode Island after teachers refused an increase in workload without extra pay (Sawchuk, 2011d).

According to an article in the *Huffington Post*, the increased workload included sacrificing a portion of teachers' duty-free lunch break to eat with students, tutoring students before and after school, and making dramatic changes in the evaluation system. Teachers felt that they were not collaborated with in regard to these changes by the district. If the school district had collaborated with teachers regarding changes in their work schedules, perhaps the outcome would have been more positive.

The Department of Education's policies regarding the linking of teacher evaluation to student performance have further strained relations between district officials and teachers even in districts in which collaboration was the norm. Collaboration was broken in various districts when the department encouraged states to include proposals (e.g., NCLB waivers and RTT grant applications) to factor in student achievement when evaluating teacher performance.

Tension mounted when experts such as the EPI, various educational officials, and unions indicated that test scores alone are unreliable in trying to determine student growth. In addition, statistical models often used to evaluate teachers were not designed to evaluate teachers based upon student performance (McNeil, 2011d; Sparks, 2011c).

SCHOOL VOUCHERS

Other popular reforms are school vouchers and charter schools. Vouchers were first supported by conservatives, but now some liberal politicians are now supporting the voucher movement as well. Currently, there is no concrete research to show that vouchers have a positive impact on student achievement. A voucher is a certificate that parents can use to pay tuition to a private school or reimbursement for homeschooling.

Usually, vouchers are associated with students who are from low-income families who are attending low-performing schools, but that is changing to include middle- and higher-income families as well (Jennings, 2011; West, 1997). Still, many educational professionals wonder that if voucher legislation is not geared toward at-risk and poverty students, then what is the purpose of vouchers other than taking resources away from public schools that serve all students (Hardy, 2011).

Public school proponents see a correlation between school vouchers and the privatization of public schools. In the past year, legislators from approximately thirty states have introduced legislation supporting using public funds for private tuition, and twenty-eight other states are looking to expand and/or formulate voucher credits for students attending private schools (Hardy, 2011).

Vouchers pose a direct threat to public schools because most vouchers allow students to attend private schools. If private school enrollment increases, logically public school attendance will decrease, which will impact the amount of revenue districts will receive. With most districts currently operating on shoestring budgets, some districts will not be able to keep their doors open.

According to Jennings (2011), private school advocates switched tactics three times to promote vouchers. First, during the 1950s, 1960s, and early 1970s, advocates complained that they were being taxed twice by paying taxes and paying private tuition, but their argument did not receive any traction. Advocates switched tactics during the 1970s and argued that vouchers were necessary to assist inner-city students in receiving a quality education. This tactic allowed voucher advocates to make a case based upon equity and doing what was in the best interest for disadvantaged students, a position progressives found hard to defend.

Current research, such as the 2011 report from the Center on Education Policy, indicates that students who use vouchers to attend private schools do not fare any better than public school students. This report was based on data collected over a ten-year span by voucher advocates from voucher programs in the following states: Wisconsin, Ohio,

Florida, and Washington, DC (Hardy, 2011). When the equity premise of those advocates proved false, voucher advocates began to support vouchers based on the premise that parents should have the right to pick the schools for their children.

The notion of allowing parents to pick their children's schools reflects the rising tide of privatizing public schools. According to Urschel (2003), the United States has made the consumer king and has blurred the lines between private and public. Choice is the value of consumerism. Now more people are taking the attitude of investing in their children's future but not in the future of other people's children.

Currently states such as Colorado, Indiana, and Wisconsin have expanded their voucher programs to include middle- and higher-income families. For instance, regardless of income, Colorado citizens can use vouchers to assist in paying for private school. Essentially, millionaires can use public dollars to send their children to private school. Under the Wisconsin voucher program, families making over seventy thousand dollars a year can obtain a voucher (Hardy, 2011).

Privatization of public schools may very well be the end goal for many critics of public education. Educational experts believe there is a concerted political effort to expand vouchers and to reduce the size of government by dismantling big governmental sectors like education. If public education becomes dismantled and school boards begin to disappear quickly, we will not have an educational institution based upon the needs of the people or society but those of private enterprise.

For instance, the industry-funded group American Legislative Exchange Council (ALEC) is supported by various top U.S. corporations and private foundations to draft legislation that has been utilized in state legislatures throughout the country (Hardy, 2011). ALEC supports vouchers, charters, and tax credits for parents who send their children to private schools. But educational experts like Julie Underwood believe that the real motive of ALEC is to dismantle public education and to create a system where education is not provided for everyone and is profit driven (Hardy, 2011).

Many school board members are banding together and fighting back against budget cuts and the privatization of schools. For instance, in Louisiana, Governor Bobby Jindal cut school funding while simultaneously advocating for the expansion of voucher programs. Governor

Jindal's action led to the formation of the Coalition for Louisiana Public Education, which was spearheaded by Jack Loup, president of the St. Tammany Parish School Board, when he called public school supporters together to discuss Jindal's educational plans (Hardy, 2011). Primarily, the coalition seeks to spread the message of the importance of local control and the negative impact of budget cuts to public education in the state.

CHARTER SCHOOLS

The charter school movement began in 1991 in Minnesota. Since that time, there has been an accretion of charter schools throughout the nation, particularly in urban areas. The original design of charter schools was to identify "best practices" in public education by operating outside of state mandates and then transfer those "best practices" to traditional public schools.

Ideally, charter schools have fewer regulatory requirements (e.g., teacher certification, school site control over finances, ability to hire staff, curriculum and mission) compared to public schools in exchange for specific types of accountability and to be more innovative than their public school counterparts (National Charter School Institute). Yet research is emerging that depicts charters schools as not being as innovative, and, in fact, utilizing many of the same instructional practices found in traditional public schools (Bulkley, 2012).

Since their creation, charter schools have expanded, but their original purpose continues to go unfulfilled. Charter schools have expanded in part due to lawmakers who believe there is too much bureaucracy or red tape in public schools (e.g., labor unions and state and federal mandates) to produce and sustain student achievement. Nevertheless, legislators themselves are responsible for drafting legislation that heavily regulates public schools.

In short, charter schools are public schools that are allowed to operate in a manner similar to that of private schools. In theory, proponents favor charter schools because they are designed to be more accountable for achievement outcomes compared to public schools since authorizers can revoke charter contracts. And proponents of charter schools believe that public schools will perform better if they are forced to compete with charter schools—a philosophy based upon business principles.

Since their inception, there has been mounting criticism regarding the success of charter schools. Bulkley (2001), professor at Rutgers Graduate School of Education, noted that during the birth of charter schools, authorizers with little to no experience in granting performance contracts were under political pressure to fast track the operation of charter schools. Initially, many authorizers were laissez-faire in granting charters to applicants as well as in revoking charters.

Currently, charter authorizers have become more adept at identifying clearer standards and guidelines in evaluating charter applications (Bulkley, 2001). Due to more rigorous application procedures, some charter schools are making a difference. Nevertheless, other components such as compliance reviews must be considered to ensure a healthy school.

Because many authorizers overemphasize the application process to ensure a good pool of quality applicants, the renewal process in maintaining a charter is often enervated. As of 2001, only 29% of states required charter schools to go through a renewal process to ensure compliance with their written charters. Of the charter schools up for renewal, most succeeded, with the exception of charter schools that had closed for financial and/or organizational reasons (Bulkley, 2001). Ultimately, many authorizers believe that the market (e.g., parental satisfaction and waiting lists) will prove whether or not their institution is effective (Bulkley, 2001).

Difference between Charter and Private Schools

Private schools differ from charter and public schools in that the former are usually founded and managed by a private group such as a church. Nevertheless, there is some overlap between private and charter schools. For instance, both private and charter schools are exempt from many legislative regulations, with the exception that charter schools are not exempt from regulations governing educational content. Private schools frequently follow a particular philosophy and typically charge tuition to cover operating costs instead of funds being derived by local, state, or federal governments.

As noted, charter schools are not only similar to private schools in regard to being exempt from regulations but can also be managed by private for-profit organizations. Educational management organizations (EMOs) have increasingly taken charge of the operation and management of many charter schools and are considered to be one of the fastest forms of public school privatization (Miron, 2007).

Public schools have long had a history of contracting out specific services such as transportation and custodial services. However, contracting out the operation and management of schools is relatively new, dating from the early 1990s. EMOs generally are for-profit organizations and typically are reimbursed for their services by charging a per-pupil fee, typically between 10 and 15%, and offer some simple guarantee such as a positive year-end balance (Miron, 2007).

Various educational critics have argued that EMOs all too often do not understand community values and needs. After Hurricane Katrina struck New Orleans, 80% of the city's school children attended charter schools administered by EMOs. This was held as the ideal school model by Secretary Duncan. Due to community issues and other problems, currently all of the EMOs were either fired or left in shame (Carr and Gilbertson, 2013). Although EMOs have an unproven track record, charter schools often managed by EMOs continue to be the flagship for many lawmakers and reformists seeking to reform public education.

Charter and Private Schools as Compared to Public Schools

Recent research shows that private and charter schools are not faring any better than public schools. According to Center on Education Policy (2007) research on private schools, the number of graduates attending elite colleges from private schools is more associated with demographics than with academic quality. Other findings include the following:

- When student backgrounds and income levels are considered, there is essentially no difference in the quality between private and public schools.
- Achievement scores in all subjects such as reading, math, science, and history are similar for private and public school students.

- Most students attend college at similar rates from both private and public schools.

Regardless of the research, there is a perception that private and charter schools are better. For instance, charter schools have been championed by the Obama administration although research clearly indicates that they do not fare any better than traditional public schools.

Under the Obama administration, states had to promise to expand charter schools in their respective states to receive RTT funds (U.S. Department of Education, 2012). Why would the Obama administration continue to promote charter schools over traditional public schools? The answer to this question is uncertain, but many critics have reason to believe that the administration's support of charter schools is strongly tied to special interest groups.

Charters and Unions

The producers of the film *Waiting for Superman* advocated for charter schools because such schools are not shackled by union contracts, which the producers claim force the schools to keep subpar teachers employed (Wheeler, 2011). However, charter schools are not exempt from negotiating with the union.

The charter school operated by Knowledge Is Power Program (KIPP) had intense negotiations with Baltimore teachers concerning the rate of hourly pay for teachers who work extended hours outside of the normal school day (Zehr, 2011b). Many teachers believe that the public does not understand the fact that tenure is not designed to protect subpar teachers but rather to protect teachers from various forms of discrimination (Wheeler, 2011).

Charter schools were established to strengthen the public school system by allowing charter schools to be more specialized in exchange for increasing student achievement. For instance, charter schools might attempt nontraditional approaches such as single-gender classrooms. Although there are some differences in state laws that regulate charter schools, most charter schools can be opened by a group or an organization (including businesses) that successfully applies for a charter (Sautter, n.d.).

Charter managers typically run a school for three to five years, during which time the charter school receives public funds. Regardless of the facts regarding charter public schools, the American public approves of them. The forty-third annual Phi Delta Kappa/Gallup Poll showed that the American public overwhelmingly approves of charter schools by much as 70% (Bushaw and Lopez, 2011).

Educators credit Albert Shanker, past president of the AFT, for establishing charter schools. Shanker believed that charter schools should be operated by professional teachers who sought solutions to a variety of complicated social issues. However, he later lobbied against charter schools as states began allowing for-profit companies to run them. More specifically, Shanker did not envision charter schools coming into direct conflict with public schools or with teacher unions.

Charter operators created conflict with unions as charter operators sought to hire and fire teachers in most cases without due process, to determine unilaterally teachers' pay schedules, to provide bonuses (merit pay) for specific teachers, to control work conditions, and to prohibit collective bargaining. And charter operators often expect teachers to work extended hours such as late evenings and weekends while refusing to allow teachers to have a voice in the governing process (Zehr, 2011b).

Unfair Advantages of Charter Schools

Charter operators also created conflict with traditional schools by taking away various resources of public schools. For instance, parents in New York, supported by the advocacy group Class Size Matters, brought a lawsuit alleging that charter schools were not paying for the use of public school buildings, which resulted in taking away resources from traditional public schools (Zehr, 2011b). Similarly, the United Federation of Teachers and the National Association for the Advancement of Colored People brought suit in New York courts in July 2011 disputing the closing of twenty-two public schools and the reopening and/or expansion of sixteen charter schools (Zehr, 2011b).

Public schools cannot afford to lose any more resources, especially in tough financial times. It is appalling, disturbing, and, in some instances unethical, for charter schools to receive resources often not afforded to public schools, such as not paying for building space, receiving general student aid, and receiving generous amounts of private donations often tied to special interests (Green, 2011).

With such key advantages, how can charter schools realistically be compared to their public school counterparts? All too often, public schools have to cut pre-K programs, summer programs, teachers, counselors, tutors, custodians, and secretaries, and raise student fees due to decreases in state aid. Additionally, districts are freezing salaries and offering early retirement incentives as alternative ways to save money (Cavanagh, 2011b).

The American Association of School Administrators noted that 65% of superintendents said they have eliminated jobs due to lack of funding (Cavanagh, 2011). Most Americans agree that the number one issue confronting schools is a lack of funding (Bushaw and Lopez, 2011).

A variety of problems are associated with the charter school movement. Traditionally, most charter schools did not service similar subgroups as did public schools. According to Hehir (2010), most charter schools operated on the premise that children with disabilities need not apply. It is unfair to judge charter school performance compared to that of public schools when resources are not the same and different populations are served.

Student Achievement Differences between Public and Charter Schools

Research is clear in showing that public schools outperform charter schools in teaching student math skills (Nelson, Rosenberg, and Meter, 2004). According to the 2010 Illinois state report card, twenty-nine out of thirty-nine charter schools did not make adequate yearly progress, and twenty-three are on the state's academic watch list for failing to meet adequate yearly progress in subjects such as math (Wheeler, 2011).

Other major research studies indicate that charter schools are not faring better than traditional public schools. Three in-depth studies of charter schools include one commissioned by the U.S. Department of Education Institution of Education Sciences entitled *The Nation's Report Card: America's Charter Schools: Results from the NAEP 2003*

Pilot Study (National Assessment of Educational Progress, 2003) and two commissioned by the Center for Research on Education Outcomes (CREDO) at Stanford University in 2009 and 2013 entitled, *Multiple Choice: Charter School Performance in Sixteen States* and *National Charter School Study*, respectively.

The NAEP is a nationally representative, standardized test given periodically that measures U.S. students' knowledge in math, reading, science, writing, and other subjects. NAEP's report is reflective of 150 national charter schools based upon the performance of fourth graders. Stanford's report focused on charter schools in the following states: Arkansas, Arizona, California, Colorado (Denver), the District of Columbia, Florida, Georgia, Illinois (Chicago), Louisiana, Massachusetts, Minnesota, Missouri, New Mexico, North Carolina, Ohio, and Texas. Key findings from the NAEP's report (2003) include the following:

- Fourth grade students as a whole did not outperform students in public schools in math.
- There was no difference in scores of white, black, and Hispanic students in math as compared to public schools.
- There was no difference in reading scores between charter schools and public schools.
- Fourth grade students receiving free or reduced lunch did not perform as well on average as their public school counterparts.

Stanford's CREDO report (2009) noted interesting data on the performance of charter schools and indicated the following in its study of charter schools:

- Charter school students on average experience a decrease in reading and math compared to public schools students.
- Charter high school students do not perform as well as students in public schools.
- Black and Hispanic students fare far worse than their counterparts in public schools.
- Poor and English-language-learner students on average perform better than their counterparts in public schools.

Stanford's 2013 CREDO report provided new data regarding the performance of charter schools that includes the following:

- There has been slow and steady progress made with charter schools since 2009.
- There are a number of charter schools whose learning gains are significantly worse than traditional public schools.
- As a group, modest improvements have been made by the 2009 CREDO charter school studies in comparison to traditional public schools.

Staff Turnover and Charter Schools

Charter schools experience high turnover in administrators, students, and teachers. Recent surveys indicate that the number of administrative turnovers, specifically charter school principals, exceeds the turnover rate in public schools (Zehr, 2010). Without strong administrative support, it would be challenging for any school to maintain educational programs. Teacher retention is not faring any better. Charter school teachers in cities such as Los Angeles are three times more likely to leave after one year than traditional public school teachers (Samuels, 2011e).

Thevenot (2010), a writer for the *Texas Tribune*, noted the following about charter schools in Texas:

- There was 79% staff turnover at the Accelerated Intermediate Academy in Houston during the 2008–2009 school year.
- There was 71% staff turnover at Peak Preparatory in Dallas.
- There was 69% staff turnover at Harmony Science Academy in College Station.
- Forty or more of the two hundred charter operators in Texas had to replace over half of their staffs.
- There was 30% or more staff turnover at established charter operators such as KIPP and YES Prep.
- The average turnover rate for charter schools is 43%, compared to 16% of public schools in the state.

Student Attrition and Charter Schools

Student attrition is high in many charter schools as well. According to Green (2011), Western Michigan University along with Columbia University commissioned a study involving student attrition at KIPP schools in Baltimore between the years of 2006 to 2009. The report noted that, on average, 15% of students leave KIPP schools annually, compared to 3% in public schools.

Furthermore, 30% of students, many of whom are black males, leave KIPP schools between sixth and eighth grades. Ironically, the KIPP schools in Baltimore target African Americans and receive more per pupil funding, along with an additional $5,760 per pupil funding from private sources. According to the *Baltimore Sun*, regardless of whether or not KIPP was successful, KIPP received more than fifty million dollars from the U.S. Department of Education to expand, in part because Secretary Duncan favors charter schools.

According to a student survey of charter schools in New Orleans, students gave charter schools a C or D rating in areas such as safety, academic rigor, counselor support, physical plant, and classroom management. And many students indicated that their charter schools were not preparing them for college and that they had minimal contacts with school counselors (Tran, 2011). Interestingly, New Orleans is on the path to becoming the first all-charter district in the country and has been championed by Secretary Duncan.

Student Discipline Differences between Charter and Public Schools

The prodigious rate of staff turnover and student attrition in charter schools is partially related to student discipline issues. Charter schools are more common in urban areas, and most of these schools serve high numbers of minority and lower socioeconomic students, which is reflective of urban communities. Urban communities experience more social problems than other communities, often spilling into the school system and making it difficult to create and sustain an atmosphere conducive to student learning.

Educational reformers who dispraise traditional public schools must understand that, until the influx of social problems is addressed in these communities, it is doubtful that any educational institution will ultimately be successful. Therefore, it is not wise to utilize temporary remedies such as randomly firing staff and administrators as prescribed in various turnaround models.

Charter schools are finding out firsthand the difficulty of addressing their discipline issues. In an effort to manage discipline problems, many charter schools simply prohibit students from attending if these students pose behavioral or academic challenges. If such students are not prohibited from attending, usually they are screened out later. However, many charter authorizers believe they need this authority and the right to set other tough disciplinary standards in order to provide a safe school, particularly in neighborhoods plagued by violence and other social issues (Zubrzycki, Cavanagh, and McNeil, 2013).

It is for this essential reason, charter authorizers contend, that parents choose charters over traditional public schools in these communities. It should also be noted that charter schools serve far fewer special education students than do traditional public schools. In short, a key advantage of charter schools is that they have a lot of autonomy in controlling student admission. Strangely, charter supporters boast that they are considered public schools although it is evident in many cases they operate as private schools.

Unlike charter schools, traditional public schools have to accept all students. And, when students are expelled from charter schools, most find their way back to public schools. For instance, it is reported in 2013 in Chicago that 1,400 out of the 1,999 students who left charter schools returned to public schools (Zubrzycki, Cavanagh, and McNeil, 2013).

Despite this reality, public schools are discredited and teachers are told they are not up to par. Ironically, although some charter schools are restricting students with behavioral and/or special education needs from attending and have other advantages, charter schools are not faring any better than traditional public schools.

Governance of Charter Schools

If charter schools had remained true to their original design, they might have improved public schools. However, because of the way in which charter schools have been used, they have yielded negative consequences. As noted earlier, states differ as to who can open a charter school, although some states have a more rigorous process for accountability than others.

Overall, it is alarming to think about the number of states that allow virtually anyone to apply for a charter and possibly get approved. Among these are corporations, universities, and schemers who are solely looking to make a profit. Ravtich (2010) described how the Alex's Academics of Excellence school was opened by a convicted rapist and how the founders of the Mandella School of Science and Math were convicted of peddling money by cashing checks from the Department of Public Instruction in Wisconsin for children who never enrolled at the school.

The *Dallas Morning News* did an in-depth study at the success and challenges of charter schools in Texas in 2010. In December 2010, the *Dallas Morning News* printed an article entitled "Funds Misuse, Nepotism Feared at Texas Charter Schools" and noted some appalling news (Holly, 2010). The article reported how administrators, some of whom were founders, earned six-figure salaries although they had small student populations and found that families of charter school owners were cashing in as well. For instance (Holly, 2010):

- Focus Learning Academy founder and superintendent Leroy McClure earned an income of $146,000 to run a school comprised of seven hundred students. His salary is more than other public school administrators with districts of similar size. Additionally, his wife earned fifty thousand dollars from the school for consulting, and his brother and sister worked there as well, earning hefty salaries.
- Children First Academy, which has 750 students, paid the Sherwin Allen family (Sherwin's wife, two brothers, and two children) nearly seven hundred thousand dollars.
- Faith Family Academy, with an enrollment of approximately fifteen hundred students, paid the Purcell family approximately a half million dollars annually to run the school. Superintendent Ted Purcell made two hundred thousand dollars; his wife earned $82,500 as program director; his daughter, the assistant superintendent, earned $115,000; and his son-in-law earned $162,720 as technology coordinator.

Charter Schools and Private Interests

Charter schools have grown rapidly in the last twenty years. Prior to this time, such schools were virtually unheard of. Currently, charters are expanding at a rate of approximately four hundred to five hundred annually and continue to grow with the support of private foundations, for-profit organizations, and the aid of state and federal governments (Stover, 2012a). Specifically, private money is the engine running the train, as there are many links to private enterprise. For instance, according to Stover (2012a):

- The Walton Foundation gave seventy-five million dollars in school choice and charter grants in 2010.
- Between 2005 and 2010, out-of-state campaign donors gave $233,000 to Florida legislators who were viewed as charter advocates.
- More than seven hundred charter schools nationwide are operated by for-profit organizations.
- Hefty donations to charter programs are provided by various foundations such as the Eli and Edythe Broad Foundation, the Bill and Melinda Gates Foundation, the Doris and Donald Fisher Fund, the Michael and Susan Dell Foundation, and the Carnegie Corporation of New York.
- The Charter School Growth Fund (an organization that helps finance new charter startups) received over eighty-six million dollars from private foundations.
- The online education company K-12 Inc. spends approximately five hundred thousand dollars a year for charter advocate political campaigns.
- The majority of Michigan's charter schools are for-profit.

Undeniably, charter schools are receiving lots of aid but they are less effective than public schools. Why is private money being spent to overhaul public education? Public school advocates believe that private philanthropic organizations, many of which have ties to big businesses, would like to see public education based upon a market approach to improve educational outcomes. Other critics believe that wealthy businessmen and women are trying to seize an opportunity to divert money from public education into for-profit ventures.

For instance, virtual public schools are exploding across the country as alternatives to traditional classrooms with little oversight. For-profit virtual school companies such as K12 Inc. have made more than $17.5 million in profits from revenue of $708 million from public funds, from while researchers agree that many students actually lose ground in core subjects. Additionally, virtual schools in states such as Ohio, Pennsylvania, and Tennessee are doing significantly worse than public schools while still making profits (Simon, 2012e).

Ultimately, we cannot afford to experiment with our children's future by allowing charter schools to expand in this matter. We need to continue to support local schools governed by school boards. School boards should be empowered and held accountable through venues such as the election process to maximize student achievement. We do not need for-profit companies, foundations, and potential scam artists to take power away from our local citizenry under the guise of promoting student achievement with little to no oversight.

HOW THE REFORM MOVEMENT NEGATIVELY IMPACTS SCHOOL BOARDS

When there are issues of school governance or the impression that schools are failing because of unfair assessments, voters become disgruntled with their school board, although many decisions are out of the school board's control. Speer (1998) stated, "Communities entrust school boards with the oversight and leadership of their schools. Thus, school board members bear ultimate responsibility for student achievement." However, school boards need to be re-empowered and govern in a way that reflects the community's values if they are to be held accountable. We cannot hold board members accountable while maintaining a system that allows various politicians to make key educational decisions.

The reform movement has created the ambience that school boards need to continuously seek new ways to bolster student achievement. School boards have encountered increasing demands—particularly from legislators, parents, and other stakeholders—to improve test scores or face some drastic action such as converting schools to charters, particularly in urban cities.

Besides resulting in friction on the governance team (which leads to board and superintendent turnover) often school boards elect to replace the superintendent and to bring in superintendents with a reputation of being a reformer (Alsbury, 2008). In part because of this, the tenure of superintendents in urban cities is a few years. All too often, these newly hired superintendents incorporate new "silver bullet" programs and discontinue previous programs. The change in rules and programs incorporated by new superintendents often creates inconsistency in accomplishing board goals, damages staff morale, and reduces student achievement.

The American public cannot sit back and allow politicians to guide the conversation as to what they feel a quality education should be. We need to reinforce our current public school systems governed by school boards to maximize student achievement. School boards govern more closely to the people and are adept at determining what the community expectations are for their schools.

However, this is not to say that there are not areas in which school boards could improve. The reality is that if school boards do not engage in professional development and facilitate the conversation about what is needed to ensure quality schools, then school boards will increasingly be the focus of criticism, and their role will continue to diminish.

SUMMARY

The reform movement has changed the direction of public education in our country. Admittedly, some reforms are very much needed, especially in larger urban communities. However, educational reforms in these communities are not enough by themselves to consistently maintain high levels of student achievement.

In order to sustain high student achievement in these communities, there has to be a mix of educational, social, political, and economic reform because these large urban communities have a variety of factors that impact student achievement, such as the high poverty and unemployment rates. It should be clear that what is not needed is a cookie-cutter reform model approach for all of the nation's public schools. Clearly, public schools in various communities have different necessities, which offer an additional reason as to the need of local school boards to represent those interests.

Educational reformists frequently cite low worker productivity and global competiveness as primary reasons to reform public schools. More often than not, employers are pressed to identify specific skills employees lack. Often, employers are more concerned with employee work behavior than with employees' math and science skills.

Concerning global competiveness, the United States enjoyed almost a decade of prosperity in the 1990s and, despite a weakened economy between 2000 and 2002, was noted as having one of the world's largest economies. The fact is that student achievement outcomes have less to do with U.S. global competiveness as compared to commerce, trade, and other factors.

Because many legislators have primarily viewed all public schools as having the same problems and needs, these lawmakers offer the same remedies for all, such as an emphasis on standardized tests, merit pay, vouchers, charter schools, teacher and principal evaluation reforms, and various school turnaround models. All of these reforms were based on little to no academic research. For instance, the EPI warned lawmakers about linking student and teacher performance because of the number of variables involved.

Other popular reforms such as charter schools, merit pay, vouchers, and school turnaround models do not fare any better. To date, charter schools have not been shown to be more effective than traditional public schools. Regarding merit pay, it was deemed ineffective in New York and Tennessee. Also, vouchers have created systems of resegregation, and most school turnaround models are based on faulty assumptions about the factors impacting student achievement.

Ultimately, all of these reforms impact the way in which school boards operate and govern. Most school boards govern in a way to appease state and federal mandates. If state and federal mandates create certain realities such as budget shortfalls and district program cuts, the public tends to blame the school board without realizing other external factors.

QUESTIONS FOR REFLECTION

1. Do school boards, superintendents, and educational researchers favor the federal approach of reforming education?

2. Explain the enigma that exists concerning worker productivity as related to employee work and behavior skills.

3. Does a correlation exist between global competiveness and student performance? Explain.

4. Identify and describe the potential problems of linking student performance to teacher performance. Are there other ways to gauge teacher effectiveness without linking student to teacher performance? Please explain.

5. Explain how the Department of Education aided the development and expansion of the Common Core Standards.

6. Explain how unions have been blamed for hampering the process of improving public education. Are these criticisms fair?

7. What does the research say about merit pay? Are PLCs a better approach? Explain.

8. Discuss the evolution of vouchers.

9. Describe the difference between charter and private schools. How are they different from traditional public schools?

10. Why do many legislators support charter schools?

11. Identify and explain some of the major issues associated with charter schools.

12. Describe the connection between private enterprise and charter schools.

13. Describe how various school reforms impacted public school boards.

CHAPTER 4

The Need for School Boards

How to best educate students has been a topic of discussion in our nation for quite some time. As noted, the current system of school board governance dates back two hundred years, when local citizens decided that the administration of towns and schools in Massachusetts should be separate, in part due to politics (Danzberger, 1994). Influential citizens led a successful movement in the late nineteenth century to break the ties between school districts, political parties, and officials from local and state government in an effort to steer politics away from the governance of schools (Kirst, 1994a).

The design of school districts, composed of a small school board and a superintendent to oversee their day-to-day operations, originated in the early twentieth century based upon the corporate structure at the time (Land, 2002). Historically, school boards primarily supported the district in a variety of ways, such as approving the budget and legal documents, campaigning for tax referendums, and providing political cover to superintendents and other educators (Kirst, 1994a).

The belief that local communities are best suited to address educational issues through local school boards and superintendents hired by those school boards is supported by statute, although the governance model, size, and process varies from state to state. Local control has long been deemed necessary to prevent state and federal politics from disrupting what is in the best interest of student learning. This tradition has met serious opposition during the past thirty years as evidenced by the following:

- The 1983 publication of *A Nation at Risk*
- The 2002 legislation of No Child Left Behind
- The 2009 Race to the Top grant authorization

It is not the makeup or structure of school boards that threatens their usefulness. In fact, there are many reasons why school boards are needed and best suited to fulfill the corporate responsibility of public education.

FOUR REASONS WHY SCHOOL BOARDS ARE NEEDED

Who actually determines what is ultimately expected from public schools, and why are school boards ideally suited to do so? There are many stakeholders with competing visions regarding the vision for public education. It is faulty to assume that public schools would excel in a culture of chaotic governance. Boyle and Burns (2011) summed up the competition for control of public schools best when they stated,

> Today we have multiple and competing visions of public education, but no national consensus about the fundamental purposes and roles of public schools. . . . Currently there is no evidence of a national consensus regarding the institutional framework in which public school operates or the larger social and cultural purposes a system of public schools ought to serve. Why we created public schools, what we expect of them, and the beliefs that frame public education are all shaped by the "invisible hand of ideology." In debates about who should be educated, what they should learn, how they should be taught, who should govern public schools, and how schools should be funded, ideology, values and beliefs matter. . . . Each generation wages a "war for children's minds" battling among itself to define the purposes and goals of public schools.

Consistent with the nation's beliefs when school boards were established, it is the author's opinion that local communities were, and remain, best suited to address educational issues through local school boards and superintendents hired by those school boards. Local school boards provide the link to the community so that constituents' voices are heard and board members are held accountable through the election process.

Whether voters approve or disapprove of board member decisions, they can voice their opinions at the ballot box. School boards allow parents and community members a place to provide input about educational issues such as curriculum and extracurricular concerns indicative of local democracy at work.

Because America is so diverse and the needs and resources of one community often are significantly different than those of another community, locally elected school boards most accurately reflect the values and expectations of their respective communities. This keeps educational decisions as close as possible to those most affected by those decisions (Shannon, 1990). And research suggests that most parents are happy with this arrangement. According to a recent Phi Delta Kappa Gallup Poll, parents are happy with the schools in their community, and they favor state and local control but would like to see less federal involvement (Bushaw and Lopez, 2011; Rose and Gallup, 2010).

The following are four primary reasons why local school boards should govern local public schools specifically:

1. School boards keep the public in public schools.
2. School boards positively impact student achievement.
3. School boards serve as trustees over district resources.
4. School boards serve as advocates for public schools.

School Boards Keep the Public in Public Schools

Local school boards play a key role in preserving our democratic republic by maintaining individual freedoms while simultaneously forging unity. Their unique perspectives allow them to balance complex community values without forfeiting the greater common good. According to Boyle and Burns (2011), "What's public about public schools? . . . It's about how we forge a sense of 'we' and of connection and belonging in a nation of individuals predicated on the principle of self-interest." Without local support, it would be challenging indeed for parents and nonparent citizens to have a genuine voice in the quality of public education for children individually and for the community at large.

Michael Adamson, director of board services for the Indiana Association of School Boards, describes the need for school boards: "Public education is governed by boards because multiple perspectives help ensure that the best decisions are reached in matters affecting a broad constituency; governance by boards provides checks and balances when individuals from different backgrounds and experiences converge, thereby discouraging the domination of leadership by a single individual; public education is governed by boards because local control is an inherent value of a free democracy" (2012). It is vital, therefore, that governing systems are in place to represent that diversity.

Local representation in school governance may be one of the greatest strengths of a democratic nation. As Albert Shanker, former president of the American Federation of Teachers, stated, "School boards are the way the public controls schools in a democracy. Abolishing school boards because they get in the way of efficient school functioning would be like abolishing Congress or state legislatures in the name of efficiency" (Capital Area School Development Association, 1990). More importantly, citizen oversight of local government has always been the cornerstone of our democracy. Our nation is built upon this premise. We use citizen control for cities, counties, states, regions, and police (California School Boards Association, 2007).

John Cassel, former field service director for the Illinois Association of School Boards, noted how school boards are instrumental in balancing community and individual rights. School boards weigh various community values in specific board decisions such as student drug policies. The board must balance community concerns and individual rights to determine who will be tested without violating student privacy (Cassel, 2010).

Of course, effective school boards should also assess such proposals and analyze the benefits and consequences in consultation with professional educators (Shannon, 1990). It then becomes the superintendent's job to investigate, collect, and analyze the necessary data from staff before offering recommendations for the school board to consider. Relying on professionals and analyzing decisions from the perspective of their community assure that the school board can make the best decision possible on critical policy matters. This reliance on district staff and expertise should not be viewed as conceding to a passive role in governance; in fact, quite the opposite is true.

Bracey and Resnick (1998) noted, "Local school boards play the central role in driving and guiding the process to establish a vision of education for their school systems. Indeed, as representatives of the community and governors of the school system, school boards are the best catalysts for stimulating the dialogue, consensus and actions that can shape a truly dynamic and responsive student achievement plan."

School Boards Positively Impact Student Achievement

School boards significantly impact student achievement when the school board's role in student achievement is clearly defined and understood by the board, the staff, and the community. But that's a tall order. The Iowa School Boards Foundation (2008) noted that "the linkages between school boards and teaching and learning in classrooms are often misunderstood. School boards do not directly cause student learning. However, it would appear from findings from the Lighthouse Research and others, the beliefs, decisions and actions of school boards directly impact the conditions within schools that enable district efforts to improve achievement to either succeed or fail."

School board training can support the school board's role in fostering student achievement. A recent national survey indicates that school board members are extremely interested in student achievement. According to the School Boards Circa (Hess and Meeks, 2010) report, school board members indicated that their time is increasingly being spent on student achievement issues, 63% of board members believe that board members should be knowledgeable about factors promoting student achievement, and 50% of board members desire more information concerning student achievement.

According to several research studies (see chapter 5), school boards impact student achievement in several ways. Primarily, districts impact student achievement by formulating and monitoring district ends (vision, mission, and goals) in partnership with administration, staff, and the community (Archer, 2006; Land, 2002). Other ways include working with various social and state agencies, engaging the community, and allocating money appropriately.

In addition to the in-depth research studies presented in chapter 5, Johnson (2005) identifies twelve school board governance principles related to increased student achievement:

1. Creating a vision (Danzberger, 1994; Delagardelle, 2008; Goodman, Fulbright, and Zimmerman, 1997; LaRocque and Coleman, 1993; McAdams, 2000)
2. Using data (Delagardelle, 2008; Goodman, Fulbright, and Zimmerman, 1997; Lamont and Delagardelle, 2009; Leithwood and Jantzi, 2008; Murphy and Hallinger, 2001)
3. Setting goals (Danzberger, 1994; Delagardelle, 2008; Goodman, Fulbright, and Zimmerman, 1997; Leithwood and Jantzi, 2008; Marzano and Waters, 2009; McAdams, 2000; Murphy and Hallinger, 2001; Rice et al., 2001)
4. Monitoring progress and taking corrective action (Delagardelle, 2008; Goodman, Fulbright, and Zimmerman, 1997; LaRocque and Coleman, 1993; Marzano and Waters, 2009; Murphy and Hallinger, 2001)
5. Creating awareness and urgency (Delagardelle, 2008; Goodman and Zimmerman, 2000; Goodman, Fulbright, and Zimmerman, 1997; LaRocque and Coleman, 1993)
6. Engaging the community (Danzberger, 1994; Delagardelle, 2008; Goodman and Zimmerman, 2000; Hoffman, 1995; McAdams, 2000; Murphy and Hallinger, 2001)
7. Connecting with district leadership (Delagardelle, 2008; Lamont and Delagardelle, 2009; LaRocque and Coleman, 1993; Leithwood and Jantzi, 2009)
8. Creating climate (Delagardelle, 2008; Goodman, Fulbright, and Zimmerman, 1997; LaRocque and Coleman, 1993; Leithwood and Jantzi, 2009; Murphy and Hallinger, 2001; Rice et al., 2001)
9. Providing staff development (Danzberger, 1994; Delagardelle, 2008; Goodman, Fulbright, and Zimmerman, 1997; LaRocque and Coleman, 1993; Leithwood and Jantzi, 2009; Marzano and Waters, 2009; Murphy and Hallinger, 2001)
10. Developing policy with a focus on student learning (Danzberger, 1994; Delagardelle, 2008; Goodman, Fulbright, and Zimmerman, 1997; LaRocque and Coleman, 1993)
11. Demonstrating commitment (Danzberger, 1994; Delagardelle, 2008; Goodman, Fulbright, and Zimmerman, 1997; Lamont and Delagardelle, 2009; LaRocque and Coleman, 1993; Marzano and Waters, 2009)

12. Practicing unified governance (Danzberger, 1994; Delagardelle, 2008; Goodman, Fulbright, and Zimmerman, 1997; LaRocque and Coleman, 1993; Leithwood and Jantzi, 2009)

School Boards Serve as Trustees Over District Resources

As the community's trustee, school boards are charged to ensure that district resources are managed appropriately and that the community understands "who is getting what for how much" (Cassel, 2010). For instance, school boards not only approve the annual budget but also establish budget parameters to ensure that the district's budget is in sync with the district's goals. More importantly, school boards monitor the budget to ensure that resources are being spent appropriately and are targeted to improve student learning (Washington State School Directors's Association, 2011).

As trustees, school boards govern on behalf of the community. In other words, the school board holds the district's mission, operations, and results accountable to the taxpayers. To govern effectively, school boards need to collaborate with the community and with district staff to establish the district's ends for student learning. School boards also establish systems and processes to formulate and monitor district ends (which are discussed further in chapter 9). This includes evaluating the superintendent, monitoring and revising policies, and evaluating its own performance (California School Boards Association, 2007).

As Shannon (1990), former executive director of the National School Boards Association (NSBA), pointed out, without school boards, who would represent the people? Who would hear the appeals of those who are dissatisfied with the district decisions? Who could object to the superintendent's interpretation of state and federal mandates? School boards are the best catalyst to ensure that the district is held accountable to the public because they are elected from the community and elected specifically for this purpose. It is this proximity to, and familiarity with, the community—regardless of its size—that gives school boards a distinct advantage over agencies and institutions that attempt to legislate from a much greater distance.

School Boards Serve as Advocates for Public Schools

The school board is the primary advocate for public education and is in a position to engage the community in support of its educational objectives (see chapter 12). School board members are the only elected officials charged with solely representing the welfare of student achievement. As elected officials from the community, school boards are also effective at lobbying state and federal legislators for support for district programs or for protection from excessive outside interference.

School board members can get involved in advocacy campaigns through their individual state school board associations. Nationally, school board members can get involved in advocacy campaigns by being a part of the NSBA's Federal Relations Network (FRN). The FRN solicits school board members to serve as advocates in making public education a top priority for the federal government. According to the NSBA, "FRN members are appointed by their state associations to attend the FRN Conference and remain in contact with their members of Congress throughout the year to discuss NSBA's and their state association's positions on key education issues (National School Board Association, n.d.)."

There are several other ways that school board members can engage in advocacy. School board members may want to write a member of Congress, write to the local newspaper editor, meet with editorial boards, use media, and call and/or write legislators (NSBA, n.d.-a). Lobbyists from various state school board associations offer the following advice for school board members willing to serve as public education advocates (Stover, 2011b):

- School board members must keep in mind that they represent the same constituents as their congressional lawmakers. School board members represent students, parents, school personnel, and the local community.
- Be persistent and consistent in their communications to lawmakers.
- Build relationships with lawmakers and invite them to school/ district functions; get to know them as individuals.
- Because lawmakers are busy, be concise and give the correct context in making points and utilize examples that impact their districts.
- Maintain communications on issues they agree and disagree with.

SUMMARY

School boards are needed for a variety of reasons. Primarily, they are the best catalyst to ensure local control of education. In other words, school boards give the local community a voice concerning the aims of public education. Specifically, school boards keep the public in public schools, have a positive impact on student achievement, function as trustees over district resources, and serve as advocates for public schools.

As a democratic country, we have valued citizen oversight to assist us in making decisions for the greater good rather than making decisions predicated on self-interests. School boards are unique because they can balance individual rights and community values better than decisions made on Capitol Hill behind closed doors. In short, school boards allow the community to stay connected to its schools.

School boards have a positive impact on student achievement. School boards ensure that districts are governed effectively and that those who oversee the day-to-day operations are held accountable for student achievement. Although school boards are not responsible for the day-to-day management of schools, their decisions and actions create the environments that enable district efforts to improve.

School boards serve as trustees over district resources. School boards ensure that taxpayer dollars are carefully and appropriately spent. Primarily, the school board approves the budget, which identifies the parameters of district spending and ensures that there is a clear alignment between the budget and district ends. School boards are also advocates for public education, having been created for the sole purpose of representing the welfare of students.

In order for the United States to remain great, we must not forget about our democratic values. As a diverse country, we have cherished citizen oversight to promote the common good. School boards are a shining example of how men and women from the community come together to govern on behalf of the community and to promote the common good. If the role of the school board continues to diminish, many citizens will be disenfranchised concerning the aims of public education, ultimately leaving a system of the haves and have-nots.

QUESTIONS FOR REFLECTION

1. Explain the evolution of school boards in governing public education.
2. Why are school boards better positioned to define the purpose of public schools?
3. Describe and explain the four reasons why school boards are needed to govern over public education.
4. What is the primary mechanism by which school boards can positively impact student achievement?

CHAPTER 5

How School Boards Can Impact Student Achievement

Since the publication of *A Nation at Risk* in 1983, there has been a national crusade to boost student achievement. Student achievement is often deemed necessary to promote the economy and to foster a competitive workforce, but recently it has been aligned with national security. Educational reformists believe that the United States must stay competitive with other nations if we are going to continue to lead the free world.

More importantly, student achievement is necessary for a democracy to thrive. All of these reasons have their own merits as to why the public should promote student achievement. However, care must be taken that schools are not simply vehicles to train student minds to serve in a fashion solely to promote business interests. Schools should provide educational opportunities that encourage students to be innovative and to provide for a more secure democracy. Countries that invest in building healthy democracies will ensure that their citizens are provided with optimal resources to be successful.

Often, educational reformists look to teachers, administrators, and policymakers to boost student achievement. Although school boards play a pivotal role in this equation, their role has been largely overlooked. How can school boards create and sustain an effective learning environment when school boards are traditionally not expected to implement educational curricula or be experts in educational pedagogy?

There are numerous ways in which school boards affect student achievement. Most importantly, school boards establish a culture in which student achievement can thrive. Building a culture is done in conjunction with the superintendent and is most effective when the district has district ends or a strategic plan in place, highlighting district priorities, as described later in this chapter.

In building an ambience in which student achievement is valued, school boards should learn from other effective districts about good governance and how policies can help the school board initiate and sustain an environment conducive to student learning. As noted, school boards impact school culture through governance. In order to affect student achievement through school governance, boards must know how to ask relevant questions related to student achievement as reflected in the goals and general expectations of the district. For instance, according to Bamford (2012) and the Nebraska Association of School Boards' (NASB) AIM document (n.d.), school board members should ask the following questions as appropriate:

- How is the district monitoring student achievement, and what data is being collected and analyzed?
- Does the data represent the entire population including all subgroups?
- What information and trends are we learning from the data?
- How are we identifying achievement gaps?
- Are we regularly discussing student achievement as a school board and district?
- What comparative data do we have on our district and other districts throughout the state, country, and world?
- Is our curriculum aligned to state standards, and how are we ensuring that teachers are using approved district curriculum?
- Are we utilizing growth model assessments to gauge student learning?
- What professional development opportunities are available for our teachers?
- How are we fostering the participation of parents in the learning process?
- What results should the school board expect, including unintended outcomes?
- What instructional supports and resources are needed for the initiative? Are these in place, and if not, when?

- Is staff able to carry out the initiative? If not, what skills are necessary and is there a plan to provide professional development?
- Does the district have the financial resources to fund this initiative?
- What policies are aligned to this initiative?
- Will a dashboard be needed to track district ends?

By periodically raising questions related to student achievement, school boards can ensure that their district is committed to student achievement and that resources are properly aligned. More importantly, school board members will understand firsthand how the district is seeking to improve student achievement.

THE INTERDEPENDENCY ROLE OF THE SCHOOL BOARD AND SUPERINTENDENT

Research is clear in indicating that district-level leadership impacts student achievement outcomes. This is primarily accomplished by the school board taking a lead role in drafting the strategic plan for the district in collaboration with administration, staff, and the community (Archer, 2006).

The strategic plan establishes the course for the district over a period based upon priority areas and is expected to be a living document (modified as needed in pursuit of district goals and community changes). For instance, many districts develop goals centered on student achievement outcomes. Because research indicates that high expectations and a caring relationship for students are critical in fostering student achievement among all students, the school board may develop goal language centered on this premise.

After the strategic plan is drafted, the school board must ensure the proper monitoring of the plan. Usually what gets monitored has a greater chance of getting done. Because district goals are the cornerstone in promoting student achievement, one of the most important decisions the school board can make is the selection of its superintendent. The superintendent is charged with the responsibility of carrying out the strategic plan of the district and overseeing the day-to-day operations of the district on behalf of the school board. Considering this aspect, it is important to realize that this is yet another way of how the school board indirectly impacts student achievement.

To successfully monitor district goals and to ensure that the board makes quality decisions, school boards must have access to information that answers key questions. Monitoring district goals assists the superintendent in his or her task of fostering student achievement. The AIM template (see the following) created by NASB is an excellent resource to assist superintendents in presenting information to the school board when school board action may be required. The NASB's AIM document (n.d.) focuses on the following:

- Provide key information needed for the governance team.
- Relate the discussion to district ends and intended outcomes.
- Address various questions frequently asked by school board members that, if not answered, may lead to tensions on the governance team.
- Ensure school board members are provided with adequate information to make the best possible decisions.
- Provide a systematic process for the school board in making decisions and participating in school-related discussions.

Sample Agenda Item Template

Date: Agenda Item:

Submitted by:

1. What is the identified need?
   a. **What is the proposed need and why?**
   b. **What is the background analysis of the problem?**

2. Proposed action

3. Authority for action
   a. **Strategic plan/board or district goal/policy reference/superintendent goal**

4. Data/alternatives assessed:
   a. **How was this need identified? What data will support this need? For example, student achievement scores, assessment results, etc.**
   b. **Scope of options reviewed**
   c. **Reasons for rejecting alternatives**

5. Administrative recommendation
   [Note: board members may consider taking action on an agenda item prior to the superintendent's recommendation.]
   a. **Advantages/benefits of this proposal**
   b. **Possible problems or disadvantages of this proposal**
   c. **Affect this action may have on other programs/system**
   d. **Consequences of not approving recommendation**

6. Stakeholder groups involved in the development of proposal
   a. **Building administrator(s)**
   b. **Other district administrator(s): (special education, curriculum, technology, etc.)**
   c. **Community members**

7. Summary
   a. **Previous board action relating to this item**
   b. **Anticipated future action**
   c. **Background information**

8. Fiscal impact
   a. **Short-term budget impact**
   b. **Long-term budget impact**
   c. **Line item budget/department**
   d. **Future/ongoing**

9. Educational impact statement
   a. **Expected results in terms of student benefit/achievement**

10. Monitoring and reporting timeline
    a. **Implementation and assessment plan**
       i. **What documents are needed to measure goals?**
    b. **Administrator responsible for evaluating the goal and/or objective**
    c. **Evaluation method and timeline**
    d. **Next scheduled report to Board of Education**

It is important to realize that the superintendent is a part of the board-superintendent team, and his or her role in promoting student achievement is somewhat similar to the efforts of the school board. This is particularly true when the superintendent and school board understand their roles and duties, maintain a good relationship, and are both held accountable for student achievement outcomes (Land, 2002).

Ironically, this is yet another paradox of the superintendent's role similar to his or her role in promoting school board training. Because the superintendent's success is an indicator of the board's success, how can a superintendent foster student achievement? Mid-Continent Research for Education and Learning's 2006 study of twenty-seven detailed research studies involving over 2,817 districts indicated three primary findings:

1. There was a positive correlation of 0.24 between district leadership and student performance.
2. Effective superintendents focused on ensuring that their districts were goal oriented such as by having promoted the use of collaborative strategic plans.
3. Superintendent longevity positively impacted student achievement.

Mid-Continent Research for Education and Learning's study indicated the significant role superintendents play in promoting student achievement. According to the study, if superintendents improved their performance by one standard deviation, this would lead to a significant increase in student achievement (Archer, 2006).

In fact, the superintendent's role is so significant in promoting student achievement that state superintendent associations, such as the Illinois Association of School Administrators, have special training programs available for superintendents aimed at maximizing their success. It is important to note that the three areas noted by Mid-Continent Research for Education and Learning are contingent upon the superintendent's relationship with his or her respective school board.

There is limited research, some of which is dated, that examines the correlation between the school board and student achievement. Although there is limited research regarding school boards and student achievement as compared to teachers and administrators, there is a consistent body of evidence that links "effective" school boards to positive student achievement outcomes. The existing research on this subject fits nicely with the National School Board Association's (NSBA's) Center for Public Education's framework for effective schools.

The NSBA's Center for Public Education report, entitled "Eight Characteristics of Effective Boards: At a Glance" (2011), identifies the following eight characteristics of effective school boards:

1. Effective school boards commit to a vision of high expectations for student achievement and define clear goals to obtain that vision.
2. Effective school boards have strong, shared beliefs and values that all students can learn at high levels.

3. Effective school boards are accountability driven and focused on policies to improve instruction.
4. Effective school boards work collaboratively with staff and other stakeholders to set and achieve district goals.
5. Effective boards frequently monitor data to drive improvement.
6. Effective boards ensure that resources are properly aligned to reach goals such as matching professional development to district goals.
7. Effective boards work collaboratively with the superintendent and maintain a high degree of trust and mutual respect.
8. Effective boards engage in professional development opportunities to learn together as a team how to become more effective as a governing body.

Just as there are indicators for effective boards, there are also indicators for noneffective boards. The Center for Public Education (2011) identifies the following "warning signs" for boards that are not governing effectively:

- Being unaware of school or district improvement initiatives
- Focusing solely on external factors related to student achievement as compared to internal variables
- Engaging in micromanagement
- Not following parliamentary procedures or the chain of command
- Lacking communication and trust between the superintendent and school board
- Being willing to blame others (teachers, parents, and students) for low performance
- Being slow in developing a mission and a vision for the district
- Being unwilling to engage in professional development

RESEARCH STUDIES LINKING SCHOOL BOARDS AND STUDENT ACHIEVEMENT

The Academic Development Institute examined existing research concerning the role of the school board in targeted improvement efforts and interviewed nineteen purposely selected educational practitioners (superintendents and school board members) regarding emerging practices in their report entitled "Moving Beyond the Killer B's" (Rhim, 2013).

The interview participants were identified by the following: participating in a school improvement initiative developed by the Academic Development Institute, utilizing federal school improvement grants or Race to the Top funds, and being finalists or winners of the Broad Prize for Urban Education. Rhim (2013) reported the following characteristics of effective boards due to the correlation between effective boards and effective districts:

- There is a link between effective school boards and effective districts.
- The most important job of the school board is to establish and monitor district ends (e.g., mission, vision, and goals).
- Effective school boards are careful in their selection of the superintendent and hold that individual accountable for achieving the district ends.
- Effective school boards establish a meaningful, trusting relationship with the superintendent.
- Effective school boards engage in ongoing professional development.
- Effective school boards orient new members to the school board.

Lee, educational leadership professor at the University of Southern Mississippi, and his graduate students conducted research to determine how the school board's management style impacts student achievement. Lee's research focused on analyzing board meetings from low- and high-achieving districts in every state hoping to establish a national research base on school board activity as well as establishing a national training model for school boards (Lee and Eadens, 2013).

The research team analyzed 115 school board meetings (using the School Board Video Project survey created by the researchers) and focused on following parliamentary protocols, determining if there was good collaboration during board meetings, observing whether the board president maintained decorum at board meetings, assessing if community input was welcomed and solicited, and focusing on student achievement issues during meetings. Based on his research, Lee discovered significant differences between low-, medium-, and high-performing school districts.

Effective districts have the following characteristics:

- The governance team works collaboratively and displays cooperation.
- Effective boards display professionalism.
- Effective boards discuss and address various items related to student achievement such as curriculum and instruction.
- Effective boards are student-centered and actively involved in the academic component.
- Effective boards display a high degree of team work with the superintendent to achieve results.

Ineffective districts have the following characteristics:

- District meetings are less orderly.
- Minimum time is spent on student achievement.
- Board members do not listen attentively and respectfully to each other.
- Board members seek solely to advance their agenda.
- Board members disregard the superintendent's advice and recommendations.
- Ineffective districts do not operate in accordance with their policies.

There are six other major research studies connecting school boards to student achievement (see summaries in the following). As noted, these research studies also link "effective" school boards to positive student achievement outcomes. These studies should serve as a guide for school boards in implementing and building a culture conducive to student achievement.

The six studies are "The Politics of Excellence: Trustee Leadership and School District Ethos" (LaRocque and Coleman, 1993); *Getting There from Here: School Board-Superintendent Collaboration: Creating a School Governance Team Capable of Raising Student Achievement* (Goodman, Fulbright, and Zimmerman, 1997); *Foundations for Success: Case Studies of How Urban School Districts Improve Student Achievement* (Snipes, Doolittle, and Herlihy, 2002); *Beyond Islands of Excellence: What Districts Can Do to Improve Student Achievement* (Togneri and Anderson, 2003); *School District Leadership That Works: The Effect of Superintendent Leadership on Student Achievement* (Waters and Marzano, 2006); and "IASB's

Lighthouse Study: School Boards and Student Achievement" (Iowa Association of School Boards, 2000).

Common themes in all of these studies concerning how school boards impact student achievement include engaging the community, formulating district ends (vision, mission, district goals), monitoring ends based upon data, governing in a fiscally responsible matter, practicing good superintendent-board relationships, and formulating and implementing effective policies.

"The Politics of Excellence: Trustee Leadership and School District Ethos" (LaRocque and Coleman, 1993)

This 1993 study by LaRocque and Coleman analyzed the effect school boards had on establishing a culture of increasing student achievement at nine schools in British Columbia, Canada. High-performing districts were described as having the following traits:

- Focusing on students and learning
- Accountability to outcomes
- Acting as change agents (policies, procedures, and practices)
- Including stakeholders in clarifying the district's purpose
- Seeking to establish shared values and commitments
- Focusing on community engagement

Similar to other research studies involving effective districts such as the Iowa Lighthouse Studies, the study found that school boards were knowledgeable about academic issues and reforms, clarity regarding how to monitor student achievement outcomes, and fiscal responsibility. They also often interacted with district administrators and other stakeholders to monitor district performance.

Getting There from Here: School Board-Superintendent Collaboration: Creating a School Governance Team Capable of Raising Student Achievement (Goodman, Fulbright, and Zimmerman, 1997)

The 1997 research study analyzed school board governance and student achievement in ten districts in ten states. Similar to Iowa

Lighthouse Studies, researchers Goodman, Fulbright, and Zimmerman noted that several school districts had a reputation for poor governance. The researchers explored the governance of school districts in various states. Specifically, they examined why some districts exhibit poor governance and others do not, why some school boards work well with their superintendent while others do not, and the nature of governance issues that hinder effective leadership.

Concerning characteristics of ineffective boards, Goodman, Fulbright, and Zimmerman (1997) noted that ineffective boards disregard the agenda process and chain of command, play to the news media, lack an understanding of their role, lack team work, micromanage the superintendent, lack motivation to improve governance, and lack communication and trust. For instance, pertaining to disregarding the agenda process and chain of command, ineffective boards discussed issues not on the board agenda and without prior notification to the school board chair or the superintendent.

In contrast, school boards that demonstrated good governance had the following qualities:

- Focused on district ends (mission, vision, board goals) addressing student achievement
- Understood and worked in their respective roles, allowing the superintendent to oversee the day-to-day operations of the district
- Focused on community engagement and served as advocates for the district
- Adopted annual budgets and approved district facilities
- Participated in board retreats with the superintendent to discuss their effectiveness as a governance team and to engage in professional development training
- Spoke with one voice regarding issues facing the district
- Conferenced (school board president) weekly with the superintendent and kept other board members informed about the affairs of the district
- Served (board members) a minimum of two-year terms and encouraged other citizens who demonstrated a commitment to serving students to run if they did not seek reelection, thus ensuring strong leadership on the governance team

Foundations for Success: Case Studies of How Urban School Districts Improve Student Achievement **(Snipes, Doolittle, and Herlihy, 2002)**

Too often, when critics discuss failing schools, they typically refer to large urban school districts where several issues, such as social and environmental factors, affect student achievement. This 2002 study showcases three large, urban school districts that increased student achievement, although they had common issues affecting achievement. These issues included the following: low expectations for at-risk students, high teacher turnover, insufficient business practices, lack of instructional clarity, and dysfunction between district staff and administration.

Similar to the Dissatisfaction Theory discussed in chapter 1, reforms started in these districts after periods of conflict in the community involving district decisions in areas such as hiring and firing of personnel and school closings. This led to changes on the governance team in each district. After acknowledging various problems, these districts pursued the following course of action to increase student achievement:

- Focusing on specific goals to foster student achievement
- Ensuring the hiring of a good superintendent who believed in the district's mission and values and holding the superintendent accountable through a performance evaluation process
- Focusing on implementing effective policies
- Engaging the community in support of district initiatives
- Engaging the school board, superintendent, district administrators, and other staff in developing a strategic plan to boost student achievement and communicating the plan to various stakeholders
- Concentrating on improving district operations to ensure that staff receive the resources they need
- Pursuing funding such as grants that were aligned to district goals

These effective districts also developed the following goals specifically related to student achievement:

- Fostering a goal-focused culture based on core beliefs about student learning

- Establishing performance goals and being held accountable to district goals
- Concentrating on at-risk schools (beginning with elementary) by providing additional resources, increasing the pool of strong teachers and principals, and assigning experts to schools to access problems
- Ensuring that middle and high school students understood the basics in reading and math
- Formulating district-wide curricula and acceptable instructional strategies to improve educational clarity across the district
- Providing professional development related to district goals and the district-approved curriculum
- Ensuring that district policies were being successfully implemented at the district schools
- Relying on data to guide district decision making and how to allocate district resources

Beyond Islands of Excellence: What Districts Can Do to Improve Student Achievement (Togneri and Anderson, 2003)

This research study, published by the National Learning First Alliance, reinforces the fact that effective districts utilize similar strategies to foster student achievement. According to the study, it is vital that districts acknowledge deficiencies and take a lead role in implementing reforms. To improve student learning, effective districts maintain a focus on district ends (mission, vision, district goals), understand and value their role as policymakers, maintain motivation to improve student achievement, and work collaboratively as a unit.

Effective districts in this study worked diligently to include a variety of stakeholders in the district planning process and encouraged staff to tackle difficult district issues and provide potential solutions. Specifically, districts in this study boosted student achievement by implementing a systematic approach to improve instruction, ensuring that district decisions were based upon data and followed appropriate policies, ensuring that professional development was tied to district goals, ensuring that staff received direct assistance with instructional experts, and redefining leadership roles so that specific groups tackled specific issues.

School District Leadership That Works: The Effect of Superintendent Leadership on Student Achievement (Waters and Marzano, 2006)

This 2006 study by Mid-Continent Research for Education and Learning of Denver analyzed over twenty-seven research studies in an effort to determine how the superintendent influences student achievement. The study involved over 2,817 districts and over 3.4 million students.

Although the study focused on how superintendents impacted student achievement, some of the findings illuminate the role of the school board. Specifically, the study found that the success of the superintendent is interdependent upon the relationship with the school board. More importantly, poor working relationships between the superintendent and school board deter the district from improving student achievement. Specific findings showed that student achievement improved when:

- All district stakeholders (superintendent, district administrators, staff, school board members, and community representatives) were involved in the development of district ends (vision, mission, nonnegotiable goals)
- The school board ensured that district ends were aggressively pursued and were top-priority areas
- The school board empowered the superintendent to monitor achievement and district goals and provide resources to meet district goals

"IASB's Lighthouse Study: School Boards and Student Achievement" (Iowa Association of School Boards, 2000)

School boards govern differently, and some yield high results while others do not. A popular research study entitled the "The Lighthouse Study" identified factors regarding effective and ineffective districts was conducted by the Iowa Association of School Boards (2000) regarding schools in Georgia. The Iowa Association of School Boards was one of the few states to study school boards in depth utilizing a mixed-methods research approach.

Among the districts examined in Iowa Association of School Boards' (2000) study, there were similarities and differences. Similarities included general concern for children, desire for peaceable relationships, school board approval of the superintendent, tension about roles in a site-based system, student categorical programs (special education), and local backgrounds of board members and staff. Differences included elevating versus accepting belief system, lacking focus and understanding on school renewal, and lacking action in buildings and classrooms.

High-achieving school districts in the Lighthouse Study consistently sought improvement rather than making excuses and were more in tune with initiatives to address student achievement. In less successful districts, board members could not recount strategies being used to enhance student achievement compared to forward-moving districts in which board members were knowledgeable about the conditions of the schools and offered solutions to address problems.

Also, in less successful districts, school staff often blamed the administration and described a lack of trust between personnel. Comparatively, in forward-moving districts, staff and administrators reported being a part of the team and working cohesively to address concerns. Moreover, forward-moving districts actively involved the community while less successful districts did not. Staff development in forward-moving districts encompassed everyone, whereas training was more individualized in stuck districts. In order for districts to be effective, school boards as designated representatives must mimic characteristics of high-performing districts.

Besides focusing on the "what" or district ends and policies connected to the board ends, there are other ways the school board impacts student achievement. To meet the diverse needs of the learner, school boards can also establish policies to work with various social agencies, local and state governments, and their respective communities to meet the social and educational needs of today's students. School boards must also approve the district's budget and ensure that money is allocated for student achievement initiatives. Finally, the school board should focus on the eight key areas identified in the NSBA's Key Work of School Boards (Gemberling, Smith, and Villani, 2000).

If these areas are not met, it is doubtful that students' academic achievement can increase. Successful districts do a variety of things to positively impact student achievement and maintain good governance. Good districts do not rely on a single strategy because effective board practices illuminated from research are often interdependent.

THE IMPORTANCE OF INTERAGENCY RELATIONSHIPS

There are many benefits to school boards collaborating with other social agencies. Student achievement will never accelerate if basic human needs such as shelter, nutrition, health care, safety, and others identified in Maslow's Hierarchy of Needs are not met. Harlem Children's Zone is an excellent example of how student achievement can improve if these basic needs are met.

In reality, school districts cannot be all things to all students, but school boards can position their districts in integrating services with social agencies through the use of policies. Schools are held responsible for serving all children, but districts often lack personnel and financial resources to deal with such issues if they work in isolation as in the past (Usdam, 1994).

Traditionally, school boards were totally separate from general purpose government and usually were not involved in coordinating activities with other agencies (Washington State School Director's Association, 2001). However, society has changed tremendously. The primary reason is the changing demographics of children and families.

Since 1979, there has been a 33% increase in children living in poverty, which in 1991 totaled more than 5.6 million children under the age of six. Also, 70% of mothers of public school students are in the workforce, along with 60% of mothers of preschool students (Usdam, 1994). In part due to this growth in poverty, agencies should work together to address the educational, health, and social needs of children, because it is unlikely that students will learn if social and health needs are unmet.

The Importance of Working with Local and State Governments

School boards originated from state statutes and are supported by state and local taxes. Due to their origin, school boards should maintain a healthy relationship with state and local governments, as well as with the community, to promote student achievement. Land (2002) argued that local and state relationships can be beneficial to school boards regarding political, economic, and community support as well.

Many school boards do not build relationships with local or state governments unless for financial reasons, because states are the primary source for funding for most public schools. School boards that are unwilling to change this behavior increase the risk of being labeled ineffective due to the increased criticisms in public education. Based upon the recent 2010 Phi Delta Kappan survey, U.S. citizens support collaboration between the school board and state government (Rose and Gallup, 2010).

There are several ways the state can assist school boards in becoming more effective in boosting student achievement. Some of these include reviewing policies to determine good governance, working with school boards as partners to develop strategies for improvement, providing legal and financial support, determining duties and responsibilities to focus on student achievement, providing technical assistance, assisting in strengthening voter turnout, and providing data to newly elected state policymakers with information that defines the duties and responsibilities of school boards (Resnick, 1999).

National School Board Association's Key Work of School Boards

To maximize student achievement, school boards should consider incorporating the NSBA's framework for good governance and/or consider their state association framework for good governance. In incorporating a governing framework, it is essential that the framework is research based.

The NSBA's framework consists of the following: vision, standards, assessment, accountability, alignment, climate, collaboration, and continuous improvement (see Appendix). These eight areas can be viewed as a part of the job description for school board members. The NSBA and the American Association of School Administrators produced a joint publication indicating how these eight areas can be implemented and its impact on student achievement outcomes (Henderson, Saks, and Wright, 2001).

SUMMARY

Often teachers and administrators are held solely responsible for student achievement. Logically, teachers and administrators are the most visible in promoting student achievement in as much as they are involved in the day-to-day operations of the district. Nevertheless, as the governing agent, the school board plays a vital role in ensuring that student achievement occurs. For starters, school boards should make sure that student achievement discussions are a focal point of board meetings by asking specific questions related to student achievement.

According to various research studies, school boards foster student achievement by engaging the community, establishing and monitoring district ends, governing in a fiscally responsible manner, practicing good school board–superintendent relations, implementing effective policies, working with other agencies, and allocating money wisely to promote student achievement.

The selection of the superintendent is one of the most significant decisions the school board must make. The superintendent's job is to carry out the strategic plan on behalf of the school board. The superintendent's impact on student achievement is directly proportional to that of the school board. Research notes that if the school board and superintendent work collaboratively on the strategic plan and the school board monitors the plan, then student achievement increases. Thus, it is vital that the school board ensure that the superintendent be a good pick for the district. This relationship is vital in positively impacting student achievement.

School boards that understand their role and duties and that practice good governance significantly improve student achievement, as evident in the Lighthouse Study (Iowa Association of School Boards, 2000). More importantly, if school boards are going to impact student achievement positively, they must demonstrate ownership of their professional development needs and continuously monitor their governance as a governance team.

QUESTIONS FOR REFLECTION

1. How do school boards create a culture wherein student achievement is a top priority?

2. Why is it vital that the district have a collaborative process in formulating a strategic plan for the district? Why is it important for the school board to monitor district goals?

3. Explain how the superintendent's role in promoting student achievement is a reflection of the school board as well.

4. How can superintendents assist school boards in the latter's task of monitoring district goals?

5. In considering the major educational research studies discussed in this chapter, identify and explain common themes related to enhancing student academic performance.

6. Explain why it is important now for school boards to develop relationships with other agencies as compared to years past.

7. In what ways can the state government assist local districts in promoting student achievement?

CHAPTER 6

Why Citizens Become School Board Members

Citizens seek to become school board members for many reasons. Most serve because they are passionate about ensuring that students are properly educated to become viable, productive citizens. Nevertheless, there is a minority of citizens who seek election to the board due to personal agendas, special interests, or political aspirations. For school boards to be effective, they must operate as a team and be student-centered in all of their decisions.

STATE AND NATIONAL DATA

There is a lack of in-depth research to describe sufficiently all the reasons citizens choose to serve on school boards. Various state school board associations have compiled survey data of their members offering some insight into the most common motives.

California School Boards Association (2009 survey):

- To ensure better educational opportunities for their own children (58%)
- To improve the effectiveness of the school district (15%)
- To give back to the community (11%)

Illinois Association of School Boards (2008 survey):

- To make improvement in the schools (19%)
- To fulfill my civic duty (15%)

- To help my children get a good education (15%)
- "I value public education" (38%)
- "I disagreed with actions of the previous board" (10%)

Michigan Association of School Boards (2008 survey):

- The majority of board members ran for the school board to give back to their districts and schools or to help improve them

Oregon School Boards Association (2008 survey):

- To give back to the community (16%)
- "I have children/grandchildren in the district" (13%)
- To help the children (12%)
- To improve education (10%)
- To help the district (8%)
- To be more active/involved in the community (7%)
- To help schools (6%)
- "I worked for schools in the past" (6%)
- To help make changes (6%)
- "I asked when there was an opening" (6%)

Pennsylvania School Board Association (2010) (major responses):

- To serve community, public service
- Dissatisfaction with present board and/or administration
- To control taxes, costs, and spending
- "I have children/grandchildren in the district"
- To improve the quality of education, standards, and/or achievement
- "I believe in the public education system"
- To share expertise and experience

School Boards Circa (Hess and Meeks, 2010):

- To ensure good schools for children (50%)
- To give back to the community (22%)

Wisconsin Association of School Boards (2011):

- To give back to the community (67%)
- Motivated by others (55%)
- To improve schools for children (46%)
- "I am interested in educational issues" (66%)

SCHOOL BOARD MEMBER DEMOGRAPHICS

School board members are somewhat diverse in respect to their backgrounds, but typically they are white males, ranging in age from forty-one to fifty, married, college educated, and live in a suburban community with children enrolled in public school (Malinsky, 1999). Specific national demographics include the following (Hess and Meeks, 2010; Michigan Association of School Boards, 2008):

- 80% white
- 12% African American
- 3% Hispanic
- 56% male
- 70% over the age of fifty
- Median income is $50,303
- 75% bachelor degree
- 95% are elected
- 50% moderate, 30% conservative, and 20% liberals

According to the School Boards Circa (Hess and Meeks, 2010) report, school boards are more diverse compared to federal and state office holders. As an example, the U.S. House is only 9.4% African American and the U.S. Senate is 1%. Regarding state offices in 2009, only 9% were African American. Tables 6.1 through 6.5 show the demographic data for school board members in various states.

Table 6.1 Illinois Demographics

Race		Sex		Age	
Caucasian	91.5%	Male	55.9%	Under 30	0.8%
African American	3.2%	Female	42.2%	30–39	10.0%
Hispanic Asian	1.2%			40–49	41.9%
Native American	1.2%			50–59	30.6%
Multiracial	1.0%			60+	15.1%

Illinois Association of School Boards, 2008.

Table 6.2 Indiana Demographics

Race		Sex		Age	
Caucasian	97.6%	Male	71%	Under 30	0.93%
African American	2%	Female	29%	30–39	14%
Hispanic Asian	0.42%			40–49	28%
				50–59	28%
				60–69	19%
				70+	8%

Indiana Association of School Boards, 2008.

Table 6.3 Ohio Demographics

Race		Sex		Age		Education	
Caucasian	97.4%	Male	66.7%	Under 26	0.6%	Grade school	0.2%
African American	2.2%	Female	33.3%	26–35	4.6%	High school	19.1%
Hispanic Asian	0.2%			36–45	20.6%	Post-secondary	9.3%
Other	0.2%			46–55	39.8%	Bachelor's	38%
				56–65	24%	Master's	21%
				65+	9.9%	Doctorate	7.6%

Ohio School Boards Association, 2010.

Table 6.4 Michigan Demographics

Race		Sex	
Caucasian	80%	Male	60%
Others	20%	Female	40%

Michigan Association of School Boards, 2008.

Table 6.5   Pennsylvania Demographics

Race		Sex		Age		Education	
Caucasian	98%	Male	62%	Under 25	0.8%	Grade school	1%
African American	1%	Female	38%	25–34	2.2%	High school	12%
Hispanic Asian	0.4%			35–44	12%	Post-secondary	15%
Other	0.6%			45–54	29%	Bachelor's	29%
				55–64	32%	Master's	28%
				65+	24%	Doctorate	15%

Pennsylvania School Boards Association, 2010.

SUMMARY

There is a variety of reasons why school board members serve. Although research suggests that a minority of board members have personal agendas, most serve to give back to the community and to ensure that students receive a quality education. While the demographic makeup of most school boards is comprised of white males who are married, college educated, and live in a suburban neighborhood, the demographics of school boards are gradually changing to reflect the diversity of their communities.

QUESTIONS FOR REFLECTION

1. Why are some citizens willing to serve on the school board? What are the major reasons citizens are willing to serve on the school board?
2. What are the demographics of school board members nationally? Describe the characteristics of an average school board member.
3. Explain how the demographics of school boards differ from federal and state elected positions.

CHAPTER 7

The Need for School Board Training

Critics of school boards argue that most school board members have little or no formal training in governance roles and responsibilities. While this is true, there are minimum qualifications to serve. According to various state school codes, no special preparation is needed to serve in these roles prior to election (see the following). According to the website Law and Legal Research (n.d.), qualifications and requirements to become a board member in other states include the following. California:

- Be at least eighteen years of age
- Be a citizen of the state
- Be a resident of the school district
- Be a registered voter

Illinois:

- Be at least eighteen years of age
- Be a U.S. citizen
- Be a resident of the school district for one year
- Be a registered voter

Indiana:

- Be at least twenty-one years of age
- Be a resident voter of the school city for one year prior to election

- Take an oath of office indicating the following:
  o Possess qualifications required under state code
  o Will honestly and faithfully discharge the duties of office
  o Will be in the selection of officers, agents, and employees only by considerations of merit, fitness, and qualification

Michigan:

- Be at least twenty-one years of age
- Be an eligible voter
- Be a district resident for at least thirty days

Minnesota:

- Be at least twenty-one years of age
- Be an eligible voter
- Be a district resident for at least thirty days prior to election or appointment
- Must receive training in school finance and management

Oklahoma:

- Be in district for six months
- Must have a high school diploma or high school equivalent
- Must complete twelve hours of training in educational issues, school finance, Oklahoma law and ethics, and duties and responsibilities of board members

Oregon:

- Must be an elector of the district
- Must reside in the district one year

In addition to qualifications, some state codes list specific powers and duties of school boards. For instance, the Virginia school code lists the following power and duties: ensure that school laws are properly explained, enforced, and observed; ensure that schools are conducted in concert with state law; oversee building and grounds; determine methods of study and teaching; perform duties prescribed by law; obtain public comments concerning district schools; and ensure schools are registered with the department of state police in order to obtain information regarding sex offenders within that subdivision (Law and Legal Research, n.d.).

State law determines the specific roles and duties of school boards. However, in most states, the school board's job description encompasses three primary areas: policymaking, clarifying the district purpose, and engaging in a two-way conversation with the community.

School boards primarily operate through policies, some of which are mandated by the state and/or federal government to ensure efficient operation of the district. As part of its administrative duties, the school board also determines the direction of the district by developing the district's mission and vision. In determining the direction of the district, the school board often engages the community.

To accomplish board goals and desires, the school board relies upon one person—the superintendent—to oversee the day-to-day operations of the district. The school board can ensure a two-way conversation with the community by having a process for community input and an avenue for the district to tell its story to the community (Rice, 2010). Information regarding individual state codes indicating the powers and duties of the school board can be found at the Law and Legal Research website (n.d.).

CONFLICTS OF INTEREST AND DISQUALIFICATIONS OF SCHOOL BOARD MEMBERS

Besides basic qualifications to run for the school board, most states have additional regulations that will either disqualify an individual for school board membership or be seen as a conflict of interest. In most states, citizens cannot serve on the school board if they have been convicted of any felonies, are registered sex offenders, serve on another educational board and/or in another incompatible public office, or are employees of the local board of education. Information available at the Law and Legal Research website (n.d.) indicates that individuals are disqualified from school board membership if they fail to meet the following qualifications

California:

- Not disqualified by the constitution or laws of the state from holding a civil office
- Not an employee of the district

Illinois:

- Not a school trustee
- Cannot hold an incompatible office
- Not a registered sex offender

Indiana:

- Not an employee of the district
- Cannot serve either in an elected or appointed office under the government of a civil city while serving on the board
- Cannot have an interest in a contract or a purchase with the school district in which they preside

Michigan:

- Not a convicted felon or sex offender
- Cannot have a financial interest pertaining to district sales or contracts
- Cannot hold another elected position except township board
- Cannot make over eight thousand dollars as an employee of the district

Minnesota:

- Cannot be a sex offender who has been convicted of an offense
- Cannot be convicted of a felony

Oklahoma:

- Cannot have been convicted or pleaded guilty or no contest to a felony under state or federal law or to a misdemeanor involving embezzlement

Oregon:

- Cannot receive compensation for services unless it is for reasonable reimbursement for expenses related to school business
- Cannot be an employee of the district or of a charter school over which the district has oversight

Besides specific rules that will automatically prohibit citizens from running for the school board, there are some general conflicts of interests of which school board members should be aware, primarily in the area of financial interests. Most states have language in state code that prohibits school board members from having a financial interest in the districts they serve. For instance, states such as Washington have laws attempting to alleviate the possibility of financial conflicts of interest between school board members and the districts they serve.

Based upon my experiences in working with school boards, I believe that the Washington State School Directors's Association's description of potential conflicts of interest, while based upon state law, is also helpful to school board members in other states. The Washington State School Directors's Association's (2007) statement regarding a general conflict of interest reads, "No municipal officer shall be beneficially interested, directly or indirectly, in any contract which may be made by, through or under the supervision of such officer, in whole or in part, or which may be made for the benefit of his or her office, or accept, directly or indirectly, any compensation, gratuity or reward in connection with such contract from any other person beneficially interested therein."

As noted, codes in most other states such as New Jersey and Colorado contain language related to conflicts of interests. According to New Jersey statute 18A:12-2:

> No member of any board of education shall be interested directly or indirectly in any contract with or claim against the board, nor, in the case of local and regional school districts, shall he hold office as mayor or as a member of the governing body of a municipality, nor, in the case of county special services school districts and county vocational school districts, shall he hold office as a member of the governing body of a country. (Law and Legal Research, n.d.)

In order for school board members to serve effectively and establish trust within the community they serve, they should attempt to avoid even the appearance of a conflict of interest. To assist school board members in determining whether or not something is a conflict of interest, school board members should ask themselves the following questions: Will my personal interests benefit as a result of my action? Would a reasonable person conclude that my personal interests may impair my independent and impartial judgment in the exercise of my official duties (Washington State School Directors's Association, 2007)?

If a school board member answered yes to either of those questions, he or she should take immediate and deliberate action to avoid a possible conflict of interest or appearance thereof. As a general rule of thumb, in order to prevent a conflict of interest, board members should not attempt to utilize their status to secure special privileges, should not accept any personal gifts or other forms of compensation connected with their position, should not accept employment or engage in business with the district in which they serve, and should not utilize confidential information obtained with their position to promote their special interests.

TRAINING IS NEEDED TO PROMOTE THE IMPORTANT WORK OF SCHOOL BOARDS

The qualifications to become a board member in most states are minimal at best and help to draw the maximum number of potential candidates. None of the qualifications requires an understanding or skill in board member roles and responsibilities. That's where professional development enters the picture. Although it may be argued that training does not ensure good governance, most educators, such as superintendents, agree that relying on untrained board members is not a good idea either (Jane, 2003).

Based upon a review of research literature by Land (2002), school board members and educators overwhelmingly agree that school board training is vital especially for newer school board members, but there is not a consensus regarding the form and scope of the training and whether such training should be mandated.

It should be noted that there are factors that interfere with school board members being trained. Often family and work schedules are obstacles for school board members to pursue rigorous training. Additionally, in some districts there is a lack of necessary leadership to promote school board training. Nevertheless, the end result is the establishment of a culture in which school board training is not deemed as necessary or vital.

ROLE CONFUSION

School management is becoming more complex as school officials struggle with evolving role expectations (Anderson and Snyder, 1980). As a result of the ambiguity that exists among local, state, and federal governments, a school board may not know exactly what it should be working on. Richard Elmore, a scholar at Harvard University, stated (2003), "The downfall of low-performing schools is not their lack of effort and motivation; rather, it is poor decisions regarding what to work on." What it takes for school districts to lead, given the vague relationship of shared governance as well as the areas in which leadership needs improvement, is a recurring question in research literature and needs further exploration.

HOW ROLE CONFUSION IMPACTS SUPERINTENDENT TURNOVER

Superintendent turnover can be attributed to many factors such as retirements, promotions, and new job opportunities, but, all too often, superintendent turnover happens when school board members are unclear about their role and duties. This is an important reason why many educational stakeholders advocate for school board training.

The Institute for Educational Leadership (2001) provides a detailed account of how the ambiguity that exists surrounding the role of the school board and superintendents often leads to micromanagement and superintendent turnover. The Institute for Educational Leadership (2001) reported that the average tenure of superintendents in urban districts fell from 2.7 years in 1997 to 2.3 years in 1999. And a 2008 Illinois survey of superintendents indicated that 48.5% of superintendents felt that their school board spent too much time on operational issues compared to determining goals and expectations of the district. (Law and Legal Research, n.d.)

There are many examples of role confusion. For instance, there are situations when school board members would like to evaluate a teacher if they have to approve that teacher for tenure. This conflict is likely to occur because school board members are authorized to make important decisions such as personnel but also want to be directly involved in the logistics of their decisions (Castallo, 2000).

Micromanagement can erode the quality of educational programs and increase staff turnover according to Jazzar (2005). A growing number of superintendents believe that the superintendency is in a state of crisis due to micromanagement from school boards, which leads to superintendent turnover (Glass, 2001). Part of the problem is that the distinction between the duties of the board and the duties of district administrators has not been studied in depth. Carver (2006) noted how management research literature on this subject is minimal and that there seems to be more research conducted on staff duties compared to that conducted on governance.

CHARACTERISTICS OF HIGH-PERFORMING SCHOOL BOARDS

School boards govern differently throughout the country and yield different results in regard to their performance. Based upon research by the Iowa Association of School Boards (2000), school boards in high-achieving districts govern quite differently from school boards in low-performing districts. If that premise is correct, what are the characteristics/behaviors of effective school boards, and could some of the characteristics be applied to other school boards through training? Goodman, Fulbright, and Zimmerman (1997) list some of the following characteristics of effective school boards:

- Establish partnerships with the community to meet the needs of students
- Ensure that the budget is fiscally responsible
- Ensure that instructional methods are based on research
- Review district policies to make sure they are aligned with the district's vision

- Engage in ongoing professional development
- Develop a mutual understanding of the superintendent's job description
- Operate through board policy and allow the superintendent to carry out the day-to-day operations of the schools
- Evaluate (annually) the performance of the school board and superintendent
- Abstain from voting on issues that impact board members either economically or personally

It may be incorrect to conclude that high-performing school districts are a direct result of effective school board governance, organization, training, and performance, but school districts with high standards of student achievement tend to be associated with boards that practice good governance (McAdams, 2002). Research suggests that most school boards intend to provide good leadership but often lack vision and the necessary skills to implement the vision. This is why training is needed (Rallis and Criscoe, 1993). Good intentions are never enough to improve school board governance; ongoing training is needed to establish and maintain competency in school board work.

No Surprises at School Board Meetings

Effective boards follow the cardinal rule of good governance, which is "no surprises." This means that neither the superintendent nor school board members should be surprised at meetings or between meetings. My former colleague John Cassel (Illinois Association of School Boards) believes that people resist this rule because they want to play "got-cha." But to govern effectively, respect is fundamental. Successful governance requires that the superintendent not surprise school board members with new information at meetings that members are unprepared to discuss. Likewise, school board members should not question the superintendent about matters that he or she is unprepared to discuss.

Therefore, to alleviate surprises, the superintendent must make sure that he or she communicates regularly with the board in advance of a meeting via e-mail or school board agenda packets. If school board members have questions or concerns about an upcoming meeting, they should meet or touch base with the superintendent in advance of a meeting as well. If surprises plague the governance team, it will lead to a lack of trust and will impact both superintendent and school board member tenure.

PREPARING FOR CHANGES ON THE GOVERNANCE TEAM: BUILDING A CULTURE OF PROFESSIONAL DEVELOPMENT

The majority of school board members are elected to office by popular vote. Others are appointed due to the form of governance or to fill midterm vacancies. No matter how members are selected, periodic changes will occur on the governance team due to the election and/ or appointment process. Although many well-intentioned citizens run for the board, sometimes unsuitable candidates get elected to office just because of a particularly low voter turnout. Occasionally, veteran school board members can be defeated at the polls by candidates who make promises of change and reform.

School board members run for the board for a variety of reasons, including personal agendas. Some school board members see winning the election as an edict for educational change and often promise various constituents improvements. These personal agendas can interfere with the governing process because not all school board members share the same concerns.

When school board members serve with personal agendas, it hampers the cooperation on the board-superintendent governance team. Citizens may be more apt to run for the school board with personal interests for a variety of reasons, but all too often it is because they fail to understand their role and duties (Land, 2002). It is one more way that training can redirect the minority of school board members who serve for personal agendas.

New Board Members and Personal Agendas

Many critics argue that it is not entirely fair to blame school board members for seeking election with personal agendas considering the fact that many states have limited qualifications for members. Critics argue that school board members are generally not provided a clear job description and will, as individuals, try to determine what their role is. In defining their role, it may be logical for school board members to include issues they are personally passionate about and not understand how their agendas can negatively impact school board governance.

School board members who govern with personal agendas hamper the governance team from reaching and supporting final school board decisions. For instance, if a member disagrees with a school board decision, he or she may be overly critical of the board's decision in public, which may create disharmony on the school board. When situations like this occur, the governance team fails to speak as one voice regarding its expectations.

School board members who do not understand their roles often do not realize that they cannot speak for the entire team or have any power outside of official meetings. New members who have personal agendas can wreak havoc on the board in terms of collaborating with other members who do not have agendas. Often, existing members are concerned about the effect of newer members being elected or appointed with personal agendas and the negative impact this may have on board collaboration (Rice, 2010).

To help control board members who are elected with personal agendas, it is imperative that the school board provide proper orientation for new members to the governance team, as discussed in chapters 8 and 9. First, the foundation must be laid for this to occur. Thus, the school board must be forward thinking by recruiting capable school board members to serve. Often, effective districts look to recruit capable school board members once they become aware of potential school board member turnover, such as by resignation (Rice, 2010).

A vital part of the orientation process should deal with board process agreements, so that school board members can understand how the governance team will operate, including how to place items on the agenda for board discussion. If newly elected school board members are not clear about how to address issues about which they are passionate, it may lead to their advocating for their positions in unintended and inappropriate ways.

Educational critics note that requirements for school board membership do not include knowledge of school board operations or provision for professional development to assist members in understanding their role. Vague powers designated to the school board often create uneven and, in some cases, inadequate board governance. For instance, the school code in Illinois vaguely authorizes the school board to adopt and enforce all necessary rules for the management of schools in its district (Braun, 1998).

In situations such as these, some school board members will take the initiative to learn their roles and duties, while others will not. This is evident in Illinois where a vast majority of school board members voluntarily participate in board training (Illinois Association of School Boards, n.d.).

BUILDING A CULTURE OF PROFESSIONAL DEVELOPMENT

It is essential for all school board members to understand that effective board governance relies on a team approach. Effective governance doesn't happen in a vacuum; it requires general maintenance through ongoing professional development. To maximize good governance, the superintendent's role in the training process is critical to the overall success of the school board. To demonstrate the value of trainings, it is wise for superintendents to play an active part in promoting professional development by establishing resources for the school board, accompanying new members to trainings, and working with school board associations to promote school board training.

Effective school boards build a culture of ongoing training to ensure good governance. If a culture of training is nonexistent, even the best of school boards will eventually experience problems. Too often, when problems emerge on the governance team, the board reacts by engaging in some sort of training. However, if the training was nonexistent prior to the problem, it may result in newer school board members feeling as though they were the target of such trainings.

Effective school boards develop a culture of ongoing professional development by aligning training initiatives with school board policy. Consistent training allows habits to form. Habits are behaviors that come into fruition because of discipline. Often, good habits for school boards develop because the governance team has taken advantage of various training opportunities that instructed the governance team in how to be successful in its work. Effective school boards believe and live by the quote in the 2011 film *The Mechanic*: victory loves preparation. In short, school boards must pay attention to how they are functioning to be successful. Stephen Covey calls this "sharpening the saw" in his book *The 7 Habits of Highly Effective People* (1990). To illustrate his point, Covey gives an example of a wood cutter:

> Suppose you were to come upon someone in the woods working fever-ishly to saw down a tree. "What are you doing?" you ask. "Can't you see?" comes the impatient reply. "I'm sawing down this tree." "You look exhausted!" you exclaim. "How long have your been at it?" "Over five hours," he returns, "and I'm beat! This is hard work." "Well, why don't you take a break for a few minutes and sharpen the saw?" you inquire. "I'm sure it would go a lot faster." "I don't have time to sharpen the saw." The man says emphatically. "I'm too busy sawing!" (287)

When school boards refuse to engage in training opportunities and/or board evaluations, they are subconsciously saying they have no time to sharpen their saw. Effective school boards engage in activities that are most relevant to their needs and utilize training opportunities to keep them on-track and focused. School boards that sharpen their saw in this capacity rarely feel overwhelmed and nonproductive (Cassel, Peifer, and Allen, 1997).

When school boards fail to establish a culture of professional development, even the best of school boards are bound to experience problems. Often these problems come as a surprise to the school board because after a period of good governance, in-fighting between members and/or the superintendent and other problems emerge. John Cassel, a former field services director for the Illinois Association of School Boards, identifies potential causes and solutions in his 2003 article, "The Hazards of Success: A Surprising Form of Board Troubles and How to Avoid Them." There are several things that Cassel notes, but a primary problem is that the board forgets its primary job.

The school board has many responsibilities, but some are more important than others. For instance, the primary mission of the school board is to ensure good governance and to clarify the district's purpose by establishing and maintaining the district ends. Effective districts have a plan to continuously monitor and modify district ends, because, as the world changes, the school board must adapt (Cassel, 2003). Often, ineffective school boards do not take the time to review their district ends. As a result, superintendents may not understand the expectations of the school board.

SUMMARY

Educational critics argue that school board members should be trained to do their jobs, especially given the fact that in most states there is no special preparation needed to become a board member. Equally important, school board members must avoid potential conflicts of interest or the appearance thereof, specifically financial conflicts of interest. Thus, many states have drafted policies in an effort to restrict public officials serving with financial positions that may impair their decision making. In order for school board members to be perceived as trustworthy by various stakeholders in the community, a school board member's character must be impeccable.

School board member training is vitally needed to assist school board members in understanding their central duties, such as implementing policy, understanding roles and duties, providing administrative oversight and direction to the district (vision), and engaging the community. Danzberger (1994) explained that school boards commonly appear dysfunctional because of internal conflicts among school board members, an inability for school boards to set a vision or direction for the school district, and a lack of understanding concerning the board's role.

There are several other issues that confront school boards that training may help to alleviate. They include loss of power to other organizations, challenging superintendent relationships, lack of community and media communication, lack of voter and candidate interest, and failure to explain to dissenters why local citizens should belong on the school board (Sell, 2006). School boards that engage in training have an opportunity to demonstrate to the community that they are credible because they are trained to do their jobs and are interested in improving their performance.

A major deficiency of most school boards is never planning for changes on the governance team. When school boards fail to prepare themselves for changes on the governance team, it creates a variety of issues such as board members serving with personal agendas. Often school board members are not provided with a clear job description of their roles and duties, and they frequently see winning the election as an edict for change.

QUESTIONS FOR REFLECTION

1. On what basis do critics believe school board training is warranted?
2. For what reasons may a board member or a board member candidate be disqualified for board service?
3. Describe some conflicts of interests that board members should be aware of when serving.
4. How does engaging in professional development positively impact the perception of the school board?
5. Explain the correlation between school board micromanagement and superintendent turnover.
6. Compare and contrast the differences between highly effective and low-performing school districts.
7. How do newly elected school board members often view winning their board seat? What possible impacts may this have on the governance team and superintendent?
8. Why should school boards invest in building a culture of professional development, and why do many boards not do so?

CHAPTER 8

School Board Member Perspectives about School Board Training

Research indicates that most school board members favor individual and/or group training. But there is not a clear consensus regarding the nature and scope of school board training. Disagreement centers on several issues such as what specific skills are needed, quality of the training, whether training should be voluntary or mandatory, and the time and expenses involved with training.

Out of these concerns, mandatory training emerges as the primary concern for most school board members. It should be noted that although most school board members do not favor mandatory school board member training in general, veteran school board members and superintendents are open to the idea of minimum training standards for newer members. Superintendents and veteran board members believe that new members should be oriented to the school board to learn their roles and duties in an effort to curb new members' serving with personal agendas and enhance teamwork on the governance team.

THE FORM AND SCOPE OF BOARD TRAINING

Most school board members acknowledge that they can benefit from formal training, but there is not a consensus regarding the form and scope of school board training. Specifically, in what subject areas should school boards receive training and how often? Most state school board associations strongly encourage and offer school board member training in critical areas of school law, finance, and governance. But how much more training and how much expertise do board members need to fulfill their role and responsibilities? Research shows that when school board members are properly trained, they are more likely to understand their roles and duties, work more effectively as a team, and learn how to engage in problem-solving strategies (Anderson and Snyder, 1980).

School board members must also weigh the value of their time and how the training specifically addresses their needs. It is essential that a school board member's time is not wasted, given the fact most school board members cite lack of time as a primary reason for not participating in professional development (Land, 2002). An additional challenge occurs between the training needs of newly elected and veteran school board members. Newly elected board members are generally more in favor of board member orientation workshops and other learning opportunities than are experienced board members (Payne, 1994; South-Eastern Regional Vision for Education, 1997).

CONCERNS AND BENEFITS WITH MANDATORY TRAINING

Research indicates there are both potential advantages and disadvantages associated with mandatory training (Capital Area School Development Association, 1990; Rice, 2010). Advantages of mandatory board training include the following: school board members will be better informed so that they can make knowledgeable decisions; the board will be more organized, allowing for more effective and efficient meetings; the board will understand its role as policymakers and overseers; there is likely to be increased collaboration between school board members and the superintendent; and school board members will feel their service is more valued.

Negative concerns associated with mandatory training include the following: the possibility that some citizens may be discouraged to seek election; the cost of mandatory training and who pays for it; who provides the training; how much training is needed; and whether mandatory training discourages additional voluntary training (Capital Area School Development Association, 1990).

A key question concerning mandatory training is whether it discourages citizens from seeking school board positions. There is no solid evidence to suggest this, although the additional requirement obviously adds another challenge to school districts where the pool of interested or qualified citizens is limited. Generally, rural communities struggle to find candidates compared to urban communities because of population shortages (Rice, 2010).

Because many education reformers and like-minded legislators are convinced that school boards must be held "accountable," more states are mandating school board member training. Twenty-two states—Arkansas, Delaware, Georgia, Illinois, Kentucky, Louisiana, Maine, Maryland, Massachusetts, Michigan, Minnesota, Missouri, New Jersey, New Mexico, New York, North Carolina, North Dakota, Oklahoma, South Carolina, Tennessee, Texas, and Virginia—mandate some form of school board training. Each of these states requires training, but each has different requirements, as shown in the following (National School Boards Association, 2010; Petronis, Hall, and Pierson, 1996; Rice, 2010; SouthEastern Regional Vision for Education, 1997):

Arkansas:

- Six hours for newly elected and reelected members.
- Curriculum includes duties of school boards and laws governing the state schools.
- Providers include the Arkansas School Board Association, Institutions of Higher Education, and the Arkansas Department of Education.

Delaware:

- All board members must receive training.
- Curriculum includes school finance and superintendent evaluation.

Georgia:

- Newly elected and appointed board members will receive orientation training (one day of training within a year of being seated on the board).
- Curriculum includes education program objectives, school finance, school law, responsiveness to the community, ethics and

duties of a board member, evaluation of superintendent, and school board effectiveness.
- Providers include the Department of Education, in collaboration with the Georgia School Board Association.

Illinois:

- Newly elected, reelected, and/or appointed board members must receive four hours of training within the first year of the board member's term.
- Curriculum includes education and labor law, financial oversight and accountability, and fiduciary responsibilities.
- School board members must be trained in Performance Evaluation Reform Act and Open Meetings Act training.
- It is also required that school districts post on their websites the names of all board members who have successfully completed the training.

Kentucky:

- School board members with zero to three years of experience must engage in twelve hours of professional development per year.
- School board members with four to seven years of experience must engage in eight hours of professional development per year.
- School board members with eight or more years of experience must engage in four hours of professional development per year.
- Curriculum includes roles and duties of a board member and school board, school finance, superintendent and staff relations, school law, and community relations.

Louisiana:

- Six hours of training per year for all board members.
- Curriculum includes governance, curriculum, trends in education, open meetings, and public records.

Massachusetts:

- Eight hours of training per year for newly elected board members.
- Curriculum includes leadership, roles and responsibilities, collective bargaining, finance, open meeting and public records law, ethics statutes, and conflict interest laws.

Minnesota:

- Newly elected board members must complete training.
- Curriculum includes finance and management. The training will be provided by the Minnesota School Boards Association.

Mississippi:

- Newly elected board members shall engage in a twelve-hour basic course within six months of being seated to the board.
- All board members will receive six hours of board training per year; providers include the State Department of Education.

Missouri:

- Sixteen hours of training for all newly elected and/or appointed board members within one year of their election or appointment.
- Curriculum includes governance roles, board-superintendent relationships, school law, finance, goal-setting, and policy.

New Jersey:

- All elected school board members must receive training.
- Curriculum includes:
  o New board members—New Board Member Orientation Conference
  o First term, second full year of service—finance
  o Third full year of service—student achievement
  o Reelected/reappointed board members in the first year of any succeeding term—legal update + Anti-Bullying Bill of Rights

- Second and/or third year board members (elected and/or appointed) must engage in training in governance and school law.

New Mexico:

- All board members must engage in training a minimum of five hours per year.
- Curriculum includes state educational law, policies and procedures, statutory powers and duties of school boards, educational legal concepts, finance and budget, and other areas deemed as important by the State Department of Education.

New York:

- Six hours of one-time training for all newly elected school board members.
- Curriculum includes fiscal oversight.

North Carolina:

- Local boards shall engage in twelve hours of professional development annually.
- Providers include the North Carolina School Boards Association, the Institute of Government at the University of North Carolina, or other approved providers.

North Dakota:

- Newly elected school board members must engage in a one-day orientation seminar.
- Curriculum includes the role of a school board member, duties of board members. and educational finance.

Oklahoma:

- Newly elected board members will engage in a two-day statewide orientation and twenty additional hours after thirteen months.

- Veteran board members shall complete fifteen hours of training during their term and may not seek reelection until hours are completed.
- Curriculum includes school finance, school code, ethics, and roles and duties of board members.
- Providers include Oklahoma School Boards Association and State Department of Education.

South Carolina:

- Newly elected school board members must take six hours of mandated training.
- Curriculum includes roles and duties, legal, superintendent relations, procedures, budget, and employee relations.

Tennessee:

- Newly elected board members are required to attend an orientation session and a seven-hour training module. All board members will attend one of six seven-hour training modules per year.
- Curriculum includes board-superintendent relations, school law, policy and board operations, planning, finance, school governance, and new school board member orientations.
- Providers include State Department of Education, Tennessee School Boards Association, University of Tennessee Center for Governmental Training, Educational Foundation, and State Department of Education.

Texas:
- Newly elected board members will receive orientation training prior to sixty days of being elected and twenty additional hours during their first year in office.
- Veteran board members shall receive six hours of training annually.
- Curriculum includes ethics, board-superintendent responsibilities, community engagement, school board policy, effective planning, instructional programs, business and fiscal practices, school law, personnel, board meeting management, and meeting mandate for training.

- Providers include Education Service Centers in Texas, private and professional organizations, school districts, governmental agencies, and colleges and universities.

Virginia:

- Each school board shall require its members to annually participate in training workshops.
- Curriculum includes personnel, curriculum, and current issues.

WHO PROVIDES THE TRAINING?

As a compromise to state mandates, the Capital Area School Development Association (1990) recommended that the state require each district to develop its own training program that focuses on the unique needs of that district. In addition to ensuring local control of trainings, school boards would have more latitude in how they choose to participate in professional development. For instance, training could be offered in a variety of ways, including workshops, working with consultants, reading professional literature, or participating in annual assessments and retreats.

Yet the question remains that if each school district is responsible for its own training program, are school boards up to the task of ensuring that their school board training is a meaningful experience? Logically, no one wants to spend his or her time on something of no value. Perhaps professionals such as school board associations and universities with professional development programs could be approved providers. Additionally, veteran board members or state departments of education could contribute.

Whatever training format is utilized, it is vital that training programs be evaluated to measure their quality and effectiveness (Institute for Educational Leadership, 2001). Various states require training, but the providers are different (see the following) (National School Boards Association, 2010; Petronis, Hall, and Pierson, 1996; Rice, 2010; South-Eastern Regional Vision for Education, 1997).

Arkansas:

- Includes the Arkansas School Board Association, Institution of Higher Education, and the Arkansas Department of Education.

Georgia:

- Includes the Department of Education in collaboration with the Georgia School Board Association.

Illinois:

- Providers include the Illinois Association of School Boards.

Minnesota:

- Training provided by the Minnesota School Boards Association.

Mississippi:

- Providers include the State Department of Education.

New Jersey:

- Providers include the New Jersey School Boards Association.

North Carolina:

- Providers include the North Carolina School Boards Association, the Institute of Government at the University of North Carolina, or other approved providers.

Oklahoma:

- Providers include Oklahoma School Boards Association and State Department of Education.

Tennessee:

- Providers include State Department of Education, Tennessee School Boards Association, University of Tennessee Center for Governmental Training, Educational Foundation, and State Department of Education.

Texas:

- Providers include Education Service Centers in Texas, private and professional organizations, school districts, governmental agencies, and colleges and universities.

TIME COMMITMENT: HOW MUCH AND WHEN?

School board members are concerned about the time commitment associated with school board training. After all, most school board members serve voluntarily on the board. Many school board members feel that those who serve voluntarily should not have excessive demands placed on them without compensation (Rice, 2010). Most school board members work full-time jobs and have significant family and other demands on their time. McAdams (2006) identifies the following time demands on school board members:

- Attend board meetings, workshops, and other committee sessions.
- Attend district events, ceremonial, and social and cultural events.
- Respond to various constituents.
- Communicate with the superintendent, other board members, and civic leaders to build relationships to support district ideas and functions.

How much time do school board members spend on school board work? California, Illinois, Pennsylvania, and a national survey sponsored by the National School Boards Association offer insight concerning the average time per month board members spend on board work.

California School Boards Association (2005):

- 6 hours (regular board meetings)
- 5.2 hours (communications with parents/community)
- 4.9 hours (preparation for meetings)
- 4.8 hours (communications with superintendent/staff)
- 4.8 hours (committee meetings)
- 4.7 hours (board-related community meetings)
- 4.5 hours (school site visits)

- 4.2 hours (advisory or parent groups)
- 3.5 hours (closed sessions)
- 3.2 hours (charter school approval, monitoring, etc.)
- 5.1 hours (other activities)

Illinois Association of School Boards (2008):

- Five hours or less per month
- Six to ten hours
- Eleven to fifteen hours
- Sixteen to twenty hours
- More than twenty hours per month

Pennsylvania School Board Association (2010):

- One to five hours
- Six to ten hours
- Eleven to fifteen hours
- Sixteen to twenty hours
- Twenty-one to thirty-five hours
- Twenty-six to thirty hours
- Thirty-one to thirty-five hours
- Thirty-six to forty hours
- Forty-one to fifty hours
- Fifty-one or more

School Boards Circa (Hess and Meeks, 2010):
Note: board members nationally

- More than forty hours
- Twenty-five to forty hours
- Fifteen to twenty-four hours
- Seven to fourteen hours
- Fewer than seven hours

It should be noted that some school board members are paid to serve. School board members in states such as Alabama, California, Florida,

Louisiana, New York, North Carolina, and Virginia receive pay and other benefits for their service. The average salary ranges from fifteen thousand to twenty thousand dollars. The state of Florida pays the highest salary for board members, with salaries ranging from twenty-three thousand to forty-one thousand dollars per year. Benefits include medical insurance, stipends for attending board meetings, compensation for travel, expense accounts, and credit cards (Council of the Great City Schools, 2005).

HOW SCHOOL BOARD MEMBER TRAINING IS FUNDED

School boards are also concerned about the increasing number of unfunded mandates that they have to implement. The cost of board training is no exception. According to the National School Boards Association (2010), states that have passed mandatory school board training requirements are funded in a variety of ways, including:

- State school board associations provide some trainings at no cost to member districts.
- The state provides the financial resources for the training.
- State and local funding.
- State grants.
- The districts pay for the training.

As noted, there is no guarantee that school boards will be reimbursed by the state for participating in mandated training programs. It is the author's opinion that, if states mandate school board member training, they should give districts the necessary resources to conduct that training. If states provide resources such as funding, this may foster more buy-in from board members to engage in professional development.

NEW BOARD MEMBER ORIENTATION

State school board associations, veteran school board members, and superintendents agree that some sort of training is beneficial to orient new members to the school board (Rice, 2010). Many new school board members are unclear about their roles and responsibilities, leading to role confusion, tension between the superintendent and the board, and tension with other school board members as well.

Formal orientation programs can assist new school board members and can aid the entire board in operating more effectively. Unfortunately, most school board members receive little to no training prior to serving on the board. In many cases, new board members are only given some reading materials and attend a meeting with the superintendent (Kunder, 1975).

When board members are properly oriented to the work of the school board and see that training as beneficial, they are likely to continue to participate in ongoing professional development. Various survey data from state school board associations indicate the importance of orientation programs for new school board members (see the following).

California School Boards Association (2005 survey):

- 67% of respondents rated training for new and first-term board members as very valuable, and 82% of respondents were aware of new board member training that the California School Boards Association offers.

Illinois Association of School Boards (2008 survey):

- 64.5% of respondents indicated that their board discussed orientation services for new board members.
- 44.3% of respondents believe in some form of mandatory board member training and believe that mandatory training of all board members may alleviate board member turnover.
- 30.3% of respondents would oppose mandatory board member training but would participate.
- 33.7% of respondents indicated that board members need all the training they can obtain.
- 33.6% of respondents indicated that every board member needs training in the basics of school governance.

Michigan Association of School Boards (2008 survey):

- 66% of respondents favor mandatory school board member training.

- 80% of respondents believe training is vital in assisting new board members in understanding their role and responsibilities.

Pennsylvania School Board Association (2009 survey):

- 55% of respondents favor new board member orientation.

Virginia School Board Association (2011 survey):

- 80.3% of respondents favor mentoring program for new board members.
- 74.6% of respondents favor training for new board members.
- 93% of respondents favor increased availability of new board member orientation training.

As part of the orientation process, newly elected board members need the opportunity to become familiar with each other and with the veteran board members. One school board member can change the dynamics of the governance team, especially if that member does not feel connected to the school board. Revisiting district ends provides one opportunity to ensure buy-in from fellow school board members.

To orient new school board members to the board, there are several methods for districts to consider. Districts may want to collaborate with state school board associations or other consultants that provide new board member orientation in areas such as roles and duties, finance, and governance. One way to train newly elected school board members is by participating in mock school board meetings. These simulations provide school board members with a glance at how to govern with other members and what to expect.

It is vital that orientation programs be structured around the needs and abilities of the local school board and that they teach school board members how to ask the right questions to govern effectively. Based upon my experience, for orientation programs to be successful, care must also be given to the site of the training, a convenient time for school board members to participate, and what materials are needed.

Although the superintendent should play a key role, that person's role in orientation should not be perceived as dictating to his or her employer.

According to Kunder (1975), an orientation program may include the following:

- Board member conduct: School board members must understand that, as individuals, they have no authority; their power only derives when they govern at a legal meeting. Members must be respectful of others and of their viewpoints. School board members should express their points of agreement and disagreement at a legal meeting but should support the overall work of the school board.
- Community relations: School boards are trustees for the communities in which they serve. In order for the community to have a voice in its schools and for school boards to be responsible to the needs of the community, a two-way conversation is required.
- Curriculum: School board members are not expected to be directly engaged in curriculum planning or to be involved in academic instruction. Nevertheless, a relationship exists between school board decisions and school curriculum, specifically in the area of financial resources.
- Development of school policies: School board members must understand that they primarily govern through the use of policies. By utilizing policies to govern the district, the school board has a system for how it will operate.
- Board and superintendent evaluation: School board and superintendent evaluations are helpful in identifying strengths and weaknesses on the governance team and aid in clarifying roles and duties of the board and the superintendent.
- Personnel: The superintendent is the school board's only employee, and the board should utilize caution in the selection, employment, and evaluation of the superintendent. In regard to other staff members, the board adopts the district salary schedule, approves final collective bargaining agreements, and hires and terminates staff based upon the superintendent's recommendation.
- Finance: The budget is a financial expression of district ends. In other words, the budget symbolizes the district's plan to accomplish the aims of the district expressed in money.
- Building and grounds: School board members are not expected to have a keen acumen when it comes to the management of

the physical plant and new construction. But in order to make wise decisions and to plan adequately for the future, members should be familiar with various educational needs and types of construction.

- School board meetings: School board members should be knowledgeable about various procedures in conducting school board meetings. This includes parliamentary rules, the role of the board president and secretary, the school board agenda, and special and/ or reconvened meetings of the school board.

SUMMARY

Although there is disagreement regarding the form and scope of school board member training, most board members support and seek training opportunities, voluntarily participate in professional development, and believe that new school board members, at a minimum, should be properly trained and/or oriented to the board. Key orientation areas include school board member conduct, community relations, curriculum, school policies, school board/superintendent evaluations, personnel, finance, building and grounds, and school board meetings.

School board members generally feel that new members should not join the board due to personal agendas, which lead to dysfunction on the governance team. Overall, disagreement is centered on which skills should be addressed, the quality of the training program, and whether or not training should be mandatory. Of these three, mandatory training is the greatest concern.

Some school board members view mandatory training as another unfunded mandate that will impact school district expenses and place further demands on volunteer school board members. More importantly, the time commitment required for board members is not a motivator for continued service and may distract other citizens from serving on the school board as well.

As a compromise in regard to specific, prescriptive state and/or federal mandates, many educational stakeholders favor a more regulatory approach. For instance, school boards can be regulated to engage in training, although the school board will have the flexibility to determine the makeup of that training based on the unique needs of their district. By working in concert with local school districts, legislators can alleviate the "one-size-fits-all" model.

QUESTIONS FOR REFLECTION

1. Generally, do school board members favor professional development? What concerns, if any, do school board members have about professional development?
2. Should there be a distinction between the training needs of newer school board members and those of more experienced school board members?
3. What are the positives and negatives associated with mandatory school board member training?
4. As an alternative to state mandates for professional development, some educational stakeholders believe regulatory guidelines are a better solution. Do you agree or disagree? Explain.
5. What concerns, if any, do school board members have about time commitments associated with school board training?
6. Who pays for mandatory school board member training?
7. Why do many tenured board members, superintendents, and school board associations favor some sort of training for newer school board members?
8. Identify and describe some ways in which school boards and districts may orient newer school board members.

CHAPTER 9

The Superintendent Role in School Board Training and the Benefits Thereof

There are many reasons why the superintendent should promote professional development with the school board. A primary reason is the fact that if school boards are not trained to understand their role and duties, then role confusion will continue to plague many districts, adversely impacting the superintendent's job and, in many cases, leading to superintendent turnover, thus negatively impacting student achievement (Glass, 2001).

Secondly, the need for school boards will continue to be called into question if boards fail to understand their role and duties. This will lead to more state and federal involvement and/or other governance models such as mayoral control of schools, which will impact the superintendent's management discretion (Rice, 2010).

The fact that superintendents are often not trained to work with school boards further complicates this problem. To demonstrate the magnitude of this problem, the Interstate School Leaders Licensure Consortium Standards, in collaboration with the National Policy Board on Educational Administration and supported by the Council of Chief State School Officers, provides six fundamental standards that superintendents must know and understand to be successful educational leaders. These standards, endorsed by thirty-five states, provide guidance for college preparatory programs that instruct future superintendents (Council of Chief State School Officers, 2008).

Although the standards are not designed to address every aspect of the role of the superintendent, they are designed to address the major roles and duties of the position. The superintendent's role in working with the school board is not addressed in the Interstate School Leaders Licensure Consortium Standards. This is unfortunate, as the superintendent's success will be largely determined by the working relationship he or she has with the school board. The six Interstate School Leaders Licensure Consortium Standards are (Council of Chief State School Officers, 2008):

- Standard 1: A school administrator is an educational leader who promotes the success of all students by facilitating the development, articulation, implementation, and stewardship of a vision of learning that is shared and supported by the school community.
- Standard 2: A school administrator is an educational leader who promotes the success of all students by advocating, nurturing, and sustaining a school culture and instructional program conducive to student learning and staff professional growth.
- Standard 3: A school administrator is an educational leader who promotes the success of all students by ensuring management of the organization, operations, and resources for a safe, efficient, and effective learning environment.
- Standard 4: A school administrator is an educational leader who promotes the success of all students by collaborating with families and community members, responding to diverse community interests and needs, and mobilizing community resources.
- Standard 5: A school administrator is an educational leader who promotes the success of all students by acting with integrity, fairness, and in an ethical manner.
- Standard 6: A school administrator is an educational leader who promotes the success of all students by understanding, responding to, and influencing the larger political, social, economic, legal, and cultural context.

UNDERSTANDING THE IMPORTANCE OF PROMOTING LOCAL SCHOOL BOARD GOVERNANCE AS COMPARED TO A MAYORAL FORM OF GOVERNANCE

In order for superintendents to promote school boards effectively, they must understand and value the belief that local communities are best suited to address educational issues through local school boards and superintendents hired by those school boards. This model works best especially when everyone understands his or her role and duties, there are no secret agendas, and everyone works as a team. However, most importantly in this model, the community is represented.

If school boards were replaced by other forms of governance such as the mayoral form, superintendents would have to consider how this would impact them as educational leaders. Instead of educational leaders, will superintendents become simply managers for the mayor? For instance, some mayors may believe that one does not need educational acumen at all, which should be disconcerting for superintendents. This was evident when Mayor Bloomberg of New York nominated Cathie Black, a businesswoman, to oversee public school operation. After three months on the job, Black and Mayor Bloomberg agreed that she should resign, due in part to an increase in parental complaints and the departure of several chancellors (Samuels, 2001).

It is evident that U.S. Secretary of Education Arne Duncan favors mayoral forms of governance as well. For instance, Secretary Duncan pressured Detroit officials to place a question on the ballot concerning turning over the operation of its schools to the mayor (McNeil, 2011a). Educational reform advocates who support the mayoral form of school governance primarily do so because they believe mayors can be more efficient in carrying out school reforms compared to school boards.

But to exchange the school board model for the mayoral form may be exchanging efficiency at the expense of public participation. Under a mayoral form of governance, the superintendent must also consider how the mayor's approval ratings are in some ways interconnected with the job of the superintendent, which may impact the superintendent's tenure in office due to the politics involved. This is evident when the voters ousted Washington, D.C., mayor Adrian Fenty, which led to the resignation of Michelle Rhee, in part due to voter concerns over educational issues.

U.S. mayors would like parents to be in control of public schools, especially low-performing public schools. During the summer of 2012, hundreds of mayors from the United States convened in part to support new laws aimed at strengthening the parent role in education through firing teachers and administrators and allowing private management companies to govern public schools. This is better known as "parent trigger" (Simon, 2012b).

Increasingly, mayors are focusing on a new direction for public education, one that is strictly consumer-centered, which many businesses and private foundations support. For instance, the Bill and Melinda Gates Foundation and the Walton Family Foundation invest in "parent trigger," although no evidence supports that this type of reform works.

Ironically, the mayors did not discuss any detailed plans of how parents can organize themselves to run public schools. Sadly, mayors criticized public schools but offered no detailed alternative plans. Simply saying that public schools should be turned over to groups of parents at random without any structured plan will lead to anarchy. More importantly, these mayors should realize that many parents already serve on public school boards to oversee education on behalf of the community.

There are other concerns associated with the mayoral form of governance as well. The Institute on Educational Law and Policy studied the mayoral forms of governance in Baltimore, Boston, Cleveland, Chicago, Detroit, Hartford, and New York. The study noted the following (Council of Chief State School Officers, 2008):

- Parents in New York were unhappy with the lack of transparency regarding various educational issues.
- Parents in Chicago and Boston were displeased because they had no voice in school closings.
- Parents and other community stakeholders voted to end mayoral control of schools in Detroit.

SCHOOL BOARDS DEPEND ON THE SUPERINTENDENT FOR THEIR TRAINING NEEDS

Superintendents must also realize that more states, such as Illinois, are mandating school board member training. Because of the superintendent's position as a member of the governance team and an educational leader of the district, school board members often look to him or her for guidance concerning their training needs. According to the School Boards Circa report authored by Hess and Meeks (2010), 88% of respondents almost always seek the superintendent's advice on making decisions and for obtaining information on educational issues.

A major reason why superintendents should promote school board training is the fact that the superintendents' effectiveness will be determined in large part by their school board. The school board approves or disapproves of how the superintendent manages the day-to-day operations of the district. In short, in order for the superintendent to do his or her job effectively, the board must do its job effectively and vice versa.

AN OVERVIEW OF THE ROLES AND RESPONSIBILITIES OF THE SUPERINTENDENT AND SCHOOL BOARD

Effective superintendents not only advocate for school board training but also educate board members directly concerning members' roles and responsibilities. There are many areas in which the superintendent could assist board members with understanding their roles and duties. But first, how do school boards govern and what exactly are their roles and duties? School boards govern through policy and decide the direction of the district, while the superintendent manages or carries out the daily operations of the district. In short, the school board governs while the superintendent administers.

A primary duty of the school board is to promote student achievement through community and stakeholder engagement (Gemberling, Smith, and Villani, 2000). The board decides the direction of the district by establishing the vision and the mission and by identifying goals and policies to support this key work or district ends (mission, vision, goals). If the board fails to establish the vision and mission of the district, often the staff will develop its own versions, creating a fragmented sense of purpose and identity. If this occurs, aligning and identifying resources to different missions and visions will be most troublesome for any governance team and will negatively impact student achievement.

School boards must realize that one of the most important decisions they will ever make is in the selection of the superintendent. Effective districts are based in part on good board–superintendent relationships, centered on a mutual understanding of their roles and duties. As stated, it is the superintendent's job to carry out the goals of the board, but the superintendent must understand board governance in order to be successful in this task.

According to Eadie (2011), the consequences of the board selecting the wrong superintendent are dire in areas such as student performance, faculty and administrator morale, administrative performance in the areas of financial planning and management, community relations, and the governance performance of the board.

To determine how familiar superintendents are in the area of board governance, a growing number of school boards are screening a candidate's knowledge about school board governance. According to Eadie (2011), screening questions include the following: identify the pros and cons of your last school board as a governing body, describe ways that you can use to determine if you have a good working relationship with your school board, identify ways you assisted your school board in improving its governance, identify practical steps you can make to ensure that your school board is active in the strategic planning for the district, and identify some ways the school board can evaluate the superintendent based on district goals.

To carry out the goals of the school board, the superintendent must focus on objectives, action plans, regulations, procedures, and monitoring. To properly meet school board expectations, it is imperative that the superintendent maintain a healthy relationship with the board. In fairness to the superintendent, the school board must speak in unison when instructing the superintendent to work on its behalf.

A TRAINED BOARD CAN EFFECTIVELY EVALUATE THE SUPERINTENDENT AND IMPROVE ITS GOVERNANCE

Generally speaking, when school boards are trained, they tend to understand their roles and duties better, work more effectively as a team, and engage in problem-solving strategies (Anderson and Snyder, 1980). Additionally, a trained school board understands the importance of establishing district ends (core values, mission, vision, and goals), but more importantly it also understands the goals to obtain them.

Clarifying the district's purpose by identifying the district ends is a primary function of the school board. In other words, the board has to be able to answer the question, "If X district did not exist, why would it be necessary to create it?" The school board should develop goals that not only serve as a part of its evaluation but also serve as part of the superintendent's evaluation as well, including mutually accepted criteria.

Superintendents should welcome evaluations from their individual school board that are based upon board priority areas so that he or she can clearly understand their marching orders. It is unfair for the superintendent to be labeled as ineffective by the board if it has not indicated or evaluated the superintendent based upon mutually agreed upon criteria that include board goals. The superintendent and the board should also want some general professional expectations as a part of the evaluation instrument. Superintendents should welcome constructive feedback because they themselves should want to grow professionally.

Many superintendents are not comfortable with the board evaluating their performance due to reasons such as a lack of trust and the board's competency level regarding the evaluation process. Trust between the board and superintendent should increase if school boards have been trained in the evaluation process, there is a shared agreement of the process, and the evaluation instrument ties superintendent expectations to school board goals. After all, the superintendent should expect the school board to monitor its ends, but it is imperative that the superintendent be an active stakeholder in determining how those ends will be monitored and evaluated.

For superintendent evaluations to be successful, there must be some other prerequisites as well. For instance, if trust is an issue on the governance team, the board may want to consider being in-serviced on board-superintendent relations prior to the superintendent's evaluation. Furthermore, the board needs to understand how to formulate an effective evaluation tool (with superintendent involvement) and to engage in a board self-evaluation to pinpoint areas of distrust. Most state school board associations are able to provide these services and/or resources. If both trust and district ends are absent, the board should reconsider its evaluation of the superintendent.

Regarding value, the board and the superintendent must understand why the superintendent evaluation is beneficial to both parties. For starters, it assists the board in governing more effectively by ensuring compliance and monitoring of its ends (assuming that a good evaluation plan was in place based upon district goals).

Regarding superintendents, the evaluation assists them by understanding school board expectations and the fact that governance teams often change, possibly impacting board expectations of the superintendent. When changes on the governance team occur, the superintendent can confidently inform the new governance team how he or she has been committed to the goals of the district but understands if the school board would like to review and/or modify those goals.

Most school boards are unclear concerning how to develop a superintendent evaluation based upon district goals and agreed upon expectations between the superintendent and the school board. There is a variety of methods school boards can utilize to develop an evaluation instrument. However, some school boards prefer a simple Likert scale entailing generally agreed upon expectations, school board goals, and superintendent objectives for meeting those goals. For example, the following is an evaluation template based upon general expectations and superintendent objectives for meeting District Z goals:

- Develop and/or enhance an inclusive process to generate feedback from all district stakeholders (staff, community, business) regarding how to improve the performance of District Z schools.
- Recruit and retain a high-quality staff.
- Develop and implement a fiscally responsible plan to reduce district operating expenses.
- Promote and market the accomplishments of District Z and its schools.

District Z: Superintendent Evaluation Form

Superintendent Name:

Evaluation Year:

School Board Member Name:

Directions: Based upon your knowledge of the superintendent's performance centered on general expectations and board goals, circle the appropriate number that responds to your rating. District Z goals are:

- Develop and/or enhance an inclusive process to generate feedback from all district stakeholders (staff, community, business) regarding how to improve the performance of District Z schools
- Recruit and retain a high-quality staff
- Develop and implement a fiscally responsible plan to reduce district operating expenses
- Promote and market the accomplishments of District Z and its schools

Rating Scale:

5. Outstanding
4. Exceeds Expectations
3. Meets Expectations
2. Does Not Meet Expectations
1. Unsatisfactory

Part One: (Agreed upon) Superintendent-Board of Education Expectations

Table 9.1

Leadership	1 2 3 4 5
• Nurtures and develops leadership in others • Collaborates with stakeholders for district improvement	
Curriculum planning and development	1 2 3 4 5
• Utilizes data as a guide to make decisions • Ensures a diverse curriculum to meet the needs of our students	
Policy and governance	1 2 3 4 5
• Provides recommendations to the board regarding policy concerns and changes • Ensures the implementation of board policy	
Knowledge	1 2 3 4 5
• Is knowledgeable about research-based practices • Participates in professional development opportunities	

Other comments:

Part Two: Board Goals and Superintendent Objectives

Table 9.2

Goal 1: Develop and/or enhance an inclusive process to generate feedback from all district stakeholders (staff, community, business) regarding how to improve the performance of District Z schools	1 2 3 4 5
• Superintendent's cabinet will develop a plan	
Goal 2: Recruit and retain a high-quality staff	1 2 3 4 5
• Work with school board to begin negotiations with the teacher's union • Work with human resources to develop a recruiting plan	
Goal 3: Develop and implement a fiscally responsible plan to reduce district operating expenses	1 2 3 4 5
• Formulate a committee to make budget recommendations • Make final budget revisions and submit proposal to the school board	
Goal 4: Promote and market the accomplishments of District Z and its schools	1 2 3 4 5
• Work with district principals to develop a newsletter for each of the district schools • Meet with the public relations director to issue district newsletters • Recognize student and staff accomplishments at board meetings	

Other comments:

TRAINING CONTENT FOR SCHOOL BOARD MEMBERS

The content of board member training programs generally consists of basic roles and responsibilities, instructional programs, district finances, superintendent-staff relations, school law, and community relations (Petronis, Hall, and Pierson, 1996). Nevertheless, board members are diverse in their training needs regarding specific issues, as shown in the following. Various school board associations acknowledge and strongly encourage school board member training, especially in the key areas of law, finance, and governance. Despite this encouragement, there are no national uniform training requirements.

California School Boards Association, 2009:
Note: Most valuable services

- Updates on pending and new legislation (88%)
- Legislative representation and advocacy (84%)
- Action alerts (76%)
- Professional development opportunities (73%)
- Policy analysis (70%)

California School Boards Association, 2005:
Note: Importance of future products need for school boards

- Evaluation of the superintendent (67%)
- Board self-evaluation (58%)
- Collective bargaining/contract development (59%)
- Curriculum and instruction methods (56%)
- Evaluation of program performance/educational outcomes (55%)
- General legal issues (53%)
- Analysis of employee benefit packages (53%)
- Develop and align budget to district/Country Office of Education goals (44%)
- Plan for bond and tax elections (40%)
- Plan and budget for capital improvements (38%)
- Suspension/expulsion (31%)

New Jersey School Boards Association, 2007:
Note: Most beneficial services

- Goal setting (approximately 49%)
- Community engagement (approximately 44%)
- Strategic planning (approximately 34%)
- Legal assistance (approximately 32%)
- Superintendent search (approximately 32%)

Oregon School Boards Association, 2012:
Note: Importance of services

- How to improve student achievement (75%)
- Common Core Standards (67%)
- Board governance (roles and responsibilities) (55%)
- How to communicate with the public (55%)
- School law (54%)
- Effective relationship with your labor union (51%)
- Conducting effective meetings (42%)
- Ethics (39%)

Pennsylvania School Boards Association, 2010:
Note: Difficult areas of school board operations to understand

- State regulations/controls (24%)
- School finance/budget   (21%)
- Personnel/negotiations (16%)

School Boards Circa (Hess and Meeks, 2010):
Note: Percentage of training received

- Board roles, responsibilities, and operations (92.6%)
- Legal and policy issues (82.7%)
- Funding and budget (82.9%)
- Leadership skills (75.2%)
- Student achievement (73.9%)
- Community engagement (65.1%)

Washington Association of School Boards, 2011
Note: Importance of Washington Association of School Boards services

- Assistance with contract reviews (41.3%)
- Policy review/assistance (46.6%)
- Government relations (48.1%)
- Individual board development programs (43.2%)
- Talking points on particular issues/board resolutions (49.9%)

BUDGETING FOR PROFESSIONAL DEVELOPMENT

The school board can demonstrate the value of its professional development needs by establishing a line item in the district budget. In short, the budget represents the district priorities. A line-item budget can include areas such as new board member orientation, team building, self-evaluation, subscriptions and resources, conferences, school board association leadership activities, work with consultants, and other one-time or regular professional development opportunities. Similar to teachers and administrators, board members need opportunities to increase their knowledge of educational trends, legal issues, and how to ensure good teamwork.

Budgeting for school board professional development needs is critical if school boards are to govern effectively. But, how much money should the school board spend on individual school board member and/ or on school board governance professional development needs? All too often, school board members are criticized by their constituents when it comes to spending taxpayer dollars, especially for various travel, food, lodging, and other incidental costs associated with professional development needs.

Yet, the answer to this question may depend on several variables such as the cost of living in the state and the unique circumstances of the board. For instance, school boards that have many new members on the governance team are likely to invest more in professional development compared to boards with little turnover. No two districts have the same training needs. Nevertheless, there are some good parameters that school boards should consider in developing their budget for professional development.

Activities that boards may want to consider when developing their professional development budget include annual state school board conferences, regional school board member trainings, mandatory school board training costs if required, yearly board self-evaluation, goal-setting workshops, and other customized in-district workshops. Additionally, the board must budget for miscellaneous costs such as hotels, meals, and mileage.

There are other issues and/or suggestions the board may consider when planning for the budget for school board professional development. For instance, according to a 2008 survey of Michigan board members, key findings related to professional development for school boards indicated the following (Council of Chief State School Officers, 2008):

- 66% believed in mandatory board member training
- 80% feel that training is necessary once members are elected to the board
- 91% support training/professional development opportunities located within one hour of their district
- 72% support local districts paying for training/professional development at a conference within the state
- 52% oppose board members attending national conferences
- 66% oppose training/professional development held at a large resort within the state
- 80% oppose training/professional development held at a large resort within the United States
- 24% of respondents feel that a local district should spend up to five hundred dollars for professional development

Realizing the value of professional development, wise school boards understand the importance of utilizing a commonsense approach in determining how much to spend on professional development. The Michigan (2008) survey provides some good parameters for boards to consider. For instance, it is safe to conclude that board members in Michigan believe in training/professional development, but training/professional development should be done in-state, preferably close to the school district, and should not include funds for expensive resorts or travel outside the state.

Similarly, according to the Illinois (2008) survey, respondents favored in-district workshops (66.5%) and/or state school board conferences such as the Illinois Joint Annual School Board Conference (79.6%) conducted in Chicago.

Linda Dawson (2003), director of editorial services for the Illinois Association of School Boards and editor of Illinois Association of School Boards's journal provides the following good advice for school boards to consider concerning their professional development needs:

- Understand and be able to explain to constituents why participation in professional development is important to your professional growth and the community.
- To maximize professional development at conferences, board members should consider attending different workshops and share their experiences with all members.
- School boards should understand that cutting board professional development is as dubious as a business decreasing advertising when it starts to lose customers.
- Be transparent and share learning opportunities with the local media and other community stakeholders. Taxpayers are more supportive of professional development once they understand the value of professional development opportunities.
- System funds should be used only to pay for board-approved expenses incurred at workshops and not for personal expenses.

As noted, there are a variety of factors that a board should consider in determining how much to spend on its professional development needs. Nevertheless, good parameters include establishing a line-item budget considering the unique needs of the school board, including in-service of new members, the approval of reasonable professional development expenses, and consideration of in-district and/or in-state workshops.

Although these are good parameters, there is no substitute for good, commonsense thinking when the school board considers its professional development budget. School boards must be able to understand and explain the benefit of workshop opportunities to constituents and to the local media

SUPERINTENDENT LEADERSHIP IN SCHOOL BOARD TRAINING

How can superintendents ensure that their boards will understand their role and duties? Superintendents must advocate for training and play a role in the training process for school board members. Superintendent leadership is critical if school boards are to improve. School board members look to the superintendent's guidance in understanding their roles and responsibilities.

Research conducted by Rice (2010) noted how the majority of school board members from southern Illinois believe that the superintendent's leadership is critical in motivating the school board to engage in professional development opportunities. According to Rice (2010), school board members and superintendents believe that the superintendent's chief responsibility is to inform and educate the school board regarding the very complicated issues of school governance.

Coincidentally, this is similar to the findings of the School Board Circa (Hess and Meeks, 2010) report in which school board members looked to the superintendent for information and guidance on educational issues. In short, if the superintendent does not value professional development, the school board will, more often than not, be disinterested as well. In promoting training opportunities, the effective superintendent should ask himself or herself the following questions (Townsend et al., 2007):

- How will you ensure that school board members are aware of their job descriptions and how the district operates?
- Have you identified a plan for continuous professional development opportunities for school board members?
- Have policies been adopted that explain the school board and superintendent's role?
- Have you formed an agreement with the school board concerning how you will operate and make decisions (board process agreements)? Conflicts arise if individual school board members attempt to modify what the superintendent believes is his or her area of responsibility.

THE SUPERINTENDENT'S ROLE IN ORIENTING NEW SCHOOL BOARD MEMBERS

Because some school board members are likely to run with personal agendas, it is vital that the superintendent play a role in orienting new school board members. A key overarching goal of the orientation process is to inform the newly elected board member that the success of the district depends on the governance team and not on one individual. To this end, the orientation process must include a strong emphasis on how the board relies on board policy and the development of a strategic plan that guides the board's work as a governance team.

To properly orient new board members, the superintendent must understand the political aspirations, interests, and backgrounds of the members so that he or she can develop a knowledge base to determine what resources may be needed to enhance success on the governance team. By encouraging training when a school board member is first elected, the superintendent creates a climate in which professional development is deemed invaluable to the success of the district.

Generally, superintendents agree that it is a part of their job to assist in educating the school board members about their roles and duties, but they must be careful about how they go about promoting this work. Because the school board is the superintendent's employer, it is vital that superintendents are not perceived as dictating to their bosses.

So, how should superintendents maneuver? They can be engaged in school board trainings in a variety of ways that would not be seen as offensive to their employer. Superintendents can promote training in a user friendly manner through the use of preorientation workshops, orientation manuals, school board meetings, retreats, the utilization of local consultants and/or state school board associations, and the use of technology.

VARIOUS WAYS THE SUPERINTENDENT CAN PROMOTE BOARD TRAININGS FOR NEW AND CURRENT BOARD MEMBERS

Preorientation Training

Superintendents should conduct preorientation trainings for school board members prior to their becoming elected or appointed to the school board. When the superintendent plays a role in the orientation trainings, the superintendent is more likely to be perceived as an educational leader and to set the tone that training is important. More importantly, the superintendent can be seen as a key resource for future school board trainings. This will minimize superintendents being perceived as dictating to their bosses.

Pretrainings may deter some citizens from running for the school board for purely selfish or personal reasons and will help build relationships with future school board members. The superintendent can facilitate preorientation workshops at the district level and/or by forming relationships with various school board associations.

There are several areas the superintendent should review with citizens interested in school board service. But many superintendents and school board associations believe it is imperative that new board members engage in professional development early in their career primarily to minimize and/or to eradicate any personal agendas they might bring to the table.

Respondents in Rice's (2010) study felt that school board members who lacked an understanding of their roles and duties were more likely to run for the school board with personal agendas such as having children in the district and ensuring that their children receive specific advantages. Due to concerns such as these, it is important that citizens attend school board meetings and pretraining prior to seeking election, which may deter some of them from running for the school board with such agendas or special interests. When school boards practice good governance, micromanagement of the superintendent is likely to decrease concerning the daily operations and being directly involved in educational pedagogy.

Other key areas that the superintendent should discuss with citizens interested in school board service include the goals of the district, current school problems, district structure, school finance, basic governance policies, and school board protocol (Goodman, Fulbright, and Zimmerman, 1997). In orienting potential members, the superintendent may consider giving a tour of the district as well.

Orientation Manuals

Superintendents can advocate for board training in a less intimidating way to their employer by establishing an orientation manual. An orientation manual is helpful in educating board members regarding their basic roles and responsibilities and the operation of the district. There may be school board members who decline participation in formal training opportunities due to reasons such as busy schedules, but they may be open to reviewing an orientation manual.

A key advantage to an orientation manual is that it allows the school board member to study at his or her own pace. Typically, these manuals are composed by the superintendent and/or other district administrators with additional resources from school board associations and other educational organizations (Rice, 2010).

By formulating a manual, the superintendent communicates a message to the school board that professional development is important. Thus, effective superintendents should assist in preparing, monitoring, reviewing, and updating orientation manuals not only for new school board members but for all of the district's school board members. It is imperative that, when new school board members take the board, the orientation manual be reviewed to assist in ensuring teamwork, positive collaboration, and a sense of common purpose. There are several things that should be included in a good orientation manual (see resources in the following).

In-district Tours

The superintendent can inform the newly elected school board member about how the district operates by providing welcoming tours. For instance, the superintendent of a school district in Pearland, Texas, orients newly elected school board members by giving them a detailed tour of the district and providing the school board member with various resources. The tour includes departmental overviews and office visits of transportation, human resources, curriculum, business, and food service.

The orientation also includes additional resources such as a school board member training video and a luncheon with the superintendent and the board president (Cain, 2002). The luncheon provides the new school board member with an opportunity to ask specific questions of the superintendent as well as of a seasoned school board member.

Training at Board Workshops and/or Meetings

Training for current school board members can occur at board meetings and/or special board workshops that school board members are accustomed to attending. Utilizing these venues for training may alleviate concerns of time commitment associated with other training programs. It should be noted that special workshops and/or retreats are most ideal for in-depth targeted trainings.

According to Eadie (2007), a board workshop and/or retreat is defined as a special work session, usually during a full day, to cover work that is not ideal at traditional school board meetings. Unlike traditional school board meetings, school board retreats often are facilitated by the superintendent. School board retreats generally focus on strengthening the governance team processes and operations, updating mission and vision statements, and engaging in problem solving regarding critical issues facing the district.

Regarding traditional school board meetings that the school board president facilitates, what role can the superintendent play in promoting school board trainings at these meetings? The key lies in the relationship between the school board president and the superintendent. For starters, the superintendent and school board president often work together to draft the board agenda.

According to McAdams (2005), school board meetings are the school board's meeting, but most school boards consider the superintendent's agenda, which makes the meeting a joint responsibility. While working with the school board president to formulate monthly agendas, the superintendent can seize this opportunity to keep members abreast of various educational topics and/or provide professional development opportunities. For instance, the superintendent can discuss various articles of interest and other literature regarding issues confronting the district and/or educational updates.

Collaborating with State School Board Associations

Superintendents can also work with state school board associations. Most school boards turn to their associations to provide in-district workshops and training at state and regional conferences. The School Board Circa (Hess and Meeks, 2010) report indicates that 81.6% of respondents cited their associations in providing in-district and regional/state trainings.

According to school board member surveys in states such as California (2005 and 2009), Illinois (2008), Florida (2010), Michigan (2008), Oregon (2008), Washington (2011), and Virginia (2011), the overwhelming majority rated their involvement with state school board associations as positive. By forming partnerships, superintendents can have access to a wealth of resources, including state board association resources.

State associations can organize trainings centered on the unique learning needs of the school board. Board members in Rice's (2010) study strongly urged school board associations to assist their efforts in learning about their role and duties. More importantly, the superintendent will not be alone in advocating for professional development. By forming relationships, the superintendent can advocate for professional development in a less intimidating manner when motivating his or her employer to participate in professional development opportunities (Rice, 2010).

Utilizing Technology to Provide Trainings

Superintendents can utilize technology to provide training for school board members. Currently, many people have access to the Internet and utilize e-mail as a tool for communications. A report on CNN indicated how e-mail has become so popular that the U.S. Postal Service is reorganizing because of revenue losses in part associated with e-mail and online billing, which does not require U.S. postage. Superintendents can utilize technology in a variety of ways such as establishing a professional development webpage with links to articles, hot topics, legislative news, and other appropriate websites.

According to the School Boards Circa (Hess and Meeks, 2010) report, 87.8% of board members utilize the Internet, half of the school board presidents send board materials electronically, more than two-thirds of districts post their policies online, and 56% of boards post board minutes online. Several state school board association survey data indicate most board members often utilize technology as well (see the following).

California School Boards Association (2009):

- 85% of respondents preferred to receive communications via e-mail compared to 68% in 2005.

California School Boards Association (2005):

- 98% of respondents have a computer.
- Seven out of ten board members prefer to receive information from the California School Boards Association via e-mail (68%).
- The majority of California School Boards Association members would order California School Boards Association materials if such materials were available in video/DVD/CD-RROM format, and half are interested in web-based trainings.

Florida School Boards Association (2010) (survey recommendations):

- Increase e-mail usage as a tool to communicate and distribute information to its members.
- Diversify Florida School Boards Association webcasts for its members that address issues such as state priority areas, reports from the Florida School Boards Association president and executive director, and training videos on topics such as sunshine laws, public records, and ethics.

Illinois Association of School Boards (2008):

- 95.7% have Internet access at home or at work.
- 95.5% of respondents have an e-mail address.
- 46.1% are interested in receiving communications from the Illinois Association of School Boards via e-mail.

Michigan Association of School Boards (2008):

- 55% of respondents support board member training online or via the Internet.
- 75.1% of respondents prefer paperless publications (online).
- 70.1% have Internet access.

New Jersey School Boards Association (2007):

- Approximately 70% of participants prefer online learning opportunities.

Oregon School Boards Association (2012):

- 99% of respondents have access to a computer, including Internet access.
- 93% of respondents favored receiving Oregon School Boards Association's information via e-mail.
- 80% of respondents indicated that Oregon School Boards Association's daily electronic clippings are helpful.

Pennsylvania School Board Association (2009):

- 86% of respondents use e-mail to communicate with each other.

School Board Circa report (Hess and Meeks, 2010):

- Over 87.8% of respondents utilize the Internet daily, and over 66.7% have e-mail.

Washington Association of School Boards (2011):

- 79.4% have home Internet.
- 72.5% have wireless connection.
- 73.9% have a desktop personal computer.
- 73.2% have a laptop.
- 32.8% prefer e-mail for board development information.

Virginia School Boards Association (2011):

- 96% of respondents are pleased with the Virginia School Boards Association website.
- 99% of respondents are pleased with the Virginia School Boards Association E-newsletter.
- 95% of respondents are pleased with the Virginia School Boards Association legislative blogs.

KEY TRAINING AREAS FOR THE BOARD

There are many areas of school board governance that the superintendent can target for training, but it is essential that the superintendent offer guidance to the school board concerning the unique issues facing their district. When training is catered to their district, school board buy-in for professional development is likely to increase. What are some common issues facing school districts today? Most districts are dealing with issues related to school funding and student achievement, as shown in the following.

California School Boards Association, 2009:
Note: Major issues facing school districts

- Achievement gap (36%)
- Curriculum and instruction (60%)
- Declining enrollment (36%)
- Local decision making (52%)
- Parent/community relations (44%)
- Public perception of schools (47%)
- School funding (88%)
- Special education (37%)
- Student academic achievement (68%)
- Student wellness (31%)
- Teacher quality/professional development (52%)

Illinois Association of School Boards, 2008:
Note: Obstacles to quality education in their district

- Funding (44.8%)
- Social problems (27.6%)
- State regulations/restrictions (41.6%)

Michigan Association of School Boards, 2008:
Note: Major issues facing school districts (top concerns only and no percentages given)

- Achievement gap
- School funding
- Student academic achievement
- Teacher quality/professional development

New Jersey School Boards Association, 2007:

Note: Major issues facing school districts (top concerns only, no percentages given)

- No Child Left Behind
- Public/community awareness
- Public/perception/involvement
- Special education

Oregon School Boards Association, 2012:
Note: Major issues facing school districts

- Public Employees Retirement System reform (20%)
- Achievement gap (16%)
- Cost drivers (e.g., health insurance, public contracting) (15%)
- Oregon Education Investment Board and achievement compacts (12%)
- Common Core Standards (7%)
- Collective bargaining reform (5%)
- Local option levy and bond campaigns (4%)
- Open enrollment (3%)
- Mandate relief (3%)
- No Child Left Behind waivers (1%)
- Charter school authorization (1%)

Pennsylvania School Boards Association, 2010:
Note: Major issues facing school districts (top concerns, no percentages given)

- Academic standards, assessment tests, No Child Left Behind, adequate yearly progress
- Mandates, state and federal regulations
- Pension crisis, Public School Employees' Retirement System
- Personnel issues (e.g., salaries, benefits, unions, and staff management)
- School funding
- Tax reform, Act 1, referendum

School Board Circa report (Hess and Meeks, 2010):
Note: urgent matters facing the district

- Achievement gap (69.8%)
- Budget/funding (89.9%)
- Community engagement (54.8%)
- Discipline/school safety (41.6%)
- Improving student achievement (79.1%)
- Quality of leadership (55.7%)
- Quality of teaching (64.5%)

As noted previously, the superintendent can target many areas for school board training that are outside the scope of this book. But some training areas are vital to the success of school boards. First, school boards exist to ensure student academic success, but many school boards are unclear about how to promote student achievement (see chapter 5).

There are other areas of governance that can wreak havoc on the school board and should be given priority as well. For instance, superintendent-board collaboration, district finances, and communications of the school board are vital areas the superintendent must review with her or his board in order for successful governance to occur (Rice, 2010). These are critical areas in which the community can either be satisfied or dissatisfied with the board, resulting in board member/superintendent turnover. Strengthening superintendent-board collaboration will be discussed in chapter 10.

Finance

Financial issues can hamper school board governance and community relations. Regarding financial issues, school boards occasionally experience poor community relations in the following areas (see the following): consolidation and/or restructuring of schools and/or districts, building and grounds issues, reduction in force, contract negotiations, class size, and tax referendums (Rice, 2010).

Consolidation/restructuring

- Citizens may be unhappy with attendance centers compared to neighborhood schools; the board/superintendent should be prepared to deal with issues concerning the bussing of students as well.

Building and grounds

- Most citizens are not aware of cost and other resources associated with building and grounds. The board needs to have a plan to communicate its message such as through town hall meetings.

Contract negotiations/reduction in force

- School employees are typically from the community and have support networks that can impact public relations if employees are unhappy.

Class size/tax referendum

- Citizens do not like recommendations involving tax referendums, program cuts, and/or sales tax; citizens usually fail to provide any direction on how to obtain money for the operation of schools; school board/ superintendent should conduct town halls and be diligent in budgeting.

Superintendents must work with their school board to ensure resources are managed properly. If resources are not used wisely and boards have to make cuts in either educational or sports programs, the community may become unhappy and choose to replace board member(s) and possibly the superintendent as well (Alsbury, 2002). Unfortunately between the two, research suggests that the community tends to be more unhappy over sport program cuts than academic cuts.

School Board Communications

Financial issues can wreak havoc for a school board and its relationship with the community, but there are other potentially problematic areas as well, such as board communications. Regardless of the issue, failure to communicate with the public is a key problem associated with community dissatisfaction (Rice, 2010).

The board and/or superintendent have to be forthcoming and explain to their constituents the state of their respective school district and any potential actions the district is likely to pursue, especially as it relates to sports and school consolidation. Effective communications also require the board to be tactful in getting its message out by utilizing methods such as talking points and building a relationship with the media. By communicating with the public, the board will help the public better understand why it is pursuing a specific course of action.

School boards can communicate with their stakeholders in a variety of venues, including hosting town hall meetings, mailing district newsletters, speaking to local Rotaries and other organizations, and presenting information at a variety of community events. Thus, school board members need training to be adept in working with the media, talking to irate citizens, and talking to other constituents regarding school board affairs. Training could also provide public speaking tips to ensure that board members are tactful and communicating clearly when discussing board affairs with the public.

Failure to communicate with the public regarding unpopular decisions will yield negative repercussions. For instance, superintendents are often dismissed if the school board is not willing to communicate frequently with the community specifically regarding controversial issues. This usually happens because the superintendent is perceived as the school board's spokesperson and as a major contributor regarding popular or unpopular decisions from the school board. Frequently, it is the superintendent who is out front and at the center of attention. Chapter 12 describes more in-depth ways the superintendent can assist the school board in communicating with the community.

ADDITIONAL RESOURCES

Table 9.3

Indicators of Highly Effective/Ineffective School Districts

Effective school districts:
- School board members serve long terms, usually two, and encourage other qualified citizens to run for board service.
- School boards should schedule monthly meetings that last a minimum of two hours.
- School boards should engage in training (including board retreats) and evaluation.
- Good school boards have a board member orientation process.
- School boards should not micromanage administrators; they must understand their role primarily as policymakers.
- There should be a communication process between board members and the superintendent.
- A special relationship should exist between the board president and superintendent (collaborate on designing the agenda for board meetings).
- School boards should support the superintendent as the leader of the school district.
- Effective school boards build community support.
- Effective school boards adopt an annual budget.
- Effective school boards approve facility updates.
- Effective school boards engage in superintendent evaluation based on mutual agreed benchmarks.
- There is a high level of trust and respect between board members of effective districts.

Ineffective school districts:
- Ineffective districts disregard the chain of command and other governance protocols.
- Ineffective districts engage in playing to the media in an effort to embarrass the district or to promote individual agendas.
- Role confusion (board members and superintendent roles) exists in ineffective districts.
- Board members engage in petty bickering over minor concerns (e.g., spelling in reports).
- The board micromanages the superintendent.
- There is a disinterest in board training and evaluation to improve board governance.
- Board members display a concern for personal interests.
- There is a lack of trust and respect on the governance team.

Goodman, Fulbright, and Zimmerman, 1997; Rice, 2010.

Table 9.4

Sample Orientation Manual Contents

- Community demographics
- General district information (e.g., district structure and school/district calendars)
- Legal definition of a school board
- Role and duties of the board and board members (job description, board president role)
- Role and duties of the superintendent (job description)
- The characteristics of effective school boards
- Preparation for board service
- Information for potential board members (election information)
- Code of conduct for school board members
- Professional development opportunities (include board associations)
- Information of the district's mission, vision, and strategic plan
- Past board minutes (helpful in identifying how polices and precedents were set at previous board meetings)
- Information on how meetings are conducted
- Copy of the district's budget
- Enrollment trend information
- Information regarding the district's curriculum program (including special education)
- Student achievement assessment data information
- Copy of the district and school improvement plans
- Copy of the technology plan
- Copy of the school's crisis plans
- Collective bargaining agreements
- Staff evaluation forms
- District facility report

Table 9.5

Miscellaneous Orientation Topics

- Identify critical issues facing the school board
- Discuss how the budget is developed and identify funding sources
- Provide a copy of the budget
- Explain how class sizes are determined
- Suggest reading materials and other resources
- Discuss the role of the school board member and the superintendent
- Explain the district's philosophy of education
- Provide a copy of the district's policy manual or provide online access
- Discuss the community's use of school facilities
- Explain how the district involves the community in its schools
- Discuss state and federal mandates
- Discuss student achievement outcomes and measurements
- Discuss and explain the condition of buildings and grounds in the district
- Review student activity programs

Kunder, 1975; Rice, 2010.

Table 9.6

Desirable Characteristics of a Good School Board Member

- Supports and believes in public schools (advocate of building community, state, and federal support for student achievement)
- Makes decisions without bias and remains open minded (all decisions are made in the best interests of students)
- Policies are endorsed which support board/superintendent goals
- Supports utilizing and monitoring of resources (including funding) that are aligned with board policies and goals to strengthen student achievement
- Abstains from voting on business contracts that may result in personal gain or may serve other personal interests
- Shows interest in school/district activities
- Values teamwork and respects diversity of people and opinions; ensures that stakeholders are involved in the decision-making process
- Represents the district and all children as a whole
- Believes in accountability (e.g., evaluation) and professional growth (commitment to ongoing training) for board members and staff employed by the district
- Supports decisions made by the school board
- Understands that a board member's role is not to oversee the day-to-day operations of the district
- Displays knowledge of educational trends
- Always punctual at board meetings and reviews board materials in advance
- Believes that all students can advance in learning and engage in critical thinking
- Demonstrates the ability to withstand criticism
- Believes in effective communications with the public and district staff

Table 9.7

Code of Conduct for School Board Members

As a member of my local school board, I will do my utmost to represent the public interest in education by adhering to the following standards and principles:

1. I will represent all school district constituents honestly and equally, and refuse to surrender my responsibilities to special interest or partisan political groups.
2. I will avoid any conflict of interest or the appearance of impropriety that could result from my position, and will not use my board membership for personal gain or publicity.
3. I will recognize that a board member has no legal authority as an individual and that decisions can be made only by a majority vote at a board meeting.
4. I will take no private action that might compromise the board or administration, and will respect the confidentiality of privileged information.
5. I will abide by majority decisions of the board, while retaining the right to seek changes in such decisions through ethical and constructive channels.
6. I will encourage and respect the free expression of opinion by my fellow board members and will participate in board discussions in an open, honest, and respectful manner, honoring differences of opinion or perspective.
7. I will prepare for, attend, and actively participate in school board meetings.
8. I will be sufficiently informed about and prepared to act on the specific issues before the board, and remain reasonably knowledgeable about local, state, national, and global education issues.
9. I will respectfully listen to those who communicate with the board, seeking to understand their views, while recognizing my responsibility to represent the interests of the entire community.
10. I will strive for a positive working relationship with the superintendent, respecting the superintendent's authority to advise the board, implement board policy, and administer the district.
11. I will model continuous learning and work to ensure good governance by taking advantage of board member development opportunities, such as those sponsored by my state and national school board associations, and encourage my fellow board members to do the same.
12. I will strive to keep my board focused on its primary work of clarifying the district purpose, direction, and goals, and monitoring district performance.

Illinois Association of School Boards, 1976.

Table 9.8

Sample Job Description: School Board Member

- Set goals and establish policy for the district with which all board decisions should align
- Practice being a skilled decision maker
- Believe, support, and actively engage in a collaborative process to make decisions
- Support and abide by decisions made by the school board
- Ensure that I am prepared for board meetings by reading materials in advance, etc.
- Participate and abide by board policies and protocols
- Respect the rights and views of others
- Ensure decisions are made with an open mind and the basis of what is ultimately best for students (independent judgment from personal and special interest groups)

Table 9.9

Sample Policy

Policies ensure stakeholders in how the board is operating the affairs of the district, inform the community of board goals, and establish a legal document (Goodman, Fulbright, and Zimmerman, 1997).

The school board employs and evaluates the superintendent and holds him or her accountable for the operation of the district in accordance with board policies and federal law. The board–superintendent relationship is based on mutual respect for their complementary roles. The relationship requires clear communication of expectations regarding the duties and responsibilities of both the board and superintendent.

The board considers the recommendations of the superintendent as the district's chief executive officer. The board adopts policies necessary to provide general direction for the district and to encourage achievement of board goals. The superintendent develops plans, programs, and procedures to implement policies and directs the district's operations.
Legal Ref: 105 ILCS 5/10-16.7 and 5/10-21.4

Sample Policy: Illinois Association of School Boards, 2006.

Table 9.10

Sample Mission/Vision Statement

A mission statement defines the purpose of why an organization exists and how it will go about fulfilling its vision. The vision outlines what the organization aims to become or an idealized view of the organization.

Our mission: Challenging all students to seek a brighter future. Our vision: Always seeking, always learning.

Mount Vernon City Schools District 80, 2008.

Table 9.11

Sample Orientation Agenda

- Welcome to board service (10 minutes)
- What an effective board looks like
- Conflict of interest and other legal matters (discuss the importance of confidentiality)
- Overview of the board orientation packet (if available)

- Governance (45 minutes)
- Law (various state and federal statutes such as open meetings)
- Finance (budget, revenue, expenditures, and audits)
- Governance (superintendent-board collaboration, policies, training, and evaluation of the board and superintendent)

- Instructional program (10 minutes)
- Student achievement data reports
- Support programs (Response to Intervention and special education)
- Professional development for staff

- District strategic plan (10 minutes)
- Overview of the district's plan to guide the mission and vision of the district

- Personnel (10 minutes)
- Labor contracts update
- Student/teacher/administrator ratio

- School community relations (10 minutes)
- Communications with the community
- School/district/community partnerships

Questions and discussion (10 minutes)

Table 9.12

Building and Sustaining an Effective School Board (New School Board Members)
Action Steps/Reflection

Have you made an effort to spend personal/business time with each board member to properly understand his or her rationale for becoming a board member, political interests, and professional backgrounds?

How do you plan to orient board members regarding their role and duties, and district and board expectations?

Have you worked with key stakeholders (board associations, administrators, former and current board members and teachers) to determine what resources and other information to include in orienting new school board members?

Have you kept disagreements centered on the issues and not on the person?

Have you assessed whether or not all stakeholders are participating in meetings to determine board member goals and priorities?

Do you know how members of your board are engaged in the community?

SUMMARY

There are several reasons why the superintendent should encourage school board training as well as play a role in school board training. Primarily, the superintendent must promote school board training because his or her success is tied to the success of the school board and vice versa. For instance, school board dissatisfaction by the community often leads to superintendent turnover. Research suggests that school boards are more apt to engage in professional development if motivated by the superintendent, especially given the fact that the superintendent is a member of the board-superintendent governance team (Rice, 2010).

Superintendents must be mindful of the fact that if the role of the school board diminishes, an alternate form of governance will take its place and will impact the role of the superintendent. A common governance system besides the use of school boards is the mayoral form of governance. The mayoral governance of schools may lead to the superintendent serving more as an educational manager than as an educational leader.

There is a variety of benefits associated with school board training. Primarily, it is imperative that school board members understand that their job is to govern and establish the aims of the district, while the superintendent is responsible for carrying out that vision. Understanding roles and responsibilities will prevent the superintendent from being micromanaged by the school board. Other key benefits include working together effectively as a team and engaging in problem solving.

Although there is no nationally agreed upon training content for school board members, most state school board associations and school board members believe that the training content, at a minimum, should include school board roles and duties, district finances, and school law. Other key training areas to avoid community dissatisfaction should include superintendent-board collaboration and school community relations.

Frequently, there will be a cost for any sort of professional development on behalf of the board. Thus, wise school boards should budget for their professional development needs. Because no two boards are alike and their training needs may be significantly different, the school board must consider several factors such as school board member turnover in determining the district's budget.

The board should primarily demonstrate ownership of its own professional development needs, but the superintendent's role in motivating the school board to engage in training opportunities is vital. There are various ways in which the superintendent can promote school board training, such as school board member preorientation, orientation manuals, school board retreats, and establishing relationships with state school board associations.

QUESTIONS FOR REFLECTION

1. Explain why the superintendent should advocate for school board training.
2. Identify and describe the differences between local school board governance as compared to a mayoral form of school governance. In which system would you assume a superintendent would like to work?
3. Explain how the school board relies on the superintendent's expertise for part of its professional development needs.
4. Identify and explain the roles and responsibilities of the school board and the superintendent.
5. Explain why a trained school board should evaluate the performance of its superintendent. Describe what, if any, prerequisites are needed prior to the school board evaluation of its superintendent.
6. Should all school boards budget the same amount for professional development needs? What factors should board members consider prior to adopting the budget for their professional development needs?
7. How can superintendents assist in orienting new and current board members regarding their professional development needs?
8. There are several areas in which the school board should receive training, but explain why finance and school board communications are vital to the success of the school board.

CHAPTER 10

Building and Maintaining Collaboration/Relationships

Superintendent and/or board collaboration is the cornerstone for effective governance. It is challenging to have eight individuals working together in meetings to engage in problem solving due to a variety of differing opinions and personality styles. However, it is essential that all members feel a part of a democratic system and, although disagreements may occur, feel that their voices were heard. As has been said, democracy is messy.

School board training is the foundation of a good working relationship among school board members and between the school board and/or superintendent. Research is clear that ineffective superintendent-board collaboration is often the result of school board members not understanding their roles and duties, which often leads to the micromanagement of the superintendent. In addition, if effective school boards do not take the time to "sharpen their saw," as Covey (1990) puts it, they will also experience problems.

ROLE OF THE SUPERINTENDENT IN FORMING RELATIONSHIPS

What role can the superintendent play in building and sustaining effective collaboration with the governance team? First, the superintendent must realize that his or her role in this process is vital. Doug Eadie, a school board consultant, stated, "These executives [superintendents] wear what I call the 'psychologist-in-chief hat.' Wearing this hat, effective superintendents aggressively pursue opportunities to strengthen their school board members' ownership of their governing work."

(2008) Good superintendents devote time to building systems to engage the school board in its work and to be reflective of that work.

Soliciting Board Members' Involvement on the Governance Team

Good superintendents help to ensure member participation and seek opportunities to strengthen relationships on the governance team. Superintendents can serve as role models for school board members in terms of fostering relationships and collaborating more effectively with other team members. Superintendents may have boards that fail to collaborate effectively due to personality differences, egos, and/or members who lack understanding of their roles and duties. Therefore, it is essential that the superintendent play a role in ensuring teamwork and collaboration with the goal of having the school board eventually take responsibility for its own behavior.

FOSTERING STUDENT ACHIEVEMENT

More than any other reason, the superintendent should assist in ensuring that an effective collaboration system exists with school board members in order to sustain and improve student achievement. As various stakeholders run for the school board, they should be made aware of the district's commitment to collaboration and teamwork. As noted, when poor board governance continues to exist, superintendent turnover rapidly increases. If there are frequent changes in administration, the ability to maintain a good instructional program will be jeopardized, negatively impacting student achievement. Moreover, the school board will not be effective in any of its fiduciary responsibilities if collaboration is absent.

FORMING AND SUSTAINING BOARD MEMBER–SUPERINTENDENT RELATIONSHIPS

Promoting superintendent-board collaboration should be an ongoing process. Targeted training in this area should be revisited when there are changes on the governance team due to reasons such as board member resignations, defeats, deaths, and other personal reasons.

As changes occur, school boards should consider engaging in self-evaluations, which allow the board to discuss process agreements and would indicate how the new school board plans to govern together. Unfortunately, some school boards do not participate in evaluations due to sunshine laws in their state that prohibit them from discussing their performance in closed session. Nevertheless, the benefits are certainly worth the investment.

Superintendent and/or board collaboration and orienting new school board members are the two most frequently cited training areas in research literature that school board members and superintendents agree are needed for successful governance to occur (Rice, 2010). When school board members do not understand their role and/or seek to promote a personal agenda, other members may not see their colleague as a team player. This leads to a lack of the respect between school board members, and respect is essential for good governance.

School board members who are not successful in promoting a personal agenda due to the resistance of other members may decide to miss meetings and not engage in additional school board activities. If teamwork is absent, the ability to meet and solve problems will be challenging if not impossible.

Forming Relationships through Retreats, Individual Relationships, and Evaluations

Maintaining effective superintendent-board collaboration entails three primary areas: school board retreats and meetings, individual relationship building, and superintendent and school board evaluation. These areas will be addressed in this chapter with the exception of school board evaluation, which will be discussed in chapter 11.

Among these three, it is important to note that the superintendent evaluation process can serve as a catalyst in forming relationships with the school board. The superintendent evaluation has key advantages. For instance, it can help aid effective communication between the school board and the superintendent, particularly concerning goals and performance. Also, the superintendent evaluation process can address differences between the superintendent and school board in a professional manner. In short, the superintendent evaluation process can assist in eliminating miscommunications between the school board and its employee, which is necessary to enhance overall relationships.

UNDERSTANDING HUMAN BEHAVIORS TO FORM RELATIONSHIPS AT BOARD RETREATS

Neil Rackham's SPIN Selling

Understanding human behavior (psychology) can assist the superintendent and/or school board president in ensuring collaboration at school board retreats and meetings. Neil Rackham (1988), a behavioral psychologist, is well known for his work in the creation of SPIN Selling, which is based upon extensive research by Rackham and Huthwaite, the company Rackham created during the 1970s and 1980s. During this time, Rackham and his company, Huthwaite, studied the art of successfully selling products for many international corporations such as IBM and Xerox over a twelve-year period.

Rackham and his company analyzed over thirty-five thousand sales interviews in more than twenty countries and identified over a hundred factors that could improve company sales. The research gave insights concerning how salespeople can identify customer needs based upon four types of questions that he called the "SPIN model." SPIN represents an acronym for situation (facts), problem (clarifying), implication (effects of the problem), and Need Payoff (buyer informs sales agent of the buyer needs and the benefits of sale agent's solutions) questions (Rackham, 1988). The research conducted by Rackham was published by McGraw-Hill in his bestselling book entitled *SPIN Selling*.

The Eleven Categories of Rackham's Interactive Behavioral Analysis

Based upon his research, Rackham invented the Behavioral Analysis (BA). The BA's premise is that what people say and do are often different. Rackham invented BA to document human behavior in hopes of identifying specific patterns of behavior that resulted in successful outcomes. In short, BA is a method for observing, categorizing, and quantifying human behavior in interactive situations such as meetings and negotiations.

Rackham and his company conducted additional research and divided human interactions into behaviors that can be measured in regard to quantity and quality, which he calls the "Success Model." The researchers identified eleven categories of interactive (verbal) behaviors necessary for effective teamwork: proposing, building, supporting, disagreeing, defending/attacking, testing understanding, summarizing, seeking information, giving information, bringing in, and shutting out (Huthwaite, 2007; *Huthwaite Coaching Skills*, n.d.). The following are definitions and examples of these interactive behaviors to aid the superintendent and/or school board president in conducting effective board retreats/meetings.

Rackham's premise is that individuals can work successfully only if they are willing to make some basic behavioral changes as individuals and as groups. If meetings are facilitated in accordance with these eleven interactive behaviors, increased collaboration will be fostered. Rackman's work is grounded in the Expectancy Theory first proposed by Victory Vroom of the Yale School of Management. The Expectancy Theory alleges that a person will behave or act in certain ways if he or she is motivated to choose specific behaviors over others. The motivation given to select a behavior is measured by the desirability of the outcome (Smith, 2009).

To understand Rackham's premise concerning the eleven interactive behaviors necessary for teamwork, one must recognize that there are strengths associated with the manner in which each individual thinks and solves problems. The key to good governance is to capitalize on the various thinking frames each individual brings to the table. Not only do we think and solve problems differently as individuals (thinking frames), but individuals may perceive and approach problems differently based on culture, ethnicity, and gender.

Because the school board governs on behalf of diverse constituents, various thinking frames should be valued. To maximize collaboration, the superintendent and/or board president must be familiar with individual behaviors and must attempt to maximize the behaviors needed for increased positive collaboration during meetings. In brief, the superintendent/board president cannot control individual team member behavior, but he or she can influence school board members' behavior through role modeling and the way in which meetings are facilitated.

THE SUPERINTENDENT/BOARD PRESIDENT ROLE IN CONDUCTING RETREATS/MEETINGS BASED ON RACKHAM'S PREMISE

By facilitating effective meetings based on Rackham's premise, the superintendent/school board president is role modeling how governance members should interact with one another to foster increased board-superintendent collaboration. When individuals model and praise desired behaviors, it increases the chances of those behaviors being duplicated. The researchers at Huthwaite and Rackham labeled nine out of the eleven behaviors as initiating, reacting, and clarifying. The other two are labeled as process behaviors as shown in Tables 10.1 and 10.2.

Process behaviors:

Table 10.1

Behavior	Definition	Exhibited Behaviors
Initiating	Brainstorm ideas, concepts, suggestions	Proposing and building
Reacting	Analyzing ideas brought forth	Supporting, disagreeing, defending/attacking
Clarifying (Comprehending)	Trading information, facts, and opinion for clarification	Seeking information, giving information, summarizing, and testing understanding

Table 10.2

Bringing in	Solicit people, ideas, and opinions
Shutting out (very rarely used except in unusual circumstances)	Decreases the opportunity for others to participate (interrupting is the common form of shutting out)

The superintendent/school board president must understand how and when to use particular behavioral skills. This is necessary in order to have meaningful dialogue on the governing team. Effective dialogue is maximized when all participants are engaged and attentive to all voices on the governance team. In conducting retreats, the superintendent/school board president must balance the three areas of initiating, reacting, and clarifying.

Simultaneously, the superintendent/school board president must use the process behaviors of bringing in and shutting out skillfully with the other behavioral areas for a successful meeting because process behaviors do not have content in regard to the other behaviors. For instance, if people use bringing in behaviors, they do so by proposing or building information such as, "Let's ask Ann to join us." Balancing these behaviors during a meeting is contingent upon the situation. The superintendent/school board president must frequently observe and analyze meetings and determine which interactive behavior to initiate because meetings are not stable.

Practicing interactive behaviors too little or too much can have negative consequences. The facilitator must be aware of the discussion, situation, atmosphere, and desired expectations. For example, if the superintendent does not apply initiating behavior enough, conversations may receive limited insights. If used too much, nothing is accomplished because there are too many ideas. If reacting is overly applied, the discussion may be perceived as close-ended compared to overly initiating, which leads to emotional debates and endless conflicts. If clarifying is seldom used during a meeting, conversations tend to be disorganized, and decisions are made without a thorough understanding of the problem. When clarifying is used too frequently, little progress is made in the discussion because participants are overwhelmed with minor details.

Table 10.3 shows different behaviors and how the interactive skill behaviors apply. The more practice the facilitator has in utilizing these skill sets, the better he or she will become in conducting meetings.

Table 10.4 shows various examples of how individuals perceive the use of these behaviors and their impact. The plus signs are used to symbolize high usage of these skill sets.

SUPERINTENDENT-BOARD MEMBER RELATIONSHIPS

The superintendent can promote collaboration with school board members by forming individual relationships. People are much more likely to be agreeable with each other if they feel a sense of relationship and know each other as people. In order to ensure good governance and promote teamwork, it is imperative that the superintendent understand school board members' motives and concerns.

Table 10.3

Seeking proposals	Asking for ideas and/or suggestions	"Tell me how you feel about closing Ford school, starting with Bob."
Building	Extending or adding on to a proposal mentioned by someone else	"We can survey our stakeholders to see how citizens feel about this issue." "Let's not worry about finances right now, but tell me what services you would like to offer."
Supporting	Agreeing or deliberately supporting a person's idea	"That idea sounds great. I trust it will work."
Disagreeing	Act of disagreeing or deliberately disagreeing with someone's idea or opinion	"We tried things similar to this, and they did not work." "I disagree with your synopsis of this problem."
Defending/attacking (should be avoided)	Attacking a person or becoming defensive on a personal level	"Those ideas are absurd!" "We tried your ideas the last time, and they did not work."
Seeking information	Attempting to clarify information by requesting facts, thoughts, opinions, and feelings	"What is your opinion about staff retreat?"
Giving information	Offering or asking for facts, opinions, and examples	"Last year our students gained in reading and math by 10%."
Testing understanding	Question requiring a response for clarification purposes; paraphrasing	"Do you mean we have to reassign five instructional aide positions?"
Summarizing	Condensing information (in a nutshell)	"We all believe that . . ." "In other words . . ."
Bringing in	Soliciting information from others	"Let's see how our teachers feel about this."
Shutting out (should be used only in rare occasions)	Restricting the right of others to participate; challenging or pressing for information to find weak points; expertise flashing	"Jo, you do not have any research to support your recommendations." "Have you done a complete cost analysis for these new projects?" "I have worked in this district for twenty years, and I know what works."

The superintendent can do a variety of things to promote healthy relationships with school board members and to understand their concerns and motives. For instance, superintendents can take school board members out for breakfast and/or lunch occasionally to learn about

Table 10.4

+ *Proposing* *(overly used by an individual)*	Disdain for the ideas of others
+ *Building*	Concerned about the ideas of others
Supporting	Sense of being cared for; the more individuals know each other personally, the more support increases
Disagreeing	Individuals are more involved; decision making is prolonged
Defending/attacking	Fosters negative behavior from others; tempers and emotions increase, decreases focus on the topic; people tend to hold grudges
+ *Giving information*	Individuals are more interested in their ideas than others' ideas; fosters confusion among individuals
+ *Seeking information*	Genuine interest in others' ideas; focuses on seeking more detailed information
+ *Testing*	In-depth conversations; civil discussions; decrease in defensive/attacking behavior
+ *Summarizing*	Assists in the arranging of ideas and discussions so individuals are clear about events
+ *Bringing in*	Shows consideration and respect for all stakeholders; encourages all participants to have a voice in the discussion and decision-making process

Huthwaite, 2007; and Huthwaite Coaching Skills, n.d.

who they are as individuals and what matters most to them concerning public education. Other avenues include sitting by board members during school events like basketball games and making phone calls to members periodically, especially during special events such as birthdays and/or holidays.

In building effective relationships with school board members, superintendents should seek ways to praise them for any achievements and/or contributions (McAdams, 2009b). After all, who doesn't value praise—especially elected officials who may not receive the attention they deserve? Forming relationships with school board members is important, but care must be taken not to establish a perception that the superintendent favors one member over the other. The superintendent should strive to treat all members equitably and should never give information solely to one member without sharing that information with other members.

As noted, there are many ways in which the superintendent can form relationships with board members. Nevertheless, it is vital that the superintendent be reflective about building relationships. Townsend et al. (2007) suggests the following guidelines for the superintendent to consider prior to forming relationships:

- Have I determined the communication style preferred by individual school board members, the entire school board, and a process for board members to communicate with me?
- Do I plan to discuss school board members' personal successes, reflections, and other ambitions?
- How will I praise school board members' accomplishments and the successes of previous members?
- How will I praise school board members for being willing to pursue training and evaluation?

Superintendents should strive to treat all board members fairly, but often superintendents have a special relationship with the school board president. The relationship between the superintendent and the board president should be only a catalyst for working with the entire school board. It must be remembered that the school board president is an equal member of the board, but he or she has other important duties as well, such as facilitating board meetings, calling special meetings, and signing important paperwork on behalf of the board (Illinois Association of School Boards, 2006a).

HOW TO WORK WITH DIFFICULT BOARD MEMBERS

The wise superintendent understands that no matter how hard he or she tries to foster good relationships with school board members, there may be some school board members with whom it is difficult to work. Superintendents should keep in mind that there will occasionally be renegade school board members through no fault of their own. Here are some suggestions in dealing with rebel school board members:

- Document behaviors that are a deterrent to the school board objectives. Discuss concerns with the school board president and allow him or her to meet privately with the board member to see if he or she can remedy the problem. If the problem persists, the superintendent may consider making this a future agenda item for the board to discuss.

- Offer to assist in finding a mentor such as a fellow school board member or someone through various school board associations. This should be done in concert with the school board president.
- Model effective behaviors.
- Demonstrate patience in working with school board members. Superintendents are not privileged to choose their employers but should value their contributions and continue to seek professional development as necessary.
- Speak to the member privately and tactfully regarding concerns.

ADDITIONAL RESOURCES

Table 10.5

Meeting Self-Assessment Form

Directions: The following are various meeting skills that we should continuously develop. Please check the appropriate column (Consistent or Needs Improvement) indicating how you perceive yourself performing that behavior. Please do not list any identifiers when completing the form. To view the overall results, consider having someone such as the board secretary formulate a tally of all the fields and share the results with board members. Also, the board president and superintendent could discuss the meeting assessment results as they prepare for future meetings.

Meeting Skill	*Consistent*	*Needs Improvement*
Building I frequently suggest helpful information such as resources, procedures, and methods to proposals made by others.		
Supporting I often support the team by validating and encouraging other people's ideas.		
Disagreeing I often note areas with which I disagree and the team should consider as well.		
Defending/attacking Periodically, I have to inform my team members that they have mentioned an impractical idea.		
Seeking information I attempt to clarify discussions by defining terms and requesting additional information.		
Giving information I contribute to the team by giving facts, background, opinions, and other examples.		

Meeting Skill	Consistent	Needs Improvement
Testing information		
I often ask questions for clarification purposes.		
Summarizing		
I contribute to my team by condensing information and then checking its validity with team members.		
Bringing in		
I often attempt to obtain feedback from others so that everyone's opinion will be considered.		
Shutting out		
I often restrict people from participating if I feel they are not knowledgeable about the situation being addressed.		
Goal setting		
I help our team stay focused on the district's goals, mission, and vision.		
Initiating		
I suggest policies, methods, and procedures to accomplish board goals as needed.		
Harmonizing		
I often try to reduce tension in meetings by finding compromises and exploring different viewpoints.		
Regulating		
I assist the group by ensuring that we stick to the agenda and that proper protocols are followed.		

SUMMARY

In order for good governance to occur, all members of the governance team must understand that each of them is interdependent upon one another. School board members have no authority as individual members, and their power derives from meetings with other elected members. In brief, engaging in good teamwork is critical and should be the board's number one priority.

If teamwork is absent, good governance will not occur, and seldom will anything worthwhile be accomplished. To enhance teamwork, the role of the superintendent is vital, primarily because he or she must understand that individual success is dependent upon the school board. When boards have a track record of poor governance, it leads to superintendent turnover and negatively impacts student achievement.

There are several ways in which the school board and superintendent can promote collaboration. A vital but often overlooked method in promoting collaboration is engaging in school board self-evaluation. This should be done annually and/or whenever there is a change in the governance team. Self-evaluations are helpful in that they identify areas of strength and areas of concern. Additionally, self-evaluations can assist newer members in understanding how the school board goes about its work.

The superintendent can promote collaboration in various ways, such as promoting collaboration during school board retreats and forming individual relationships. During board retreats and/or meetings, the superintendent and/or school board president can model Rackham's (1988) eleven categories of interactive behavior, which identify various ways that individuals engage with one another, a necessity for good teamwork. In short, the superintendent and/or board president can model these traits to foster collaboration on the governance team.

Superintendents can also form individual relationships with school board members. It is imperative that superintendents understand members' concerns, points of view, and their preferences regarding communication. By forming relationships with individual school board members, the superintendent can assist in ensuring that they feel part of the governance team. Although forming individual relationships is important, care should be given to treat all school board members fairly and equally.

When establishing relationships, it is not uncommon for the superintendent to experience problems with a school board member. When dealing with a difficult school board member, the superintendent can utilize different strategies to form a healthier relationship, like having a one-on-one discussion to discuss problems and concerns and/or to document specific behaviors that are a deterrent to reaching board objectives.

QUESTIONS FOR REFLECTION

1. Identify the root cause of poor superintendent-school board relationships.
2. Why should the superintendent be involved in promoting positive relationships on the governance team? Why should he or she

not? What role can the superintendent play in promoting positive relationships on the governance team?

3. How can the superintendent and school board president utilize Rackham's premise to ensure collaboration on the governance team?

4. In what ways can the superintendent form individual relationships with board members, and why is this important?

5. Explain why training should be ongoing in enhancing superintendent-board collaboration.

6. How can superintendents deal with difficult school board members?

CHAPTER 11

How School Board Evaluations Ensure Accountability and Good Governance

Consider this: school boards evaluate the superintendent, the superintendent evaluates administrators, principals evaluate teachers, and teachers evaluate students. So, shouldn't school boards model what they expect from others and engage in school board self-evaluations as well? Evaluations aid the school board in becoming highly effective by identifying areas in which the school board is efficient and areas in which it is deficient. Put another way, "The evaluation process should serve as a road map assists a driver. It shows the lay of the land and gives alternatives for the best course" (Capital Area School Development Association, 1990).

According to Henderson et al. (2001) and Capital Area School Development Association (1990), key reasons why school boards should engage in self-evaluations include the following:

- Self-evaluations inform the school board of how well it is governing.
- They focus on areas of strengths and concerns.
- Self-evaluations assist in addressing public concern about elected officials in regard to their performance.
- They model good expectations for accountability for all staff in the district.
- They determine key areas of school board focus.

DEMONSTRATING BOARD ACCOUNTABILITY

Few states that have written policies regarding school board evaluations, a practice that educational critics argue has to change if school
boards want to continue to promote student achievement (Fridley,
2006). Without systematic assessment, it is unlikely that school boards
can ensure that they are meeting the needs of the district.

There are many ways in which a school board is held accountable, including the ballot box. Utilizing an evaluation tool to
measure school board performance can lead to improvement by
identifying the board's strengths and weaknesses (SouthEastern
Regional Vision for Education, 1997). Evaluations also can assist
school board members in understanding their roles and duties and
guide the board toward professional improvement in the areas of
goal setting and monitoring of goals (Capital Area School Development Association, 1990).

SELF- AND EXTERNAL SCHOOL BOARD EVALUATIONS

There are two types of formal evaluations often used by school boards:
self-evaluations and external evaluations. Self-evaluations are subjective and are based on school board members' perceptions of their own
effectiveness. The other type of evaluation is more objective. Generally, external evaluations are conducted by an external person or group
utilizing interviews, observations, review of data, focus groups, and
surveys. School boards that employ external evaluations may be seen
as being more accountable than those that use only self-evaluations,
because assessment is not based solely on school board member perspectives (Glass, 2000).

It is the author's opinion that school boards should primarily engage in self-evaluations. These are commonly done at school board
workshops where school board members discuss board goals and
student achievement test data. In conducting self-evaluations, there
will always be a certain degree of subjectivity because they are primarily based on school board members' perspectives. In an effort
to increase accountability, generate school board member buy-in,
and remove the superintendent from the evaluation process, school

board associations and/or other trained facilitators should assist with these self-evaluations.

The superintendent should not facilitate the school board's evaluation but should encourage the school board to evaluate itself. Superintendents will create a conflict of interest if they facilitate the school board's evaluation, because the school board is the superintendent's employer. However, school boards should include the superintendent in the evaluation process as long as the results are anonymous. The superintendent can provide some important insights regarding the strengths and weaknesses of the board.

Besides utilizing a formal evaluation model such as self- and external evaluations, there are implicit evaluations the school board can utilize such as elections, surveys, forums, and citizen complaints. But there is no consensus as to how evaluations should be conducted. For instance, the Capital Area School Development Association (1990) noted that parents, students, teachers, administrators, custodians, secretaries, community members, and others should play a role in the evaluation process. Regardless of the type of evaluation utilized, it should be tied to district goals aimed at increasing student achievement (Land, 2002).

School board elections are the most common form of an implicit evaluation, which may be why some school board members feel that formal evaluations are not necessary. Some members view the election process as the ultimate evaluation, because school board members can be replaced if they are deemed ineffective. While the election process and public perception tell us something about board member effectiveness, they should not be the primary means of evaluating school boards.

Research is clear that the public seldom involves itself in issues of school board governance unless the governance cycle is interrupted by a negative event of great magnitude for the community, such as raising local taxes (Alsbury, 2004). More importantly, elections do not provide consistent feedback regarding the school board's performance.

School board meetings are a form of an implicit evaluation. Although a board meeting may tell us something about dissatisfaction with the board, it is not a good indicator concerning the effectiveness of the school board. For instance, frequent high attendance at board meetings generally implies that the community is dissatisfied with the board. School board members and other stakeholders must realize that the board meeting is a meeting in public, not a meeting of the public. Although state laws allow citizens the right to observe and comment at public board meetings, it is not an appropriate venue regarding board dissatisfaction.

Some school boards may also be reluctant to conduct board self-evaluations because of state "sunshine" laws that require all school board sessions to be open to the public (Goodman and Zimmerman, 2000; Land, 2002). Additionally, some boards typically believe that evaluations are not needed because they assume that evaluations are only for school boards that are in "trouble." Failure to engage in healthy "checkups" often results in school boards being reactive rather than proactive regarding future governance issues.

ALIGNING EVALUATION TO SCHOOL BOARD TRAINING AND GOALS

One of the goals of any evaluation is to ensure that identified goals are met (Land, 2002). Logically, there should be a certain degree of interconnectivity between training areas and areas of assessment. Evaluations can serve to improve a school district's performance by evaluating goals and the process to implement goals. Because boards are consistently being called into question regarding their performance, evaluations can illustrate the degree of school board effectiveness in particular areas such as superintendent-board collaboration. Yet, it is still up to the school board to determine if training is making a positive difference in their governance.

As its primary task, the board must develop ends for the district. Effective districts ensure that their schools are aligned to the ends articulated by the school board. If the school board fails to determine accurately the mission of the district, it will result in a fragmented sense of purpose for staff and community alike. Only after the board establishes the direction for the district can it accurately monitor progress toward district ends through vehicles such as school board self-evaluations.

When school boards evaluate their progress regarding district ends, the process also aids the superintendent in receiving clear direction in the accomplishment of district goals. It should be noted that this evaluation process contributes to building and maintaining a healthy relationship between the school board and superintendent because the school board has spoken with "one voice" in clarifying the district purpose.

KEY SCHOOL BOARD EVALUATION AREAS

In addition to school board member training and priority areas of the school board, other key areas in which school boards should evaluate themselves are school board member roles and duties and superintendent-board collaborations (Rice, 2010). A lack of understanding concerning the difference in roles and duties between the school board and the administration creates havoc even for the most experienced school boards; therefore, this area must be continuously evaluated.

Defining and limiting roles and duties ensures that the board can focus on the big picture—the "what"—and not the "means"—or the "how." If school boards are too involved in the day-to-day operations of the district, the resulting superintendent turnover often brings about instability in the instructional programs of the district (Glass, 2000).

Superintendent-board collaboration includes following board protocols and/or process agreements such as board member attendance at school board meetings and other district events. If board members violate their process agreements and are not participating in school board activities, it contributes to a dysfunctional governance team. For effective governance to occur, school boards must evaluate how they operate and govern compared to their process agreements.

In a nutshell, there are many areas that the school board should evaluate. At best, there should be discussion centered on the unique needs of the school board, such as evaluating school board performance toward its goals, understanding roles and duties of the board, fostering good superintendent-board collaboration, and assessing the impact of professional development opportunities.

ADDITIONAL RESOURCES

Table 11.1 Board Self-Assessment Sample Questions

	We frequently do this (may substitute: strongly agree, agree, disagree, and strongly disagree).	*We need to do more of this (may substitute: strongly agree, agree, disagree, and strongly disagree).*
Our school board makes decisions based on what is ultimately best for students.		
This board strives to reach consensus regarding major decisions.		
Board members govern according to their roles and duties.		
Members of our board are familiar with the role and duties of the superintendent and allow him or her to handle the day-to-day operations of the district.		
Members of our board do not represent special interest groups or allow personal agendas to influence our decision making.		
This board governs through district policies and board protocols.		
We regularly communicate board decisions with all stakeholders.		
Members of our board continuously pursue professional development.		
Our board annually evaluates our performance.		
This board annually evaluates the superintendent.		
This school board supports overall board decisions.		
This board is prepared for board meetings by doing such things as reviewing the board agenda.		
We maintain effective school-community relationships.		

	We frequently do this (may substitute: strongly agree, agree, disagree, and strongly disagree).	We need to do more of this (may substitute: strongly agree, agree, disagree, and strongly disagree).
Our board actively recruits effective citizens to run for the board.		
Members of our board are confidential when confidentiality is needed.		
Our board cares more about academic achievement than sports.		
This board provides funding and other resources that are aligned with district goals.		
Our board is current regarding educational trends.		
Members of this board are knowledgeable about the different instructional programs of our district.		
There is a process for board members to place items on the board agenda.		
Our board maintains a healthy relationship with other members and with the superintendent.		
There is a healthy communication system established between board members and the superintendent.		
There are few if any surprises at meetings of which board members are unaware.		
During meetings, members of our board stick to the agenda format.		
Members of our board do not make commitments outside of official meetings.		
Our board governs collectively and not as individuals.		
Our board governance is aligned with our district's mission and vision.		
This school board has a process for evaluating, formulating, and updating policies.		
This board understands key areas of finance, government, and law.		

Table 11.2

The school board will engage in a goal-setting workshop for the upcoming school year.	*Summer*
The superintendent will develop action plans (goals) and submit those to the school board.	*August*
The school board will approve final board goals.	*First meeting in September*
The superintendent will update the school board on the progress of board-adopted goals.	*October*
The school board will review the self-evaluation process.	*January*
Board members and the superintendent will complete the evaluation instrument.	*February/March*
An evaluation report will be submitted to the school board.	*March*
The school board will meet to discuss the evaluation report.	*March/April*
The school board shall report to the public regarding the progress of board goals.	*May/June*
The school board shall revisit the goal-setting process.	*May to July*

SUMMARY

School boards establish the overall direction of the district and therefore must monitor the district's compliance in meeting board goals. There are several ways in which school boards can ensure compliance with district goals, such as developing policy that aligns the superintendent evaluation to district ends. Likewise, the superintendent ensures that other staff members are carrying out the district goals through utilizing tools such as evaluations as well.

Considering the fact that in most districts the school board evaluates the superintendent, the superintendent evaluates other administrators, principals evaluate teachers, and teachers evaluate students, school boards as the top governance overseers should engage in school board evaluations as well. The school board should model its expectations. Additionally, evaluations can highlight areas of strengths and of weaknesses to improve overall school board governance.

Two common forms of evaluations that school boards use are self-evaluations and external evaluations. Self-evaluations are subjective and based upon the board rating its own governance. External evaluations, on the other hand, are evaluations conducted by third parties such as parents, teachers, and community members. It should be noted that there is no consensus regarding how school boards should evaluate their performance, but, at minimum, school board evaluations should be aligned to school board training areas. Other key evaluation areas the school board should consider include school board role and duties and superintendent-board collaboration.

Although board evaluations are invaluable in improving the work of school boards, many boards refuse to evaluate themselves because of sunshine laws that mandate that they evaluate themselves publicly. Additionally, some school boards refuse to participate in evaluations based on the faulty premise that board evaluations are only for those boards that are in trouble.

If school boards engage in evaluations, it is wise that the superintendent does not play a dominant role in critiquing the school board. The superintendent should not be placed in a position where the school board views the superintendent as evaluating its employer by facilitating the evaluation. However, the superintendent should be involved in the evaluation process because he or she can provide important insights.

QUESTIONS FOR REFLECTION

1. Identify and explain reasons why a school board should evaluate its performance.
2. Besides evaluation tools, what are some other ways school boards can monitor their performance?
3. Why should the school board utilize other indicators besides the "ballot box" and school board meeting attendance to determine its effectiveness?
4. List and describe key evaluation areas on which the school board evaluation should focus.
5. Why should school board evaluations be aligned to training opportunities?
6. Why are some boards reluctant to engage in school board evaluations?
7. Describe the role of the superintendent in the board's evaluation process.

CHAPTER 12

Building Community Support
for School Boards

A district can be governed by an effective school board that engages in and practices good governance and works together as a high-functioning team, yet that board can still be deemed ineffective or irrelevant. How could it be possible for a school board to practice good governance, play by the rules, make decisions that are student-centered, yet still be viewed as ineffective or irrelevant? Simple. Public education is at war for its reputation as schools are increasingly becoming the targets of politicians and special interest groups. As the saying goes, perception is reality—and voter support often hinges on public perception. To change the negative tides, school boards must aggressively interact and collaborate with the community. After all, school boards sit in trust for the community.

The effective school board engages in a two-way conversation with the community: the community tells the district its story, and the district tells its story to the community. School boards must assist the public in understanding why local control of school boards is vital to keeping "the public" in public schools. As Mark Twain puts it, "The public is the only critic whose opinion is worth anything at all."

WHAT PUBLIC ENGAGEMENT IS AND WHY IT IS ESSENTIAL IN BUILDING COMMUNITY SUPPORT

What exactly is public engagement, and why is it necessary for school boards to invest in good community relations? Public engagement goes by many names, such as community engagement and community involvement. Regardless of the names (some of which I use inter-changeably in this chapter), it entails collaborating with the commu-nity. Michael Resnick (2000) defines public engagement in his book *Communities Count: A School Board Guide to Public Engagement*:

> Public engagement is a two-way communication between a school dis-trict and the community it serves. Although the most visible form of that communication may occur in meetings, public engagement is not about a single meeting or even a series of meetings. Nor is it about public rela-tions, defending or seeking ratification for existing programs, or other strategies primarily aimed at shaping public opinion. Instead, public engagement is an ongoing collaborative process during which the school district works with the public to build understanding, guidance, and ac-tive support for the education of the children in its community.

School boards that invest in public engagement will experience more community support toward district programs as well as a shared pas-sion to ensure that the students in their community become success-ful, productive, and viable citizens. It can be argued that many school boards have not been successful in engaging the community as a part-ner in improving its public schools. Too many citizens are still unclear about the role and purpose of school boards and who serves as trustees representing community interests (Adamson, 2012; Howell, 2005).

Because school boards have not been very visible, they bear some of the responsibility for not having been included in the conversation concerning how to improve public schools. However, with great prob-lems come great opportunities. When most of a school board is trained, is held accountable for its governance, maintains a positive relationship with the superintendent, and engages the community as a partner, the school board can revitalize its reputation. Research is clear that effec-tive school boards demonstrate these key traits.

The Importance of Community Engagement

It is imperative that school boards view community engagement as a way of life or simply a way of doing business. Community engagement should not reflect simple issues campaigns but a collaborative process whereby the school board seeks community input to guide its decision making. Although the community does not make the decisions for the board, community engagement is an important factor in helping the school board make decisions. As trustees, school boards must value and understand the importance of engaging the community to foster and maintain support for effective local governance.

There are several reasons why a relationship with the community is vital to the school board, but the primary reason is to assess what the community wants and is willing to support toward the overall direction of its schools. The school board's primary job is to clarify the district's purpose or district ends. Savvy boards understand the importance of involving parents, teachers, business officials, and other community stakeholders in the establishment of district ends.

When stakeholders have a role in crafting district ends, they will provide the resources to support those expectations (Cunningham, 2002). By including stakeholders in the development of district ends, the school board taps into the values of various stakeholders as well as sending a message that education is indeed a community issue. As Resnick (2000) states, "Motivationally, an engaged public sends the message that what students learn and how well they learn it isn't an issue just for teachers and administrators but is a real priority for the community as well. . . . Beyond its impact within the system itself, public engagement can also raise student achievement because of its ability to energize a community."

Although it would appear that the need for community engagement is obvious, it is not commonly practiced. Many school boards and districts operate on the premise that school officials alone should determine the mission, vision, goals, and values for their schools. Beliefs such as this are exactly why many school boards are not perceived as relevant in their communities. Therefore, a public engagement process may first have to include steps to tackle this belief. Resnick (2000) identifies the following questions for school boards to consider in analyzing how connected the community is with the district:

- Is the community a partner in student learning?
- Have key stakeholders been involved in district goal setting?
- Is there a process to engage the community in discussing student achievement?

- What do the stakeholders and the media know about the district ends?
- Do districts provide opportunities so that community stakeholders can establish a sense of ownership?

There are many other reasons why community engagement matters to the success of the district. When school boards actively engage their community, not only will school boards find more support for district programs, but they will also find fewer angry constituents at board meetings. When the community engagement process is weak or absent, school boards will spend an enormous amount of time dealing with angry citizens over recurring "customer" issues that prevent the school board from dealing with larger citizen and district concerns (Carr, 2008b).

Effective community engagement should also solicit staff input. If staff is neglected and not consulted in the affairs of the district, staff morale will suffer. Often employees treat their customers based upon how they are treated by their employer (Carr, 2008b). If staff feels demoralized, it is likely that the district staff will not work as hard to promote student learning or the aims of the district.

BUILDING THE FOUNDATION FOR COMMUNITY ENGAGEMENT

In order to develop a community engagement process, a school board must be deliberate and strategic about the process of engaging the public and its expectations for stakeholder involvement. Resnick (2000) identifies the following foundational questions for boards to consider prior to engaging the community:

- What are the benefits and outcomes of convening the community?
- What stakeholders should be included?
- What are the financial costs of our community engagement approach?
- What is the time commitment of staff and board members?
- What are the obstacles we foresee in convening the community?
- What is the extent of school board member involvement?
- How will we evaluate the effectiveness of our program?

HOW TO SOLICIT COMMUNITY INPUT

There are several ways in which the school board can engage the community. Although the board should try a variety of methods, over time school boards will become adept at finding best practices that work well within their community. Examples of how the school board can engage the community include the following:

- Building partnerships with local libraries
- Partnering with colleges and universities
- Establishing a relationship with businesses
- Visiting senior citizen facilities
- Surveying/polling parents during in-district activities
- Utilizing social media such as Facebook and Twitter
- Visiting service clubs such as Kiwanis and Rotary
- Establishing a relationship with church organizations
- Establishing communication tables that people frequent such as grocery stores, food banks, and outlet/indoor malls
- Hosting public forums
- Facilitating focus groups
- Organizing study circles

ENHANCING DISTRICT COMMUNICATIONS

When engaging the community, the school board must understand that the task of getting out a meaningful community message is vital to the success of the district. Effective messages entail speaking with one voice and utilizing data.

Speaking with One Voice

If school boards are going to be successful in communicating with the public, they have to speak with one voice. In other words, they must support one clear message. Although board members should express their concerns and vote their conscience, school board members must support final school board decisions in order to govern successfully without internal conflicts.

Wise school board members realize that they will be on the winning and losing side of many issues, but school board member disagreements do not give them permission to bash final school board decisions. When board members speak with one voice or a clear message, it sends a message to the community that the school board governs collectively and not as individuals.

Data Driven

Data, both qualitative and quantitative, should drive district decisions. If school board decisions are not based upon research, it opens the door to criticism. The school board should be able to communicate effectively regarding board decisions, but those decisions must be supported by data. Without data, even the most skilled communicators will have trouble explaining why a particular course of action was chosen. Using data informs the community that decisions were made based upon current information compared to the possibility of making alternate decisions based upon perceptions and limited information.

THE IMPORTANCE OF ALIGNING STUDENT ACHIEVEMENT TO DISTRICT COMMUNICATIONS

There are many ways in which the school board can engage and listen to its stakeholders. As noted, it is vital that the board understand why and what it hopes to accomplish in engaging the community. Student achievement is unique because it is the major function of public schools and is the standard for which school boards and other educators are primarily held accountable. If school boards are to win the war on public opinion concerning public schools, they must rally the community in support of student achievement.

Student achievement soars if students feel valued and are given recognition for school accomplishments by adults, parents, community groups, and businesses within the community (Price, 2011). Hugh Price, a visiting professor in the Woodrow Wilson School of Public and International Affairs at Princeton University, notes in his 2011 article "Community Mobilization: A Missing Link in School Reform" that there are many ways school boards can promote a culture of student achievement within the community by facilitating things such as:

- Staging achievement day parades when students achieve specific milestones such as graduating from various grade levels or passing state exams
- Visiting churches and other organizations to honor student successes
- Partnering with businesses to conduct giveaways for students who read a designated number of books

School boards must demonstrate to the community that student achievement is important and must serve as cheerleaders to rally the community in support of student achievement.

USING COMMUNITY ENGAGEMENT TO BUILD COMMUNITY SUPPORT FOR BOARD MEMBER PROFESSIONAL DEVELOPMENT

Some school board members do not participate in professional development workshops and conferences because they feel that the community may see it as wasteful spending given the fact that many districts struggle to find ways to balance their budgets. There may be some validity to this perception, as many citizens are not knowledgeable about the role of the school board and may view money spent on professional development as less important than money spent in the classroom. However, the reality is that citizens tend to support board member professional development when they understand how school board training impacts student achievement (Yackera, 1999).

To explain the need for school board professional development, board members should be transparent regarding professional development opportunities and explain how school board training benefits the district, the board, and the community. Primarily, professional development is needed because it assists school board members and the superintendent to understand their respective roles.

More specifically, school board training will assist the school board with its most important task: crafting district ends (vision, mission, and board goals) or establishing the direction for the district in collaboration with the community. Investing in school board training ensures that board members possess the knowledge base to provide good governance on behalf of the community.

After participating in professional development opportunities, wise boards should be transparent in sharing with the community how training will benefit them in doing their jobs successfully and how this investment is vital to good governance. To assist governance teams with this task, many state school board associations offer sample press releases that districts can utilize.

CORE ELEMENTS IN A GOOD PUBLIC ENGAGEMENT PROCESS

To foster good community relations, school boards would be wise to utilize best practices as identified in research. Key principles of good community relations include planning and preparation, understanding when to respond to negative attacks, fostering transparency, and building a culture of ongoing community engagement.

Planning and Preparation

Before engaging the community, not only must the school board be clear about why it is engaging the community, but it should also have some notion as to what success looks like. After this occurs, the school board should rely on the superintendent's expertise in carrying out the desires of the board. But to maximize community engagement, there should be a discussion about the appropriate role the school board plays in community relations. Citizens rely on school board members, their elected officials, to communicate with them. If school boards over rely on the superintendent to communicate with the public, it may make him or her overly exposed, leaving the perception that the board is not totally transparent. After all, no individual knows it all.

District Ends and Public Engagement

During the planning and preparation phase, school boards should be able to connect the dots concerning the correlation of district ends and district public relations. Aligning district ends to district public relations sends the message that the district governs effectively because it has a working plan by which it operates. For instance, what would happen if a school board engaged the community regarding the rebuilding and/or the renovating of several schools without having district ends in place? More than likely, the school board would receive push back from the community because the school board would be unable to explain to stakeholders the priorities of the board. Similarly, what wise person prepares to build a house without first calculating a budget? A good plan is essential if the school board is to govern efficiently.

Public Engagement and the Need for Various Stakeholders

Good planning requires the conditions that would bring about successful community engagement. Initial planning should include various stakeholders discussing things such as the purpose of engaging the community, specific stakeholders that should be targeted, time of meetings, and what tactics will be utilized in engaging the community.

If community engagement programs are poorly planned, the end result will be frustration and/or disappointment, and perhaps doing nothing would have been better in maintaining the image of the school (Johnson, 2008). Public engagement activities can be unorganized and reactive unless they are driven by the district plan, which addresses specific objectives, outcomes, audiences, and messages (Moore, 2005).

It is also critical that the school board develop its public relations program around stakeholder-owner needs instead of stakeholder-customer needs. Stakeholder-owner needs consider different perspectives and are motivated by the desire to act on behalf of all district stakeholders. In comparison, stakeholder-customer needs address the needs of specific customers. For instance, a parent requesting a different teacher is an example of a customer need. When the school board serves district-owner needs, it acts in the best interests of the collective good as opposed to getting overly involved in the daily operations of the district.

When organizing a range of stakeholders, various and opposing viewpoints will emerge, but it is essential that everyone's voice be heard and that all are made to feel a part of the process (Johnson, 2008). If the conversation is limited to the insights of a few people, issues will not be explored in depth, thus minimizing the best possible outcome. To arrive at a shared purpose and one that is reflective of community values, it is vital that differences be explored and valued rather than trying to suppress differences for the sake of reaching an expedited consensus.

To establish an inclusive process, the role of the facilitator is vital. Facilitators should be skilled at fostering trust with stakeholders and know how to identify areas of agreement in order to reach a consensus in an efficient manner. Moreover, facilitators should not view themselves as the ultimate authority or have already decided on a particular course of action (National Coalition for Dialogue and Deliberation [NCDD], International Association for the Public Participation [IAP2], Co-Intelligence Institute [CII], et al., 2009).

Concerning who should be sitting at the table representing the community, districts should consider individuals and/or organizations such as:

- Parents
- Community partnership teams such as Rotary
- Business partnerships
- Retirees and other community volunteers
- Alumni
- Public school foundations
- Board member involvement
- Teachers, administrators, and staff

Soliciting Inclusion of Demographic Diversity

In order to effectively engage the community, the school board must know and continuously redefine its district's stakeholders. For instance, as a result of Hurricane Katrina, many New Orleans citizens found themselves enrolled in other school districts throughout the United States. In other communities, there may be an increase in the Hispanic population. Because of ongoing population changes in many of our communities, a district must know the demographics of its community and make plans to reach out to those stakeholders.

Effective public relations require input from representatives of all district stakeholders. Commonsense thinking informs us that people often have different opinions, but different opinions should be welcomed so that the district can understand the depth of particular issues. It is vital that all stakeholders' opinions and suggestions are valued and have equal status. School boards must be cautious in inviting token "participants" and consider this to be effective community engagement practices (NCDD, IAP2, CII, et al. 2009).

Engaging Stakeholders in the Implementation Process

In order to maximize any school board plan developed as a result of the community engagement process, it is vital that districts consider asking stakeholders to be involved in some aspects of the implementation. According to Johnson (2008), many districts simply thank volunteers for their input and implement a plan only to find out that the implementation was not successful. Often this happens because there was no follow up from stakeholders.

More importantly, individuals need to know that their contributions mattered, and they need to clearly see evidence as to how their engagement influenced district decisions (NCDD, IAP2, CII, et al. 2009). By engaging stakeholders in the process, it aids the successful implementation of the plan and enhances community support by having individuals who will more than likely serve as cheerleaders for the plan.

Evaluating the Public Engagement Process

During the planning process, the board must reach consensus as to how to conclude the community engagement process and how to evaluate the effectiveness of the process. Thus, the school board must start with the end in mind. So, the board must continually ask the question, "Why are we engaging the community, and what is the payoff?" School boards must be able to answer this question in order to know when they will reach their destination (NCDD, IAP2, CII, et al. 2009).

As noted, school boards must determine whether or not their public engagement campaign is meeting its intended outcomes. Evaluation measures should monitor whether the campaign increased awareness and changed perceptions and attitudes. A popular tool to measure the impact of public engagement campaigns includes the use of surveys. However, the board can analyze output measures such as media inquiries, attendance at district forums and events, and the ratio between positive and negative news stories (Carr, 2007a).

How to Respond Effectively to Negative Attacks

No matter how transparent the school board is and operates, boards are always subject to attack from internal and/or external stakeholders. The key is to know when and how to respond to negative perceptions before they foment into outright opposition. Because some minority dissenters cannot be appeased, every community issue should not warrant community engagement but should instead be discussed.

When should school boards respond to negative attacks? School boards must individually decide when they should respond to negative criticisms. As noted, some attacks are not worth responding to. But if an issue may have widespread appeal, it may be wise for school boards to respond but to do so in a diplomatic and strategic way.

Wise school boards communicate with various stakeholders through the superintendent, who can relay messages on behalf of the school board and ensure that all stakeholders are receiving information in a fair and deliberate manner. It should be noted that often the school board president is the spokesperson for the school board, while the superintendent is the spokesperson for the district.

According to Carr (2008b), school boards should not respond in ways in which their message would primarily reach a limited audience, such as writing to the newspaper editor or engaging in a he said, she said fight with dissenters. As an alternative, boards should consider combating negative attacks by directly communicating with stakeholders such as teachers, administrators, business owners, and parents (Carr, 2008b).

In addition, boards should seek only to inform stakeholders of any misinformation and its source and provide appropriate facts. In order to communicate directly with stakeholders, the school board can do this in a variety of ways, such as sending out e-mails to stakeholders, sending home district and/or school newsletters, and updating the district/school's website.

FOSTERING TRANSPARENCY

Effective communication with the public requires a culture of transparency. If the community believes that the district is not being honest and/or transparent, it decreases community support of district programs. If a school board has a reputation for being dishonest, it would be challenging for the board to alter its reputation even after changes on the governance team. As Abraham Lincoln puts it, "Character is like a tree and reputation like its shadow. The shadow is what we think of it; the tree is the real thing." The board should ensure that the district is communicating in a truthful, open, and reliable manner even when the news is unpleasant. When school boards are honest, display integrity, and take full responsibility for their actions, it increases people's faith in the school district (Carr, 2007a).

BUILDING A CULTURE OF ONGOING COMMUNITY ENGAGEMENT

In order for the school board to ensure a culture of good public engagement, the school board must establish a system as to how the community and school board will engage in a two-way conversation. District programs and other community events that seek to engage the community must be viewed as a part of the overall district community engagement program.

Goble (1993) notes, "School boards and administrators cannot implement broad-based strategies or manage educational programs without communication, and it's not good policy to manage today and communicate tomorrow." To maximize the success of engaging the community, school boards must periodically analyze and make appropriate changes to their community engagement efforts.

Building relationships is the key to establishing a culture of ongoing community engagement. As Carr (2007a) notes, "At its core, effective communications is about systematically and strategically building mutually beneficial relationships between your organization and the people who matter most to your success." A major indicator of district and community relations is how accessible district leaders are. If district leaders are not accessible to their constituents, constituents will feel that the district does not value their ideas and opinions. As with any good relationship, relationships take time to build, and time must be spent between district leaders and the constituents they serve.

The Need for Advocacy

School board members must serve as advocates for public education with the community they serve as well as with state and federal legislators. More importantly, school board members must advocate for local control by speaking with one voice to their elected officials. The primary message to state and federal legislators should always be "Don't take away local control of education." Advocacy entails a process wherein individuals or a group attempts to influence public policy within political, economic, and social systems, and requires activities such as media campaigns and lobbying.

The time may be ripe for school boards to lobby in favor of local control as more citizens desire a balanced, but limited, role for the federal government. Perhaps some of the intrusion of the government into local education matters could be avoided and/or eliminated if school board members raised public perception about this concern.

How could school boards and school board members advocate for local control of public education and other public education concerns? First, as noted in chapter 4, the majority of school boards are members of statewide school board associations that lobby on their behalf. Thus, school board members should get involved in the process of advocacy with their state association as most have a process for determining how the organization will lobby on behalf of its members. As shown in the following with the examples of Illinois and Texas, state school board associations have various ways in which districts can advocate for public education.

It is the author's viewpoint that most state school board associations should have a resolution process for member districts that operate in a similar fashion. Usually, proposed resolutions are submitted to their delegate assembly for full consideration. The delegate assembly is generally comprised of representatives from member districts who convene at the association's yearly conference to vote on the passage of new resolutions.

Illinois Association of School Boards (IASB; www.iasb.com):

- Resolutions aimed at guiding the lobbying efforts of the IASB may be proposed by any active member, association division, association council, association board of directors, and/or the resolution committee. The resolution may be a position or belief statement.
- The IASB's resolutions committee reviews all proposed resolutions and distributes a final draft to the IASB membership forty-

five days prior to the annual meeting of the delegate assembly. The resolutions committee determines which proposals will be presented to the delegate assembly (comprised of a representative from each member district).

- The delegate assembly votes on which resolutions the IASB will lobby on behalf of its membership.

Texas Association of School Boards (TASB; www.tasb.org):

- Each year, member districts can submit resolutions that will guide TASB's communications before the state legislature.
- Each proposed resolution is reviewed by TASB's resolutions committee and thereafter by the TASB board.
- After proposals are reviewed, resolution proposals are presented at the delegate assembly for full consideration.

There is not a single preferred message for advocacy, but it is pivotal that school board members advocate for local control of education in traditional or creative ways. For instance, Bobby Rigues of the Aledo Independent School District of Texas was creative in raising awareness for stronger financial support for public schools in Texas. Rigues parked his truck under a big white tent off a farm road in Texas and asked motorists to sign a petition to increase state support of local schools. The response was overwhelming, and the state received over 5,600 letters urging a funding increase to public education and over 618 districts passed resolutions urging lawmakers to put education first (Stover, 2011b).

SUMMARY

Engaging in public engagement with the community is vital to the success and stability of school boards. Community involvement entails the school board engaging in a two-way conversation with the community regarding the direction and purpose of its schools. Also, boards have to be clear and consistent with their message to the community regarding why school boards are needed to maintain local control of education.

School boards have to be aggressive in communicating this message to the public because many citizens are unaware of the functions and duties of the school board. If boards fail to promote themselves, they will be increasingly defined through the eyes of special interest groups and various legislators who often do not have a favorable view of public schools.

To effectively engage in public engagement with the community, the board must be deliberate regarding its intention of engaging the public and utilize district communications to that end. The board must also realize the importance of forming partnerships and relationships with other organizations in the community because there is strength in numbers.

A school board should engage the public regarding its own professional development needs. Unfortunately, many boards refuse to engage in professional development opportunities because they believe the community will not support it, especially during tough economic times. Contrary to this perception, research suggests that the community supports professional development for school board members, especially when it understands the school board's role and how professional development will assist in creating good governance so that student achievement can flourish.

Key components of a good community engagement process include planning and preparation, aligning community engagement to district ends, evaluating the community engagement plan, and understanding how to respond to negative attacks. Equally important, the school board must ensure that it is transparent with the community regarding the establishment and monitoring of district ends and fostering and sustaining a culture of ongoing community engagement.

School boards must advocate for local control of public education. They must not watch passively while public education is being severely scrutinized by special interest groups and various legislators. School boards can serve as advocates in a variety of ways, such as engaging stakeholders in the community, speaking with other elected officials (both state and federal), and working with state school board associations.

QUESTIONS FOR REFLECTION

1. Explain why it is important that school boards engage the communities they represent.
2. Why is it important that the community be involved in establishing the district's strategic plan?

3. What are some ways in which the school board can engage the local community?
4. When engaging the community, why is it important that school board members speak with one voice?
5. How can school boards encourage their communities to support professional development for the board?
6. List and describe some core elements of a good public engagement strategy.
7. Explain why school boards must build a culture of ongoing public engagement.
8. Why is it essential that school board members serve as advocates for public education? In what ways can board members advocate for public education?

References

Adams, C. & Sparks, S. (2013). Grad Rate At Highest Since 1970. *Education Week, 32 (19),* 1 & 18.

Adamson, M. (2012). Fulfilling its purpose: Why board governance? *IASB Journal, March/April,* 11-13.

All Education Schools (2011). *Basic Skills Pass/Fail Data.* Retrieved from: http://illinoisbasicskillstest.com/bstestpassfaildata/

Alsbury, T. (2004). Does school board turnover matter? Revisiting critical variables in the Dissatisfaction theory of American democracy. *International Journal of Leadership in Education, 7(4),* 357-377.

Alsbury, T. (2002). *Superintendent turnover in relationship to incumbent school board member defeat in Washington from 1993-2000: a quantitative and qualitative analysis.* Paper presented at the Annual Meeting of the American Educational Research Association, New Orleans, LA.

Alsbury, T. (2008). *The Future of School Board Governance: Relevancy and Revelation.* Lanham, Maryland: Rowman & Littlefield Publishers.

Anderson, R., & Snyder, K. (1980). Leadership training for the school board members: one approach. *Education, 100,* 227-35.

Angelis, J., & Wilcox, K. (2011). Poverty, Performance, and Frog Ponds: What Best-Practice Research Tells Us About Their Connections. *Phi Delta Kappan, 93 (3),* 26-31.6)

Archer, J. (2006), Synthesis Finds District Leadership-Learning Link-Superintendents' Actions Can Boost Achievement Study Finds. *Education Week,* 26 (7), 8.

Associated Press. (2011a). Montana Chief Rejects Testing Goals. *Education Week,* 30 (31), 4.

Associated Press. (2011b). Tennessee Educators Dropping Union Ties. *Education Week, 31 (14),* 2.

Bamford, J. (2012). What Are We Learning From the Data. *School Leader, 43 (1).*

Banchero, S. (2012, February 25-26). Teacher Ratings Aired in New York. *The Wall Street Journal,* p. 1 & 2.

Barnoski, L. (2013). School Leaders: Make Sure Your Teachers Don't Lose Heart. *Education Week, 32 (27),* 23.

Beckel, M. & Russ, C. (2012). Super PACs, Nonprofits Helped Romney Narrow Obama Fundraising Edge. *The Center for Public Integrity/The Center for Responsive Politics.*

Benjamin, S., & Trout, J. (2011). Fulfilling its Purpose: Why Public Education. *The Journal,* 24-31.

Berman, S., & Camins, A. (2011). Investing in Turnaround that Endures. *Education Week, 31 (10),* 22 & 28.

Blankstein, A., & Noguera, P. (2012). What Really Works in Turning Schools Around? *Education Week,* 31 (17), 26 & 32,

Bracey, G. W., & Resnick, M. A. (1998). *Raising the bar: A school board primer on student achievement.* Alexandria, VA: National School Boards Association.

Barkan, J. (2011). Got Dough? How Billionaires Rule Our Schools. *Dissent,* 58 (1), 49-57.

Boyle, P., & Burns, D. (2011). *Preserving the Public in Public Schools.* Lanham, Maryland: Rowman & Littlefield Publishers.

Braun, B. (1998). Illinois School Law Survey, 10th edition. *Illinois Association of School Boards*

Bulkley, K. (2001). Educational Performance and Charter School Authorizers: The Accountability Bind. *Education Policy Analysis Archives,* 9(37). Retrieved from: http://epaa.asu.edu/epaa/v9n37 .html.

Bulkley, K. (2012). Charter Schools-Taking A Closer Look. *Kappa Delta Pi Record.* 110-115.

Bushaw, W., & Lopez, S. (2011). The 43rd Annual Phi Delta Kappa/ Gallup Poll of the Public's Attitudes Toward The Public Schools. *Phi Delta Kappan.*

Cain, B. (2012). Orienting New Board Members Quickly. *School Administrator, 59 (3),* 40-41.

California School Boards Association, 2005. 2005 Member Survey-Final Summary Report of Results. Prepared by: *Aurora Research Group.*

California School Boards Association. (2007). School Board Leadership. California School Boards Association, pp. 1-7.

California School Boards Association, 2009. 2009 Member Survey-Final Summary Report of Results. Prepared by: *Aurora Research Group.*

Cantor, D. (2012). Improving Student Achievement: Whose Responsibility Is It? *Education Week,* 31 (20), 23.

Capital Area School Development Association. (1990). *A view from inside: The roles and responsibilities of school board members.* Albany, NY: Author.

Carr, N. (2007a). Research and P.R. *American School Board Journal, August,* 44-45.

Carr, N. (2007b). The Art of Spokesmanship. *American School Board Journal, February,* 43-44.

Carr, N. (2008a). Setting the Record Straight. *American School Board Journal, April,* 56-57.

Carr, N. (2008b). Why Communications Matters. *American School Board Journal, August,* 44-45.

Carr, S., & Gilbertson, A. (2013). Skeptics: Profit and Education Don't Mix. *The Hechinger Report.* Retrieved from http://news.ca.msn.com/top-stories/skeptics-profit-and-education-dont-mix

Carver, J. (2006). *Boards That Make a Difference-A New Design for Leadership in Nonprofit and Public Organizations (3rd ed.).* San Francisco, CA: Jossey-Bass.

Cassel, J., Peifer, A., & Allen, J. (1997). Keeping the Saw Sharp-Stephen Covey's 7th Habit of Highly Effective People. *IASB Journal, November/December,* 1-4.

Cassel, J. (2003). The hazards of success: A surprising form of board troubles and how to avoid them. *IASB Journal, January/February,* 1-3.

Cassel, J. (2010). Citizen School Boards-School Boards reflect the values of their communities and that's where their great strength lies. *American School Board Journal, December,* 34-35.

Castallo, R. (2000). Clarifying roles through self-evaluation and periodic checks. *School Administrator, 57 (8),* 50-1.

Cavanagh, S. (2011a). Districts Face Painful Cuts as School Year Begins. *Education Week,* 31 (1), 1, 19.

Cavanagh, S. (2011b). States Urged to Promote Cooperation. *Education Week, 31 (12),* S13-S14.

Cavanagh, S. (2011c). Vote Looms On Ohio Union-Rights Law. *Education Week,* 31 (10), 14-15.

Center on Education Policy (2007). *Are Private High Schools Better Academically Than Public High Schools?* Washington, D.C. Available at: http://www.edline.com/uploads/pdf/PrivateSchoolsReport.pdf

Cody, A. (2010, September 25). Re: Education Week article writing on behalf of teachers. [The Real Thieves of Hope: America's War on Teachers]. Message posted to http://blogs.edweek.org/teachers/living-in-dialogue/

Conley, D. (2003). *Who Governs Our Schools? Changing Roles and Responsibilities.* New York, New York: Teachers College Press.

Council of the Great City Schools. (2005). Urban School Board Survey. *Council of the Great City Schools, author.* Available at: http://eric.ed.gov/?id=ED498843

Council of Chief State School Officers. (2008). *Educational Leadership Policy Standards: ISLLC 2008.* Washington D.C. Available at: www.ccsso.org/isllc.html

Covey, S. (1990). *The 7th Habits of Highly Effective People.* New York, New York: Fireside.

CREDO (2009). *Multiple Choice: Charter School Performance in Sixteen States.* Stanford, CA: Stanford University. Available at: http://credo.stanford.edu/

CREDO (2013). *National Charter School Study.* Stanford, CA: Stanford University. Available at: http://credo.stanford.edu

Cuban, L. (2004). Making Public Schools Business-Like...*Again. Political Science and Politics.* Available at: https://www.apsanet.org/imgtest/MakingPublicSchoolsBusinessLike.pdf

Cunningham, C. (2002). *Engaging the Community to Support Student Achievement.* Eugene, OR: Eric Clearinghouse on Educational Management.

Danzberger, J. P. (1994). Governing the nation's schools: The case for restructuring local school boards. *Phi Delta Kappan, 75 (5),* 367-373.

Dawson, L. (2003). Reconciling Expenses for Board Development. *Illinois School Board Journal.* July/August 2003: Article 6.

DeBray, E. (2005). NCLB Accountability Collides With Court-Ordered Desegregation: The Case of Pinellas County, Florida. *Peabody Journal of Education, 80,* 170-188.

Dufour, R., DuFour, R., Eaker, R., & Many, T. (2006). *Learning by doing: A handbook for professional learning communities at work.* Bloomington, IN: Solution Tree.

Dunn, J. (2011). Set Up to Fail? Sweeping Changes are Proposed for No Child Left Behind. *Illinois Issues, 37,* 20-22.

Eadie, D. (2007). Advancing by Retreating (2007). *National School Boards Association,* 40-41.

Eadie, D. (2011). Make the Right Choice. *American School Board Journal,* 40-41.

Economic Policy Institute. (2010, August 30). *News from EPI: Leading experts caution against reliance on test scores in teacher evaluations* [press release]. Retrieved from http://www.epi.org/publications/ entry/news_from_epi_leading_experts_caution_against_reliance_ on_test_scores_in_te/

Elder, M., & Obel-Omia, M. (2012). Why Bother With Recess? *Education Week, 31 (30),* 27.

Engel, M. (2000). The Struggle for Control of Public Education-Market Ideology vs. Democratic Values. Philadelphia: Temple University Press.

Fiori, Lindsay. (2011). Under budget, teachers with revoked licenses could teach at charter schools. *Journal Times.* Retrieved from: http:// www.journaltimes.com/news/local/article.

Florida School Boards Association. (2010). FSBA School Board Member Survey Results: May 10, 2010. *Florida School Boards Association.*

Foster, A. (2012). Too Much Emphasis on Testing? Available: www .parents4publicschools.org.

Fridley, C. M. J. (2006). Study of the relationship between school board evaluation and Illinois State Board of Education indicators of effectiveness (Doctoral dissertation, Southern Illinois University Carbondale). Dissertation Abstracts International, 67 (08), 118A.

Gemberling, K.W., Smith, C. W., & Villani, J.S. (2000). *The key work of school boards guidebook.* Alexandria, VA: National School Boards Association.

Gewertz, C. (2011). Local Massachusetts School Board Seeks Standards Rollback. *Education Week.* 30 (19), 6.

Glass, T. (2000). Better boards, better schools. *American School Board Journal, 187 (11),* 42-4.

Glass, T. (2001). Superintendent Leaders Look at the Superintendency, School Boards & Reform. *Education Commission of the States,* Denver, CO.

Goble, N. (1993). School-Community Relations: New for the 90's. *Education Digest,* 59 (4), 45-49.

Goodman, H., Fulbright, L., & Zimmerman, W. (1997). *Getting there from here. School board-superintendent collaboration: Creating a school governance team capable of raising student achievement.* Arlington, VA: Educational Research Service.

Goodman, R. H., & Zimmerman, W. G. (2000). *Thinking differently: Recommendations for 21st century school board/superintendent leadership, governance, and teamwork for high student achievement.* Arlington, VA: Educational Research Service.

Green, E. (2011). National Report Says Charter School Has High Student Attrition. *The Baltimore Sun.*

Greenblatt, A. (2011). Billionaires in the Classroom. *Governing, 25 (1),* 27-35.

Grier, T. (2011). In Houston, a Steppingstone to Better Teacher Evaluations. *Education Week, 31 (12),* 28-30.

Hammond-Darling, L. (2012). Value-Added Teacher Evaluation The Harm Behind the Hype. *Education Week,* 31 (24), 32.

Hardy, L. (2011). Coming Around Again. *American School Board Journal, 198 (11),* 14-18.

Hasan. (2010, September 16). Re: Article on how outsourcing jobs leads to unemployment in the U.S. [How Outsourcing Affects The U.S. Economy!] Message posted to http://www.dirjournal.com/business-journal/

Hawley, W., & Irvine, J. (2011). The Teaching Evaluation Gap. *Education Week, 31 (13),* 30-31.

Hehir, T. (2010) Charters: Students With Disabilities Need Not Apply? *Education Week, 29,* 18-19, 21.

Heitin, L. (2011). Evaluation System Weighing Down Tennessee Teachers. *Education Week,* 31(8), 1 & 14.

Henderson, E., Henry, J., Saks, J., & Wright, A. (2001). *Team Leadership for Student Achievement.* Alexandria, VA: National School Boards Association.

Hess, F.M., & Meeks, O. (2010). School Boards Circa 2010; Governance in the Accountability Era. *The National School Boards Association; The Thomas B. Fordham Institute; The Iowa School Boards Foundation.*

Holly, H. (2010). Funds Misuse, Nepotism Feared at Texas Charter Schools. *The Dallas Morning News.*

Hong, J. (2009). The Influence Game: Bill Gates Pushes Educational Reform. *USA Today,* pp. 1-2.

Howell, W. (ED.). (2005). Besieged: School boards and the future of education politics. Washington, D.C.: The Brookings Institute

Huthwaite Coaching Skills (n.d.). Available from: http://logic-consulting.com/logic/pages/index

Huthwaite. Know the Psychology of Sales, 2007. *Huthwaite.* Available: http://www.candogo.com/search/insight

Illinois Association of School Boards. IASB Delegates Reject Concept of Mandatory Board Member Training, 2008. Springfield, Illinois: *Illinois School Board Newsbulletin.*

Illinois Association of School Boards. (n.d.) Board Training. Springfield, Illinois: *Illinois Association of School Board.* Available: http://www.iasb.com/training/

Illinois Association of School Boards. (2006a). Coming to Order A Guide to Successful School Board Meetings. Springfield, IL: Illinois Association of School Boards

Illinois Association of School Boards. (2006b). Illinois School Code (2006 edition). Charlottesville, VA: Matthew Bender and Company

Illinois General Assembly (n.d.). Illinois General Assembly. Available: from http://www.ilga.gov/

Illinois General Assembly (n.d.). Governor Quinn Signs Bill to Strengthen Illinois' 'Race to the Top' Application Law Will Improve School Principal Certification Requirements. Available: http://www3.illinois.gov/PressReleases/ShowPressRelease.cfm?SubjectID=25&RecNum=8495

Illinois Statewide School Management Alliance. (2013). Alliance Legislative Report (98-12). Illinois Association of School Boards, Illinois

Principals Association, Illinois Association of School Administrators and Illinois Association of School Business Officials: Author.

Indiana Association of School Boards. (2008). Educational Statutes. Available at: http://law.onecle.com/

Institute for Educational Leadership. (2001). *Leadership for student learning: Restructuring school district leadership.* Washington DC: Author.

Iowa Association of School Boards. (2000). IASB's lighthouse study: School boards and student achievement. *Iowa School Board Compass, 5 (2)*, 1-12.

Iowa School Boards Foundation. (2008). Information Briefing. *Iowa School Boards Foundation, 2 (2).*

Jacobson, J. (2011). Supplemental Educational Services-An Unregulated and Unproven NCLB Training Program. *Education Week, 31 (14),* 28 & 31.

Jane, E. (2003). School board form elusive. *Pittsburgh Post-Gazette*, 1-8.

Jazzar, M. (2005). Curbing micromanagement. *American School Board Journal.*

Jennings, J. (2011). School Vouchers: No Clear Advantage in Academic Achievement. *Huff Post.* Available from: http://www.huffingtonpost.com/jack-jennings/school-vouchers-no-academic-advantage_b_909735.html

Johnson, M. (2011). A parting view... Helping school leaders be effective leaders. *The Illinois Association School Board Journal,* 79 (5), 8-9.

Johnson, P. (2008). *Community Engagement? Let's Dance!* Arlington, VA: Educational Research Service.

Jones, A. (2013). Schools for Other People's Children-I want to Send My Grandson to Sidwell. *Education Week,* 32 (18), 21.

Kay, K. (2011). Unleashing Locally Driven Innovation. *Education Week,* 31 (11), 27 & 32.

Kelleher, M. (2011). Race to Top Initiative Sparks Assessment Fears. *Education Week,* 31 (1), 20.

Kirst, M. (1994a). A changing context means school board reform. *Phi Delta Kappan, 75,* 378-81.

Kirst, M. (1994b). The future for local school boards. *Education Digest; 59,* 3pg.

Kirst, M. (2004). A History of American School Governance. In Epstein, N. (Ed.), *Who's In Charge Here? The Tangled Web of*

School Governance and Policy (pp. 15). Denver: Education Commission of the States & Washington D.C.: Brooking Institution Press.

Klein, A. (2011a). ESEA Bill Clears Panel in Senate. *Education Week,* (31), 1, 21.

Klein, A. (2011b). GOP Candidates Line Up to Slam Education Department. *Education Week, (31) 5,* 4.

Klein, A. (2011c). Outlines Emerging for ESEA. *Education Week.* 30 (31), 1, 23.

Klein, A. (2012a). After Early Progress, SIG School Struggles to Improve. *Education Week,* 32 (35), 12 & 13.

Klein, A. (2012b). Obama Budget Plans Selective Boosts in Education Aid. *Education Week,* (31), 22 & 23.

Klein, A. (2012c). Obama Finding Teacher Support Secure, if Tepid. *Education Week,* 32 (9), 1 & 22.

Klein, A., & McNeil, M. (2011). Waiver Plan Generates Relief, Fret. *Education Week,* 21 (1), 1, 23.

Koppich, J. & Humphrey, D. (2011). Getting Serious About Teacher Evaluation-A Fresh Look at Peer Assistance and Review. *Education Week,* 31 (07) 25,28.

Kraus, L. (n.d.). *The Impact of No Child Left Behind on IDEA'S Guarantee of Free, Appropriate Public Education for Students with Disabilities: A Critical Review of Recent Case Law.* Available:http://www.luc.edu/law/academics/special/center/child/childed_forum/pdfs/2009_student_papers/kraus_impact_no_child.pdf

Kunder, L. (1975). Orientation Programs for New School Board Members. *Educational Research Service,* 1-33.

Land, D. (2002). Local school boards under review: Their role and effectiveness in relation to student's academic achievement. *Educational Research, 72 (2).*

LaRocque, L. and Coleman, P. (1993). The Politics of Excellence: Trustee Leadership and School District Ethos. *The Alberta Journal of Educational Research XXXIX*(4), 449-475.

Law and Legal Research (n.d.). Law and Legal Research. Available from: http://law.onecle.com/.

Lee, D., & Eadens, D. (2013). Developing Midcentury School Boards. *University of Southern Mississippi.*

Lieberman, M. (1994). *Teacher Unions: Is the End Near? How to End the Teacher Union Veto over State Education Policy.* Rhode Island University, Providence; Urban Field Center.

Liptak, A. (2010). Justice Defends Campaign Finance Ruling. *The New York Times.* Available from: www.nytimes.com/2010/02/04/us/politics/04scotus.html

Malinsky, S. (1999). A case study of good practice of selected school boards in Illinois (Doctoral dissertation, Illinois State University, 1999). Dissertation Abstracts International, 60 (04), 132A.

McAdams, D.R. (2002). Leading City Schools Challenge and Change in Urban Education Strengthening Urban Boards. *American School Board Journal.*

McAdams, D.R. (2003). Training Your Board to Lead-The Board-Savvy Superintendent. *School Administrator.*

McAdams, D.R. (2005). The Short, Productive Board Meeting. *School Administrator.*

McAdams, D.R. (2006). Administrative Support for Board Members. *School Administrator.*

McAdams, D.R. (2009a). Surviving Board Transitions. *School Administrator.*

McAdams, D.R. (2009b). Top 10 'Guarantees' for A Great Relationship. *School Administrator.*

McKenzie, K. B., & Scheurich, J. J. (2004) The Corporatizing and Privatizing of Schooling: A Call for Grounded Critical Praxis. *Department of Educational Administration and Human Resource Development, Texas A&M University,* 54 (4), 431-443.

McNeil, M. (2011a). Politics K-12: Duncan Takes Sides in State, Local Education Debates. *Education Week, 30 (37).*

McNeil, M. (2011b). More States Asking For NCLB Waivers. *Education Week, (30) 37,* 20.

McNeil, M. (2011c). New Leeway on Horizon Under NCLB. *Education Week, 30 (35),* 1.

McNeil, M. (2011d). Ohio Vote to Scrap Bargaining Law a Labor Victory-For Now. *Education Week, 31 (12),* 1 & 26.

McNeil, M. (2011e). Study Gives First Round of 'i3' Mixed Grades. *Education Week, (30) 37,* 20.

McNeil, M. (2011f). Waiver Plans Would Scrap Parts of NCLB. *Education Week, (31)* 13, 1 & 28.

McNeil, M. (2012a). NCLB Waivers for Districts No Easy Sell With States. *Education Week, 31(27),* 19 & 19.

McNeil, M. (2012b). Race to Top Promises Come Home to Roost. *Education Week,* 31 (15), 1 & 14.

McNeil, M. (2012c). Recipients of RTT Aid Struggling. *Education Week,* 31 (17), 1 & 22.

McNeil, M. (2013a). Duncan Gets Earful on How Agenda Plays in Districts. *Education Week, 32 (20),* 21.

McNeil, M. & Klein, A. (2011b). Obama Outlines NCLB Flexibility. *Education Week, 31(5),* 1 & 20.

McNeil, M. (2013). Rifts Deepen Over Direction of Education Policy in U.S. *Education Week, 32 (30),* 1,14, 16 &17.

Michigan Association of School Boards. (2008). MASB Member Survey 2008. *Michigan Association of School Boards.*

Miron, G. (2007) Education Management Organizations. Available at: http://a100educationalpolicy.pbworks.com/f/Miron_EMO_Chpt27.pdf

Mitchell, R. (2006). High-Stakes Testing and Effects on Instruction: Research Review. Available: http://www.centerforpubliceducation. org/Main-Menu/Instruction/High-stakes-testing-and-effects-on-instruction-At-a-glance/High-stakes-testing-and-effects-on-instruction-Research-review.html

Mount Vernon City Schools District 80 (2008). District 80 Strategic Planning. *Mount Vernon City Schools, District 80.*

Myers, N. & Rafferty, Ed. (2012). Moving Up From Mediocre. *School Administrator,* 1(69), 21-26.

National Assessment of Educational Progress (2003). *The Nation's Report Card-America's Charter Schools-Results From the NAEP 2003 Pilot Study.* U.S. Department of Education Institute of Education Sciences.

National Charter School Institute (n.d.) National Charter Schools Institute. Available: http://nationalcharterschools.org/governing-breakthrough-results/

National Coalition for Dialogue & Deliberation, International Association for Public Participation, Co-Intelligence Institute and others (2009). *Core Principles for Public Engagement.* Retrieved from: www.ncdd.org/pep/

National School Boards Association. (n.d.). Mandated Training for Local School Board Members Survey—Sept. 2008. Alexandria,

Virginia: *National School Boards Association*.Available:http://
www.nsba.org/MainMenu/ResourceCenter/SurveyStudiesandEval-
uations/MandatedTraining_1_2aspx

National School Boards Association. (n.d.). Key Work of School
Boards. Alexandria, Virginia: *National School Boards Association*.
Available: http://www.nsba.org/keywork

National School Boards Association (n.d.). *Advocacy*. Available:
www.nsba.org/advocacy

National School Boards Association (n.d.). *Mandated Training for
Local School Board Members Survey*. Available: www.nsba.org/
Board-Leadership/Surveys/MandatedTraining.pdf

Nelson, F., Rosenberg, B., & Meter, N. (2004). Charter School Achievement on the 2003 National Assessment of Educational Progress.
American Federation of Teachers, AFL-CIO. [On-Line]. Available:
http://www.asu.edu/educ/epsl/EPRU/articles/EPRU-0408-63-OWI.pdf

Nemir, B. (2010) The Primary Obligation. *TABB-Texas Long Star*.

New Jersey School Boards Association. (2007). 2007 Member Survey:
Final Results and Analysis. *New Jersey School Boards Association*.

Ohanian, S. (2002). Collateral Vomitage. Available: http://www.
susanohanian.org/show_atrocities.php?id=5

Ohio School Board Association. (2010). Ohio Voters Value Board
Experience. *Ohio School Board Journal*, 20-21.

Olson, L. (2001). Study Questions Reliability of Single-Year Test
Score Gains. *Education Week*.

Oregon School Boards Association (2008). Oregon School Boards Association Benchmark Survey Summary. *Davis, Hibbitts, & Midghall Inc*.

Oregon School Boards Association (2012). Oregon School Boards Association Online Membership Survey Research Report. *DHM Research*.

Pennsylvania School Board Association (2009). Board Operations.
Pennsylvania School Board Association.

Pennsylvania School Board Association. (2010). A profile: Pennsylvania school directors. *Pennsylvania Bulletin, 35-39*.

Parents Public Schools. (2012). *Too Much Emphasis on Testing?*
Available: www.parents4publicschools.org.

Payne, J. D. (1994). Mandated school board member training for local boards of education in Tennessee as perceived by local boards
of education members and superintendents of schools (Doctoral

dissertation, East Tennessee State University, 1994). Dissertation Abstracts International, 55 (09), 2670A.

Payne, R. K. (2003). Framework for Understanding Poverty. *Texas: Aha Process, Inc.*

Petronis, J., Hall, R., & Pierson, M. (1996). *Mandatory school board training: An idea whose time has come?* (ERIC Document Reproduction Service No. ED 400625)

Price, Hugh. (2011). Community Mobilization: A Missing Link in School Reform. *Education Week,* 31 (2), 22.

Rackham, N. (1988). SPIN Selling. *New York: McGraw-Hill Book Company.*

Rallis, S.F., & Criscoe, J. (1993, April). *School boards and school restructuring: A contradiction in terms?* Paper presented at the annual meeting of the American Educational Research Association, Atlanta, GA.

Ramirez, A. (2010). It's Time to Reform Federal Education Policy. *Education Week.* 29(30), 32.

Ravitch, D. (2010). *The Death and Life of the Great American School System-How Testing and Choice Are Undermining Education.* New York, NY: Basic Books.

Rebora, A. (2011). South Korea Cracks Down On Late-Night Tutoring. *Education Week,* (31), 10.

Rebora, A. (2012). Teachers Place Little Value on Standardized Testing. *Education Week, 31 (26),* 14),

Resnick, M. (1999). *Effective school governance: A look at today's practice and tomorrow's promise.* Denver, CO: Education Commission of the States.

Resnick, M. (2000). *Communities Count: A School Board Guide to Public Engagement.* Alexandria, VA: National School Boards Association.

Rhim, L. (2013). Moving Beyond the Killer B's- The Role of School Boards in School Accountability and Transformation. *Academic Development Institute.*

Rice, P. (2010). An Analysis of the Impact of School Board Training and Evaluation As Perceived by School Board Members and Superintendents (Doctoral dissertation, Southern Illinois University, 2010). Available from Pro-Quest database. (UMI No. 3408650).

Robelen, E. (2011a). Frustration at Heart of Washington Rally. *Education Week,* 30 (35), 1 & 14.

Robelen, E. (2011b). Urban Districts Post Gains on NAEP Math But Reading Flatlines. *Education Week, 31 (14),* 6-7.

Robelen, E. (2012). More States Retaining 3rd Graders. *Education Week, 31 (26),* 1 & 15.

Robelen, E. (2013). U.S. Students Exceed International Average, But Lag Some Asian Nations in Math, Science. *Education Week,* 32 (15), 8 & 9.

Robinson, E. (2013). The Test Score Racket. *St. Louis Post Dispatch.* Available: http://www.stltoday.com/news/opinion/columns/eugene-robinson/eugene-robinson-the-test-score-racket/article_317628cb-896e-55e7-8e02-3b6d8e2971f1.html

Roby, P. (2011). What Catholic Schools Can Teach About Educating the Whole Child. *Education Week,* (31), 18.

Rochholz, M. (2012). The Problem School Boards Have With the Public. *The Illinois School Board Journal, January-February,* 28-29.

Rose, L., & Gallup, A. (2010). The 42nd Annual Phi Delta Kappa/ Gallup Poll of the Public's Attitudes toward the Public Schools. *Phi Delta Kappan.*

Rossi, R. (2011). *Only 1.5 Percent of State Public High Schools Met Federal Progress Mark.* Available: http://www.suntimes.com/news/education/8328197-418/only-15-percent-of-state-public-high-schools-met-federal-progress-mark.html

Ryan, J. (2004). A History of American School Governance. In Epstein, N. (Ed.), W*ho's In Charge Here? The Tangled Web of School Governance and Policy* (pp. 15). Denver: Education Commission of the States & Washington D.C.: Brooking Institution Press.

Samuels, C. (2001). NYC Chancellor Cathie Black Out After Three Months. *Education Week,* 30.

Samuels, C. (2011a). Districts Created to Steer 'Turnarounds.' *Education Week, 31 (14),* 1 & 18.

Samuels, C. (2011b). Foundation Gives $75 Million to Bolster Principal Training. *Education Week,* 31 (2) 10.

Samuels, C. (2011c). Principals' Performance Reviews Are Getting a Fresh Look. *Education Week,* 30 (37), 14.

Samuels, C. (2011d). School Board Members' Focus Shifting, Survey Says. *Education Week, 30 (20)* 1.

Samuels, C. (2011e). Studies: Teacher Retention Lower at Charter Schools. *Education Week, (30) 37, 5.*

Samuels, C. (2013). New Scrutiny as Head Start Centers Re-compete for Aid. *Education Week, 32 (19), 6-7.*

Sautter, C. (n.d.) Charter Schools: A New Breed of Public Schools. *Policy Briefs.*

Sawchuk, S. (2010a). Administration Pushes Teacher-Prep Accountability. *Education Week, 30 (23), 1,14.*

Sawchuk, S. (2010b). AFT Chief Promises Due-Process Reform. *Education Week, 29, 11 & 12.*

Sawchuk, S. (2010c). Study Casts Cold Water On Bonus Pay. *Education Week, 30, 1, 12.*

Sawchuk, S. (2011a). Collaboration A Never-Ending Process. *Education Week, 31(12), S10 & S12.*

Sawchuk, S. (2011b). Multiple 'Curriculum' Meanings Heighten Debate Over Standards. *Education Week, 30 (26), 1, 15.*

Sawchuk, S. (2011c). New Attitudes Shaping Labor-District Relations. *Education Week, 31 (12), S2 – S5.*

Sawchuk, S. (2011d). New Groups Giving Teachers Alternative Voice. *Education Week, 31 (3), 1, 16.*

Sawchuk, S. (2011e). Teacher Entry Criteria on Agenda of Merged NCATE. *Education Week, 31 (14), 12.*

Sawchuk, S. (2011f). Wanted: More Diverse Teaching Force. *Education Week, 32 (7), 1 & 14.*

Sawchuk, S. (2012). As Membership Plummets, NEA Tries to Boost Political Clout. *Education Week, 31 (36), 1 & 18.*

Sawchuk, S. (2013a). Diversity at Issue in Teacher Selection. *Education Week, 32 (30), 1 & 20.*

Sawchuk, S. (2013b). High Ratings for Teachers Are Still Seen. *Education Week, 32 (20), 1& 6.*

Sawchuk, S. (2013c). Union Sues Over Basis of Appraisal. *Education Week, 32 (29), 1 & 15.*

Schniedewind, N., & Sapon-Shevin, M. (2012). *Educational Courage; Resisting the Ambush of Public Education.* Boston, Massachusetts: Beacon Press Books.

Sell, S. (2006). Running an effective school district: School boards in the 21st century. *The Journal of Education,* 71-97.

SERVE: SouthEastern Regional Vision for Education. (1997). *School Board Member Training in the Southeast. Second Edition.* Office of Educational Research and Improvement (ED), Washington, DC.

Shannon, T. (1990). *Local Control of the Public Schools and Education Reform.* Alexandria, VA: National School Boards Association.

Simon, S. (2012a). Has Teach For America Betrayed Its Mission. *Reuters.*

Simon, S. (2012b). Mayors Back Parents Seizing Control of Schools. *Reuters.*

Simon, S. (2012c). Online Schools Face Backlash as States Question Results. *Reuters.*

Smith, B.D. (2009). Maybe I will, maybe I won't: what the connected perspectives of motivation theory and organizational commitment may contribute to our understanding of strategy implementation. *Journal of Strategic Marketing,* 17 (6), 473-485.

Smith, M., Turner, J., & Lattanzio, S. (2012). Public Schools: Glass Half Full or Half Empty? *Education Week,* 32 (7), 22 & 25.

Snipes, J., Doolittle, F. & C. Herlihy. (2002). *Foundation for Success: Case Studies for How Urban School Districts Improve Student Achievement.* Washington, DC: Council of Great City Schools.

Sparks, S. (2011a). 'Value-Added' Formulas Strain Collaboration. *Education Week, 31 (12), S8-S11.*

Sparks, S. (2011b). Rules Raise Bar for Head Start Centers. *Education Week, 31 (12),* 20 & 25.

Sparks, S. (2011c). N.Y.C. Ends Merit-Pay Program. *Education Week, (30) 37,* 5.

Speer, T. (1998). *Reaching for excellence, what local school districts are doing to raise student achievement.* Alexandria, VA: National School Boards Association.

Stover, D. (2011a). School Boards Work. *American School Board Journal,* 198(6), 17.

Stover, D. (2011b). Stand Up, Speak Out. *American School Board Journal,* 22.

Stover, D. (2012a). Pay to Play? *American School Board Journal,* 199(3), 14-18.

Stover, D. (2012b). Stories. *American School Board Journal,* 12-21. Available: www.asbj.com.

The Albert Lea Tribune. (2011). *Minnesota seeks waiver to No Child Left Behind*. Available: http://www.albertleatribune.com/2011/08/09/minn-seeks-waiver-to-no-child-left-behind/

The Center for Public Education. (2011). Eight Characteristics of Effective School Boards-At a Glance. *The Center for Public Education.* Available: http://www.centerforpubliceducation.org/Main-Menu/Public-education/Eight-characteristics-of-effective-school-boards/default.aspx

Thevenot, B. (2010). Charter Schools Battle High Teacher Turnover. *The Texas Tribune.*

Tisdale, D. (2013). School Board Management Style, Student Achievement Correlation Examined. *Southern Miss Now.* Available: http://www.usm.edu/news/article/school board-management-style-student-achievement-correlation-examined

Todras, E. (1993). The changing role of school boards. Eugene, OR (ERIC Document Reproduction Service No. ED 357434)

Togneri, W., & Anderson, S.E. (2003). *Beyond Islands of Excellence: What Districts Can Do to Improve Student Achievement.* Washington, DC: Learning First Alliance.

Townsend, R., Johnston, G., Gross, G., Lynch, P., Garcy, L., Roberts, B., & Novotney, P. (2007). *Effective Superintendent School Board Practices-Strategies for Developing and Maintaining Good Relationships with Your Board.* Thousand Oaks, CA: Corwin Press.

Tran, L. (2011). Inside New Orleans' Education 'Miracle.' *Education Week, 31 (10),* 21.

Ujifusa, A. (2013). Standards Draw Heat in States. *Education Week, 32 (20),* 1 & 26.

Urschel, J. (2003). Communicating education takes public involvement. *The Illinois School Board Journal, 18-22.*

Usdam, M.D. (1994). The relationship between school boards and general purpose government. *Phi Delta Kappan, 75,* 374-377.

U.S. Department of Education. (2012). District-Level Race to the Top Focus on the Classroom, Provide Tools to Enhance Learning and Serve the Needs of Every Student. Available: http://www.ed.gov/category/program/race-top-fund

Valentine, J. (2005). The Instructional Practices Inventory: A Process for Profiling Student Engaged Learning for School Improvement.

Available: http://education.missouri.edu/orgs/mllc/Upload%20 Area-Docs/IPI%20Manuscript%208-05.pdf

Vu, P. (2008). Do State Tests Make the Grade? Available: http://www. pewstates.org/projects/stateline/headlines/do-state-tests-make-the-grade-85899387452

Walsh, M. (2012). Education Spending Raised in Arguments On Health-Care Law. *Education Week, 31(27),* 19.

Washington State School Director's Association. (2011). Serving on your local school board: A Foundation for Success. *Washington State School Director's Association* pp. 1-62.

Washington State School Director's Association. (2007). Avoiding Conflicts of Interest: A Guide for School Board Members and Superintendents. *Washington State School Director's Association-Policy and Legal Services.* pp. 1-32.

Waters, T. &Marzano R. (2006). *School District Leadership that Works: The Effect of Superintendent Leadership on Student Achievement.* Denver: Mid-continent Research for Education and Learning.

West, E. (1997). Education Vouchers in Principle and Practice: A Survey. The World Bank Research Observer, 12, 83-103.

Wheeler, G. (2011). School reform: Beyond silver bullets, capes. *The Illinois School Board Journal,* 79 (4), 12-18.

Whitehurst, G.J. (2010). Did Congress Authorize Race to the Top? Education Week. 29 (30), 24.

Winerip, M. (2011). In Tennessee, Following the Rules for Evaluations Off a Cliff. *The New York Times,* A18. Available: http://www.ny-times.com/2011/11/07/education/tennessees-rules-on-teacher-evalu-ations-bring-furstration.html? r = 1&ref=education

Winkle, Matt. (2010). 'That's Not the Way It Works in Education' (What Not to Tell a New School Board Member). *Education Week, 30,* 1, 12.

Wisconsin Association of School Boards. (2011). 2011 WASB Member Survey. *Wisconsin Association of School Boards.*

Yackera, T. J. Jr. (1999). A survey of attitudes toward training mandates for school board members: Views by Keystone State (Doctoral Dissertation, Widener University, 1998). Dissertation Abstracts International, 60 (01), 41A.

Zagursky, E. (2011). "Smart? Yes. Creative? Not So Much." Available: http://www.wm.edu/research/ideation/professions/smart-yes.-creative-not-so-much.5890.php

Zehr, M. (2010). Study Looks at Turnover of Charter Principals. *Education Week,* 30 (13), 5.

Zehr, M. (2011a). Charter Operators Spell Out Barriers To 'Scaling Up.' *Education Week,* 31 (1), 2, 17.

Zehr, M. (2011b). Teacher's Union Go Toe to Toe in Baltimore. *Education Week,* 30 (24), 1, 14-15.

Zubrzycki, J. (2011). Common Core Poses Challenges for Preschools. *Education Week, 31 (13),* 1 & 10.

Zubrzycki, J. (2012a). Debates Over School Shutdowns Heating Up. *Education Week,* 32 (8), 1 & 12.

Zubrzycki, J. (2012b). Indiana Grapples With Impact of Voucher Law. *Education Week,* 31 (15), 1 & 14.

Zubrzycki, J. (2013). New Teachers Search for Place in New Orleans. *Education Week, 32 (29),* 1 & 14.

Zubrzycki, Cavanagh, & McNeil (2013). Charter Schools' Discipline Policies Face Scrutiny. *Education Week, 32 (21),* 1, 16, 17, 19 & 20.

ADDITIONAL REFERENCES

Alfen, V. (1992). A Challenge for School Boards' Leadership in Rural America. *Brigham Young University,* 1-11.

Arcrement, B. (2007). The Catalyst. *American School Board Journal, August,* 30-32.

Boyle, P. (2003). Balancing in a democracy-The true work of school boards. *Illinois Association of School Boards, September/October,* 12-17.

Bushweller, K. (1998). Under the shadow of the state. *American School Board Journal,* 185 (8), 16-19.

Calvert, B. (2004). Mandated training for public board members (Doctoral dissertation, Southern Illinois University, 2004). Dissertation Abstracts International, 65 (09), 3224A.

Canciamilla, L. S. (2000). From many to one: The intragroup behaviors of high-performing school boards (Doctoral dissertation, University of La Verne, 2000). Dissertation Abstracts International, 61 (01), 35A.

Carr, N. (2006). New Rules of Engagement. *American School Board Journal, April,* 66-68.

Carr, N. (2006). Winning the War for Public Education. *American School Board Journal, March,* 51-52.

Cizek, G. (2001). Unintended Consequences of High Stakes Testing-P-12. *Educational Measurement: Issues and Practice.*

Conzemius, A., & O'Neill, J. (2002). *The Handbook for Smart School Teams.* Bloomington, IN: National Educational Service.

Cook, G. (2003). The Perception Challenge. (2003). *National School Boards Association.* Available at: http://www.asbj.com/specialreports/1203Special%20Reports/S4.html

Daily Kos. (2010). *The problem with NBC's Education Nation-where are the voices of parents and teachers?* Available at: http://educationpolicyblog.blogspot.com

Danzberger, J. P., & Usdam, M. D. (1994). Local education governance: Perspectives on problems and strategies for change. *Phi Delta Kappan, 75,* 366.

Dowd, K. (2010). School Board Advocacy: Ready, Aim, Inspire! *Strategies: A Journal for Physical and Sport Educators, 23,* 35-36.

Eadie, D. (2008). The Board-Superintendent Rx. *National School Boards Association,* 44-45.

Hadderman, M. (1988). *State vs. Local Control of Schools.* Eugene, OR: Eric Clearinghouse on Educational Management.

Johnson, P. A..(2012). School Board Governance: The Times They Are A-Changin. *Journal of Cases in Educational Leadership,* 15 (2), 83-102.

Kolodner, M. (2011). Students, Teachers, Sweating High-stakes Tests as Parents Rebel Against Constant Prep. *Daily News.*

Looney, A., & Greenstone, M. (2012). The Importance of Education: An Economics View. *Education Week, 32 (11),* 32.

Maxwell, L. (2011). OCR Pace On Probes Quickens. *Education Week, 31 (14),* 1 & 14.

Moscovitch, R., Sadovnik, A., Barr, J., Davidson, T., Moore, T., Powell, R., Tractenberg, P., Wagman, E., & Zha, P. (n.d.). Governance and Urban School Improvement: Lessons for New Jersey From Nine Cities. *The Institute on Education Law and Policy Rutgers-Newark.*

National School Boards Association. (n.d.). *Dealing With Conflict. Available:* www.nsba.org/sbot/toolkit/Conflict.html

National Collaborative on Diversity in the Teaching Force (2004). Assessment of Diversity in America's Teaching Force-A Call to Action. Washington D.C.: *National Collaborative on Diversity in the Teaching Force.*

Odden, A.R., & Archibald, S. (2000). Investing in Learning: How schools can reallocate resources to support student achievement. *In School spending 2000-Investing in learning* [On-line]. Available: http//www.asbj.com/schoolspending/odden.html.

Picus, L. O. (2000). Setting budget priorities. *In School spending 2000-Investing in learning* [On-line]. Available: http://www.asbj.com/schoolspending/resourcespicus.html

Quercus. (2006). *The Greatest American Speeches.* London: Author.

Rice, A. (2011). Poll Finds Americans Trust Teachers, Divided on Unions. *Education Week,* 31 (1), 16.

Robelen, E. (2010). States Change Policies with Eye to Winning Federal Grants. *Education Week,* (29) 1, 21.

Rose, L., & Gallup, A. (2006). The 38th Annual Phi Delta Kappa/Gallup Poll of the Public's Attitudes Toward the Public Schools. *Phi Delta Kappan.*

School Board News. (2011, April 9). Rice: Local districts can provide solutions. *National School Boards Association,* p. 2.

Stallings, D. T. (2002). A Brief History of The U.S. Department of Education, 1979-2002. *Phi Delta Kappan, 83,* (9) 677.

Stein, L. (2012). The Art of Saving a Failing School. *Phi Delta Kappan,* 93 (5), 51-55.

Texas Association of School Boards. (2012). *Advocates for Kids.* Available: https://www.tasb.org/about/schools/role/school_boards/understanding.aspx

Texas Association of School Boards. (2012). Why *Is It Important for School Board Members to Become Advocates.* Available: https://www.tasb.org/legislative/sban/handbook/importance.aspx

Thomas, R. G. (1993). *Learning needs of school board presidents in the central region.* (ERIC Document Reproduction Service No. ED 362 481)

Toppo, G. (2011). When Test Scores Seem Too Good to Believe. *USA Today.*

Ujifusa, A. (2013). 'Parent-Trigger' Laws Catching Fresh Wave. *Education Week, 32 (26),* 23 & 27.

Wagner, H. (2010). "If you're going to make us do it, then help us fund it": Schools often have no way to pay for mandates. *Herald-Whig.* Retrieved from http://www.whig.com/search?vendor=ez&qu=unfunded+school+mandates

Washington State School Director's Association. (2001). Serving on Your Local School Board, a Guide to Effective Leadership. *Washington State School Director's Association* pp. 1-51.

Appendix

California School Boards Association, 2005 (CSBA)

In 2005, Aurora Research Group was contracted by the California School Boards Association to conduct a membership survey. According to CSBA records, Aurora utilized an online electronic survey with CSBA members who had e-mail addresses and a mail survey for those who did not. Out of 2,964 qualified respondents, 629 or 23% completed the online survey. An additional 212 respondents, or 10%, completed the mail survey. The survey databases were merged and the total number of respondents from both surveys came to 841.

According to Aurora Research Group, the margin of error for a completed sample of 841 surveys was + or − 3.1%, at the 95% confidence level. The research company was 95% confident that these numbers represented the true population parameters within +/- 3.1%. The overall response rate totaled 17%, which the researchers considered average for similar research studies and the respondents' membership was reflective of all districts under CSBA membership. Survey responses were analyzed using univariate, bivariate, and multivariate techniques, and statistical significance within cross tabulation tables were calculated using $(x2)$ statistics.

California School Boards Association, 2009 (CSBA)

In 2009, the CSBA recontracted with Aurora to provide an in-depth member survey similar to the survey it conducted in 2005. According to

CSBA records, Aurora again utilized an on-line electronic survey with CSBA members who had e-mail addresses and a mail survey for those who did not. Out of 3,733 qualified respondents, 714 or 19% completed the online survey. In regard to the mail surveys, 86 respondents or 6% out of 1,398 completed the mail survey. The survey databases were merged and total number of respondents from both surveys came to 800.

According to Aurora Research Group, the margin of error for a completed sample of 800 surveys was + or − 3.2%, at the 95% confidence level. The research company was 95% confident that these numbers represented the true population parameters within +/- 3.2%. The overall response rate totaled 16%, which the researchers considered average for similar research studies, and the respondents' membership was reasonably reflective of all districts under CSBA membership. Survey responses were again analyzed using univariate, bivariate, and multivariate techniques, and statistical significance within cross tabulation tables were calculated using ($x2$) statistics.

Illinois Association of School Boards, 2008

The Illinois Association of School Boards (IASB) commissioned a membership survey in April 2008, and worked with Western Illinois University Computer Center for assistance in tabulating survey responses. The IASB issued a survey to approximately 5,895 Illinois school board members. Out of that group, 1,699, or 28%, responded.

Florida School Board Association, 2010

The Florida School Board Association (FSBA) surveyed members in its database in February, 2010. The overall purpose of the survey was to measure the effectiveness of FSBA in achieving its mission. The mission of the FSBA is to "Support and assist school boards in shaping and improving student achievement in Florida by impacting legislation and providing proactive leadership and training through a network of services and information." Respondents could participate in the survey either electronically and/or using pencil/paper format. The number of surveys received totaled 103 or 30.7% of FSBA's membership, and the survey represented a total of 46 districts or 73%.

Michigan Association of School Boards, 2008

The Michigan Association of School Boards (MASB) conducted a survey in 2008 of its members. The 2008 survey involved 353 participants or 42% out of 846. The national and state demographic data was based upon MASB's membership files.

New Jersey School Boards Association, 2007

The New Jersey School Boards Association (NJSBA) conducted a survey of its members during 2007. NJSBA mailed out 2,500 surveys across the state. Out of the 2,500 surveys sent out, 247 respondents or 9.9% participated in the study. Zip codes of these members indicated that respondents were spread out across north, south, and central New Jersey.

The NJSBA worked with Aelera Analytics who oversaw the sampling of the surveys. Aelera Analytics indicated that the margin of error for the study was +/- 5.9% at the 95% confidence level. Aelera validated that the survey sample was a representative sample of the targeted population.

Ohio School Boards Association, 2010

The Ohio School Boards Association (OSBA) conducted a biennial survey of board members in its state. The survey conducted in 2010, was done electronically via e-mail and was sent to board treasurers to complete on behalf of their respective school boards. The response rate was 63%, which was the highest to date of similar surveys from OSBA. There were a total of 392 districts participating --representing city, exempted village, local, and municipal schools systems and educational service centers.

Oregon School Boards Association, 2008 and 2012

The Oregon School Boards Association (OSBA) contracted with Davis, Hibbitts, & Midghall (DMH Research) to conduct an online survey of its members in October 2012. OSBA invited 1,335 school board members and superintendents to participate in the survey. Out of this number, a total of 247 school board members and 85 superintendents participated.

The Oregon School Board Association (OSBA) conducted a membership survey of its members in November 2008 through DMH Research. The phone and/or electronic survey were based upon a random sample of OSBA's members. A total of 400 respondents completed a phone survey, compared to 116 who completed the survey online. According to DMH Research, the margin of error for a sample size of 400 is +/- 4.9% at the 95% confidence level. Specifically, there was a 95% probability that the sample size for this survey was a true representation of the targeted population given the margin of error of 4.9%.

Pennsylvania School Board Association, 2009

The Pennsylvania School Board Association's (PSBA) Research Inquiry on School Board Organization and Operation collects membership survey data every three to four years to compile information on how boards operate, engage the community, and provide various opportunities for students. The survey data included in this book references statistics from this survey and other information such as years of service based upon PSBA membership files. The 2009 survey were based upon 324 responding school districts out of a total of 501. The percentages listed in this book are based on the total number of participant responses and not on the total number of school districts.

School Board Circa, 2010

The School Board Circa 2010 survey respondents derived from the National School Board Association's (NSBA) database of school boards and superintendents from 7,100 districts across the United States out of a total of 13,809 districts. NSBA's database was reflective of 51% of districts across the U.S. The sample taken from NSBA's database was stratified as follows: 100 out of 118 urban districts belonging to NSBA's Council of Urban Boards of Education (CUBE), and board members and superintendents from a random sample of 400 non-urban districts with student enrollment of more than 1,000.

The web-based survey was sent to 3,805 board members and 534 superintendents in the fall of 2009. Out of 3,805 surveys sent out, 900 board members or 23.6% and 120 superintendents or 22.5% from 418 districts participated. The web-based survey had a total of 90 questions, out of which 23 were directed to all respondents, 26 specifically for board members, 12 specifically for the board president, and 29 specifically for the superintendent.

Wisconsin Association of School Boards, 2011

The Wisconsin Association of School Boards (WASB) authorized a membership survey of its members in 2011. WASB sent out surveys to all 2,638 school board members and administrators in the state and reported a 40% response rate. Respondents represented the various district sizes throughout the state of Wisconsin.

Virginia School Board Association (2011)

The Virginia School Board Association (VSBA) conducted an annual opinion survey of its members in 2011. VSBA's survey was e-mailed to all 834 school board members in the state, which 9% of board members responded. VSBA notes that 9% was less than the average desired response rate. However, VSBA's data is similar to those of other state school board surveys in terms of the findings presented in this book.

NSBA'S KEY WORK OF SCHOOL BOARDS

Vision
Agreed upon vision for student achievement endorsed by various stakeholders (community, parents, staff)

Role of the School Board	Role of the Superintendent
Approves and adopts the strategic plan with participation of stakeholders	Recommends a process for formulating the strategic plan (creating the vision); presents findings from stakeholders for the board to consider; recommends performance indicators to monitor the plan
Approves board goals that align with the strategic plan	Assists the board with clarifying its role in support of the strategic plan; works with the board to determine how the goals of the plan will be executed

Role of the School Board	Role of the Superintendent
Communicates the strategic plan	Shares information to the board concerning progress towards the strategic plan
The strategic plan (vision) is the guide for board actions.	Identifies how the strategic plan relates to superintendent recommendations
Formulates and adopts necessary policies which support the strategic plan	Facilitates policy review meetings with the board to determine policies that need to be revised, deleted, or added
Aligns resources to support the strategic plan	Facilitates review meetings with the board to determine resources needed to implement areas of the strategic plan
Continuously monitors progress toward the strategic plan	Shares data with the board to determine the effectiveness of the strategic plan; recommends changes as needed

Standards
Standards that guide the process to ensure student achievement

Role of the School Board	Role of the Superintendent
Approves learning standards for student achievement (recommends that standards be aligned to state standards)	Recommends and discusses learning standards with the board
Ensures that learning standards are aligned with district resources such as staff, resource materials, and assessment	Informs the board concerning how various resources (learning materials and staff) and professional development will be utilized to support learning standards
Monitors and modifies standards to support learning standards	Facilitates discussions and meetings with the board to identify policies that need to be revised, deleted or added
Periodically reviews learning standards and other programs to ensure student achievement	Reviews data with the board to determine if students are making continuous progress toward various learning goals; submits proposals for students not making progress toward learning standards
Ensures that parents, staff, students, and the community are kept informed of progress toward the learning standards	Develops a plan of how learning standards will be communicated to various stakeholders; works with the board on how to interpret and communicate efficiencies/ deficiencies of the learning standards to the public

Role of the School Board	Role of the Superintendent
Builds community support for learning standards	Develops materials to assist board members in advocating for learning standards
Ensures resources are made available so that students can meet/exceed learning standards	Recommends budget proposals and other resources needed to meet learning standards
Guarantees that instructional programs will be evaluated to ensure effectiveness of promoting student achievement and to provide accountability to stakeholders	Reviews data with the board to determine if students are making continuous progress toward various learning goals; recommends additions, deletions, and modifications as needed to improve student achievement based on the learning standards

Assessment
The process of measuring student achievements that are aligned to learning standards

Role of the School Board	Role of the Superintendent
Commits to on-going training to increase knowledge of various assessment techniques that are aligned to local, state and national standards	Assists in explaining styles and functions of standardized tests
Verifies that student assessment data will be evaluated by professional experts to determine proper conclusions	Recommends assessment programs to measure student achievement including alternative assessments for students with disabilities, etc; reviews assessment data with the board; uses assessment data as the basis for making recommendations concerning changes or other modifications to the curriculum to ensure student achievement
Ensures professional development opportunities for staff concerning assessment measures and analyzing data on student achievement	Identifies various resources necessary for professional development
Ensures that parents, staff, students, and the community are kept informed of various assessments and progress	Develops a plan of how assessment information will be communicated to various stakeholders;
Ensures resources are made available to support the assessment program	Recommends budget proposals
Formulates, revises, and, if necessary, deletes policies in order to have an effective assessment program.	Recommends policies to be added, modified; and/or deleted to ensure a healthy assessment program

Alignment
The school board must ensure that all resources including funding are aligned to improve student achievement

Role of the School Board	Role of the Superintendent
Engages in professional development to further understand how various resources are related to student achievement	Assists the board in understanding how the alignment of various resources improves student learning
Guarantees that the district curriculum will support district policies and goals aimed at increasing student achievement	Reports and recommends to the school board various modifications necessary to improve alignment
Supports and encourages the superintendent to draft district-wide initiatives toward aligning resources to increase student achievement	Reports to the board a plan for ensuring alignment of resources geared at increasing student achievement; reports progress and any concerns or changes
Monitors policies and superintendent initiatives aimed at aligning resources to student achievement; evaluates school and district improvement plans	Recommends and periodically discusses policies with the board that needs to be added, deleted, or modified to support student learning; provides and discusses student data; initiates, reviews, and recommends adoption of school and district improvement plans
Ensures that students' social, emotional and learning needs are addressed while promoting student achievement	Communicates with the board on various resources available to students needing assistance; discusses how social, emotional, and learning needs are addressed and students needing assistance are identified; reports success or failure of policies, curriculum, and other programs geared toward increasing student achievement; recommends modifications to district programs as needed to sustain higher student learning
Approves staff development opportunities necessary to increase student achievement	Reports to the board professional development opportunities available to staff members and how they align with board goals
Approves a system of analyzing and selecting district curriculum	Recommends text books that need to be adopted based upon stakeholder input; reports progress or failure of textbooks
Supports technology initiatives to advance student learning	Recommends grant programs to purchase technology; drafts and reviews a technology plan including staff training and placement of technology

Role of the School Board	Role of the Superintendent
Maintains school facilities to promote student learning	Prepares, reviews, and suggests a facilities plan in collaboration with stakeholders; identifies funding opportunities for the board to consider
Approves the district budget based on district goals	Prepares, monitors, reviews, and suggests a budget for the board to consider
Monitors (at least biannually) district-approved curriculum, instructional techniques, and student achievement data to maximize student learning	Monitors, reviews, and recommends various changes necessary to strengthen the district-wide curriculum plan
Ensures on-going communications with the public regarding how aligning district resources can improve student learning	Reports to the board how stakeholders are informed of district initiatives and progress in aligning resources to maximize student achievement

Climate
Formulating and sustaining a positive learning environment to maximize student achievement

Role of the School Board	Role of the Superintendent
Believes that all students can maximize their learning. which is supported by employing superintendent who shares this belief and modifying and/or creating policies that are aligned to this belief	Recommends staff personnel be hired who believe all students can learn at higher levels; reports on assistance given to staff who are deficient in student achievement expectations; recommends revisions, additions and deletions of policies
Assists in the orientation process for new school board members regarding student achievement expectations	Prepares and seeks approval for a district board orientation handbook which addresses district expectations
Reviews, monitors, and approves various programs for students who need additional support	Recommends modifications, deletions, and other changes needed to ensure that all students receive support in reaching learning goals
Reviews, monitors, and allocates resources in the budget to promote student achievement	Prepares, monitors, and seeks approval of a budget; regularly reviews the budget with the school board
Acknowledges administrators, staff members, students, and teachers for accomplishments in increasing student achievement	Assists in the planning and implementation of acknowledging administrators, staff members, students, and teachers in increasing student achievement

Role of the School Board	Role of the Superintendent
Considers student curriculum and instruction needs a primary concern at all board meetings	Assists in planning the board agenda with the board president with a focus on student curriculum and instruction
Demonstrates and models professionalism to all stakeholders	Models respect and professionalism at board meetings and with staff, students, and other stakeholders
Advocates for community, state, and federal support for student learning	Provides training and sharing of user-friendly data with board members; serves as an advocate for district goals
Periodically analyzes the climate in the district by reviewing staff turnover, retention, promotion, discipline, various surveys, attendance, and enrollment trends	Recommends, initiates, analyzes, and reports on various surveys utilized to determine district climate; recommends policy modifications and participates in discussions with board regarding district climate
Guarantees a healthy learning environment	Recommend district and school-wide crisis plans; revises, modifies and deletes policies; periodically updates the board concerning the overall learning environment
Increases community support for public education and regularly communicates with the public	Reports to the board on issues regarding the district's communication plan; creates a system of acknowledging stakeholder participating in public schools

Continuous Improvement
Ensures a system in place to guarantee high student achievement for all students

Role of the School Board	Role of the Superintendent
Establishes a process of ongoing review of student-achievement data	Formulates, recommends and reviews systems to the board for sustained improvement; seek changes in instructional programs based upon data
Participates in training opportunities regarding the use and analysis of data	Facilitates and participates in board training regarding student achievement; provides district personnel with professional development aimed at utilizing and analyzing information
Participates in training opportunities regarding curriculum alignment based on student-achievement data	Explains student-achievement data in a user-friendly matter for the board to review

Role of the School Board	Role of the Superintendent
Provides resources to ensure student learning	Submits budget recommendations to the board to ensure that they reflect student improvement
Formulates, adopts and modifies board policies for student achievement	Formulates, adopts, modifies, reviews and recommends policies to the school board needed for continuous improvement
Advocates on behalf of the community for student achievement	Reviews the process of communicating with the community regarding student achievement